The War Schools of Dobrinja

Reading, Writing, and Resistance during the Siege of Sarajevo

DAVID M. BERMAN

Caddo Gap Press

The War Schools of Dobrinja:
Reading, Writing, and Resistance during the Siege of Sarajevo

David M. Berman

Published by Caddo Gap Press
3145 Geary Bolulevard PMB 275
San Francisco, California 94118 USA

Copyright 2007 by David M. Berman

$29.95 USA

ISBN 1-880192-55-1

Book and Cover Design by Heather L. Hazuka

Library of Congress Cataloging-in-Publication Data

Berman, David M.
 The War schools of Dobrinja : reading, writing, and resistance during the siege of Sarajevo / David M. Berma.
   p. cm.
 Includes bibliographical references and index.
 ISBN 978-1-880192-55-9 (alk. paper)
 1. Education--Bosnia and Hercegovina--Dobrinje. 2. Sarajevo (Bosnia and Hercegovina)--History--Siege, 1992-1996--Education and the war. 3. Yugoslav War, 1991-1995--Bosnia and Hercegovina--Dobrinje. 4. Dobrinje (Bosnia and Hercegovina)--History. I. Title.

 DR1313.32.D63B47 2007
 949.703--dc22

2007023455

DEDICATION

To
Jessica and Joshua

and to
Smail Vesnić
and all the teachers and students
who endured
"the Siege within a Siege"
of Dobrinja

CONTENTS

List of Tables vii

Notes on Pronunciation viii

Notes on Orthography and Terminology ix

Maps x

Foreword xiii

Preface xv

Prologue
Journey into a State of Fear (*8 March 1995*) 1

Chapter One
Dobrinja—Otpisano Naselje
Dobrinja—Settlement Written Off
The Siege within a Siege of Dobrinja 9

Chapter Two
Ubice u Školskim Klupama
Killers in School Benches
The War for Dobrinja and the Dobrinja War School Center 47

Chapter Three
Drsko i Hrabrost
Cheek and Courage
The Stairway Schools of Dobrinja and Elementary Education 83

Chapter Four
Rođena je u toku Rata
Born During the War
Gimnazija Dobrinja and Secondary Education 113

Chapter Five
Mirani Ratni Dani
Peaceful War Days
The 1992-1993 War School Year 143

CHAPTER SIX
Naselje Nastavnika i Učenika Heroja
A Settlement of Teacher and Student Heroes
War School Years and War School Legacies 177

EPILOGUE
The Struggle for "Common Schools" 207

References 225

Index 237

About the Author 255

TABLES

1.1. Composition of the Population by Local Communities of Dobrinja and the Airport Settlement. *Page 16*

3.1. Number of Elementary School Students in Grades 1-4 and Grades 5-8 in the Stairway Schools by Regions of Dobrinja and the Airport Settlement, and Regional Coordinators, prior to the Official Beginning of the 1992-1993 School Year (November 1992). *Page 106*

3.2. Number of Elementary Students, Teachers, and Classes in the Stairway Schools of Quadrant C5 of the Airport Settlement (November 1992). *Page 107*

4.1. Number of Secondary School Students by Regions of Dobrinja and the Airport Settlement, and Regional Coordinators, prior to the Official Beginning of the 1992-1993 School Year (November 1992). *Page 119*

4.2. Data on Secondary School Students in Dobrinja and the Airport Settlement, Their Secondary Schools of Register, and School Coordinators, in the 1992-1993 School Year. *Page 134*

4.3. Secondary School Obligation for the Organization of Instruction by Sarajevo Local Community in the 1992-1993 School Year. *Pages 137-138*

6.1. Number of Students and Classes in Dušan Pajić-Dašić (Osman Nuri Hadžić) Elementary School at the Beginning of the 1993-1994 School Year. *Page 180*

6.2. Number of Secondary School Students by Regions of Dobrinja and the Airport Settlement at the Beginning of the 1993-1994 School Year. *Page 181*

6.3. Data on Secondary School Students in Dobrinja and the Airport Settlement and their Secondary Schools of Register during the 1993-1994 School Year. *Page 183*

6.4. Number of Students and Classes in Osman Nuri Hadžić (Dušan Pajić-Dašić) Elementary School at the Beginning of the 1994-1995 School Year. *Page 201*

NOTES ON PRONUNCIATION

c = *ts* as in cats
ć = *tj* (soft) as in tune
č = *ch* (hard) as in chamber
đ = *j* (soft) as in bridge
dž = *j* (hard) as in jet
j = *y* as in yes
lj = *lli* as in million
š = *sh* as in show
ž = *s* as in pleasure

NOTES ON ORTHOGRAPHY AND TERMINOLOGY

Throughout the narrative, and in both the text citations and reference list, I have adhered to the traditional Serbo-Croatian orthographic style. In this regard, all Serbo-Croatian references and terms, with the exception of proper names, are marked by capitalization of the first word only, as in, for example, *Treća gimnazija*. Thus the reference, *Ratni nastavni centar Dobrinja* is marked by the capitalization of the first word, *Ratni*, with the succeeding words in small letters, *nastavni centar*. Because *Dobrinja* is a proper name, it is, of course, capitalized. When these terms or references are used in English, however, all terms or references are capitalized, as in, for example, the Third Gymnasium, or the Dobrinja War School Center.

The language here is identified as Serbo–Croatian, although references in the text sometimes identify the language as Bosnian which is, of course, a result of the breakup of the Socialist Federal Republic of Yugoslavia and the establishment of Bosnia and Herzegovina as an independent state. Although texts and grammar books for the Bosnian language now appear in Sarajevo bookstores, the languages are, for the most part, one and the same.

MAPS OF DOBRINJA

Map of Dobrinja
on page xi

Map of Dobrinja and the Airport Settlement with street names as they existed at the onset of the siege. Located within Novi Grad Municipality on the southwest edge of Sarajevo city, Dobrinja lies in the shadow of Mojmilo Hill to the north and is connected to the city proper by Lukavička cesta, the single roadway that runs between Mojmilo and Nedžarići into Novi Grad. To the south lies Aerodrom Sarajevo, the Sarajevo Airport, where the airport runway separates Dobrinja and the Airport Settlement from the village of Butmir. The Airport Settlement is the complex directly across from Aerodrom Sarajevo, bounded by Rosa Hadživuković Street to the west and north, and includes the complex immediately adjacent to the east bounded by USAOJ-a Street. Map courtesy of JD Geodetski zavod BiH (1993).

Map of the Siege within a Siege of Dobrinja
on page xii

Map of Dobrinja and the Airport Settlement during the siege. An approximation of the siege lines that ran through Dobrinja and the Airport Settlement courtesy of the United Nations Protection Force (UNPROFOR) which drew the lines on an old city map. The siege lines cut through Dobrinja 1 and 4 on the east edge of the settlement, then ran along its southern boundary parallel to the airport runway, and then curved northeast along Prištinska Street through Quadrant C4 of the Airport Settlement cutting it off from Quadrant C5 and the rest of Dobrinja. The line curved northeast to cut off the settlement of Nedžarići from Dobrinja which made travel into Sarajevo proper extremely dangerous. Territory outside the siege lines, with the exception of the airport which was under control of French UNPROFOR troops, was in the hands of the Bosnian Serb Army which manned checkpoints at either end of the airport runway. The siege line parallel to the airport runway marked Bosnian government territory to the southwest side of the airport to include the village of Butmir. Map courtesy of JD Geodetski zavod BiH (n.d.).

Map of Dobrinja

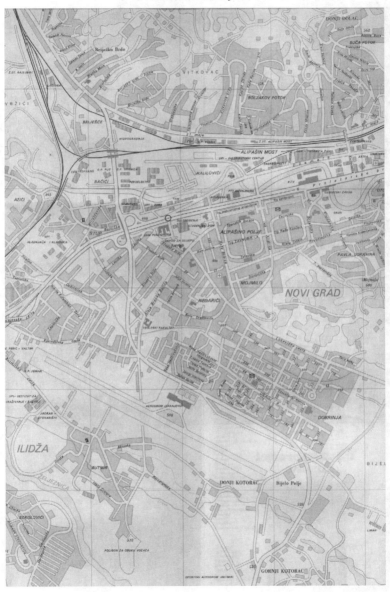

Map of the Siege within a Siege of Dobrinja

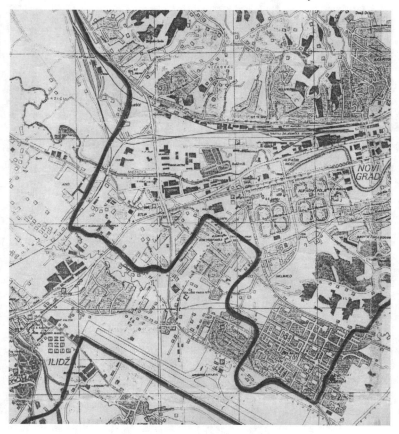

FOREWORD

The beginning of 1992. In so many words, Sarajevo is in hell. It is most difficult in Dobrinja.

In such circumstances, the educational workers of Dobrinja propose that military and civil authorities issue a directive concerning the formation of a Teaching Center, with the assignment that they initiate and organize instructional activities as securely as possible in the field of preschool, elementary, secondary, and higher education, as well as other cultural and public activities.

Hundreds of educational and cultural workers become involved in the work of the Teaching Center: elementary teachers, secondary teachers, professors, engineers, physicians, graduate students, doctors of science, and other professions and occupations.

Already in July 1992, a number of groups of preschoolers were active in Dobrinja, the "stairway schools" and secondary schools were operational, and preparations for the establishment of the General Gimnazija were underway. The Gimnazija officially began with work on 25 January 1993. The newly-established Gimnazija works today in the same premises and very successfully at that.

In collaboration with the Ministry of Education, Science, Culture, and Sports of the Republic of Bosnia and Herzegovina and the Chair of the Pedagogy Department of the Faculty of Philosophy of the University of Sarajevo, the instructional process for students of secondary schools was realized by the course of a linear program of instruction. During the 1992-1993 school year, Dobrinja's gimnazija produced over 20,000 programmed materials, i.e., instructional sheets, which were distributed by predetermined arrangements. The stairways and basements hummed from physics, chemistry, math, and Latin.

Around 800 secondary school students from 25 Sarajevo secondary schools in Dobrinja successfully realized their obligations in acquiring knowledge and completing particular classes.

The significant role of the Teaching Center was enacted in the offering of assistance to students. Consultations and instructive teaching were held on a regular basis and so were examinations.

Thus, up until June 1993, in a grace period, student-fighters stood for 352 examinations before their professors.

At that time, exhibitions, public taping of TV broadcasts, theatrical performances, etc., were organized in the Teaching Center. During the blockade of Dobrinja, the Teaching Center was visited by many prominent persons, scientists, and the highest representatives of the city and the Republic, as well as by many officials of different countries of the world. While performing instruction and other activities in shelters and safe areas, the educational workers of Dobrinja actually watched over and in effect rescued Dobrinja's youth from certain death.

Dobrinja is a settlement of teacher and student heroes. They take pride in how they organized themselves during the war, in how they defended themselves, and in their Teaching Center.

In the Teaching Center, the students learned that tolerance is the highest level of strength and that revenge is the first sign of weakness.
In effect, they learned that love is the antidote for all illness and adversity.

To be writing these lines after 14 years from the time of the establishment of the Teaching Center in Dobrinja, and in the name of the students and teachers, I wish to express sincere gratitude to Professor David Berman, a great man, educational worker—enthusiast and friend, who with this book pulled one piece of war truth about our children and ourselves from oblivion.

Professor, many thanks!

—Smail Vesnić
Sarajevo, July 2005

PREFACE

"Dobrinja was a special place," said Behija Jakić, a teacher at Treća gimnazija, the Third Gymnasium, who was trapped in her Dobrinja residence during the siege of Sarajevo. An apartment complex approximately two kilometers square in the shadow of Mount Igman, set alongside the airport in Butmir, Dobrinja was separated from Sarajevo proper by Mojmilo Hill, connected to the city by a single road below Mojmilo that ran by Nedžarići settlement, controlled by the enemy. Completely cut off from the city proper by enemy forces during the first months of the Bosnian war, and "written off" by political and military leaders, Dobrinja was the siege of Sarajevo at its most severe, often referred as "a siege within a siege" (*opsada u opsadi*). The severity of siege conditions created in those who were trapped there a determined resistance to the enemy and, in the process, Dobrinja became "a symbol of resistance" for all Sarajevo as well. During this time, the educational system became "a function of defense," in the eyes of the military commander, and "the war schools of Dobrinja" became a story in their own right.

When I first began research on schooling during the siege of Sarajevo, I took the bus out to Dobrinja to interview Professor Jakić (the title by which secondary teachers are referred to) about her experiences as a teacher during the war. I thought we were going to talk about her experience as a teacher at Treća gimnazija, located along the banks of the Miljacka River in the center of the city, but we talked instead about her work as a coordinator of secondary education in Dobrinja. Our interview was conducted during a walking tour of the area known as Dobrinja 2, one of the apartment complexes of the settlement, where she located for me the war school classrooms that functioned in the absence of secondary school buildings. Professor Jakić was one of approximately 200 teachers who lived in Dobrinja, many of whom were employed in schools throughout Sarajevo city but trapped within the settlement at the onset of the siege unable to travel to their schools. The September 1993 entry in the "Školski ljetopis" (School Annals) of Treća gimnazija includes the employees' roster, with an asterisk by the names of eight teachers, including Professor Jakić, who are referred to in the following manner:

> Teachers in a permanent working relationship in the Third Gymnasium, but teach in other local communities in the 1993-1994 school year (Treća gimnazija, 1992-1995).

Although employed as a full-time teacher at Treća gimnazija, Behija Jakić nevertheless taught in the local community of Dobrinja during the siege. This particular entry in the "School Annals," and the corresponding interview with Professor Jakić, offered the first insight into the organization of schooling in besieged Dobrinja, not to mention the complexity of the organization of schooling throughout Sarajevo city.

Behija Jakić was one of several teachers whose stories are told in my previous book, *The Heroes of Treća Gimnazija: A War School in Sarajevo, 1992-1995* (2001), a case study of a war school during the siege of the city. This book, *The War Schools of Dobrinja: Reading, Writing, and Resistance During the Siege of Sarajevo*, is a case study of the war schools of the Dobrinja community during the siege, but much of the story of "the war schools of Sarajevo" is relevant here in order to provide a sense of context for schooling throughout the entire city. In this regard, I have integrated passages from my first book into the story of "the war schools of Dobrinja" to provide this wider sense of context so that the reconstruction of schooling in besieged Dobrinja might be better understood.

Since my initial research on Dobrinja schools began with research on Treća gimnazija, there is one section in the earlier book, "The Schools of Bjelave and Dobrinja as Forerunner to the Local Community War Schools," that specifically refers to schooling in Dobrinja as a model for schooling throughout Sarajevo city (2001: 60-67). I wrote these words at the time:

> We might also note the case of Dobrinja, which had no gimnazija prior to the war but where one was created given the numbers of secondary students trapped in the siege within a siege and unable to attend their schools of registration. The local community responsibilities for Gimnazija Dobrinja were simply assigned to the Dobrinja Educational Center (Nastavni centar Dobrinja), referred to also as the Dobrinja War School Center (Ratni nastavni centar Dobrinja), which had coordinated instruction at both elementary and secondary levels throughout the besieged suburb. The story of the reconstruction of education in the

besieged settlement of Dobrinja, not to mention the story of the siege of Dobrinja itself, remains as but another story to be told of the siege of Sarajevo. (2001: 90)

Six years later, thanks to the support of Alan H. Jones and Heather L. Hazuka, the publisher and associate publisher at Caddo Gap Press, I am now able to tell "the story of the reconstruction of education in the besieged settlement of Dobrinja." Here in this book, the story will focus primarily upon those early efforts to reconstruct the schools under the most difficult of wartime conditions. In a particular sense, I am here to tell the story of the war schools of Dobrinja as they struggled to function during the early months of the siege and the story of the Dobrinja War School Center as it assumed primary administrative responsibility for organizing and integrating these schools. Indeed, the story begins with the beginning of the siege of Sarajevo in spring 1992, with the destruction of the three elementary schools in the settlement, with no secondary school in existence, and Dobrinja totally cut off from Sarajevo proper. The difficult and courageous decisions made by Dobrinja educators during this time determined the course of school events over the years of the siege, and this story will highlight those decisions and the adaptations made by Dobrinja educators in response to wartime conditions.

With the 1993-1994 school year beginning on time, and the routine of the regular school year set in motion, the Dobrinja War School Center faded out of existence in November 1993 as the responsibility for schooling was returned to the respective schools themselves now under the administration of the Sarajevo City Secretariat for Education. At this juncture, the story changes significantly, in my view, where the routine of the regular school year suggests another stage of education and adaptation during the war. Here in these pages, my hope is that the story of the war schools of Dobrinja serves to complement the story of Treća gimnazija, a war school in Sarajevo, offering one additional study as educational researchers seek to piece together the story of the war schools of Sarajevo during the siege of the city. Together, perhaps these two books will provide a greater understanding of schooling under siege, along with an appreciation for the work of Bosnian students and teachers, whose adaptations to wartime conditions might provide us all with a greater understanding of how school educators might respond to a similar set of conditions should we have to face them ourselves.

With the completion of the Treća gimnazija book, the research on schooling in Dobrinja began in spring 2001 under the auspices of a Fulbright Scholar Award where I was located in the Department of

Pedagogy, Faculty of Philosophy, University of Sarajevo. The initial results of the Fulbright research, and a forerunner to this book, recently appeared as "The War Schools of Dobrinja: Schooling under Siege in a Sarajevo Community," a title in *The Carl Beck Papers in Russian and East European Studies*, published by the Center for Russian and East European Studies of the University of Pittsburgh (2005). I must offer gracious thanks to Robert Hayden, professor of anthropology and director of the Center for Russian and East European Studies (REES) at the University of Pittsburgh, for his continuing support of my research. Bob's wife, Milica Bakić-Hayden, has assisted me on numerous occasions as well, and Stefan Hayden, their son, assisted me with translations of school documents. Eileen O'Malley, associate director of REES, deserves my heartfelt thanks as always for her support of my work in a variety of ways whether I am off to Sarajevo or to Priština.

For assistance during my research under the Fulbright award, special thanks go to Professor Adila Pašalić-Kreso who served as my host and colleague on the Faculty, and who opened doors for me that otherwise were inaccessible. I would add that, with the renaming of Sarajevo streets during the war, there is now a street in Dobrinja named after her father, a distinguished professor on the Faculty of Philosophy, Ulica Esada Pašalića, or Esad Pašalić Street which, prior to the war, was called Salvador Allende Street, where the First Stairway School Dobrinja 2B, cited later in this book, was located. Professor Pašalić-Kreso and her husband, Mirsad, were wonderful hosts to me and deserve special mention for their courtesy over the years as Mirsad "organized" events for me, my daughter Jessica, and my good friend, Gaye Burkett, whether in Sarajevo, Travnik, Jajce, Mostar, or Dubrovnik.

Mirjana Mavrak, now a docent (the equivalent of assistant professor) in the Department of Pedagogy, Faculty of Philosophy, and her husband, Ranko, became special friends as well, and I knew that I could always count on them if needed. Indeed, I first met Mirjana when she worked for the United Nations Children's Fund (UNICEF), during the war, and, to this day, I still vividly remember the tour she offered, in March 1995, of Sarajevo under siege and, in particular, her story of the *Inat kuća* (the Spite House) that exemplified the spirit of the *Sarajlije* trapped inside the siege lines.

Amir Pušina, the higher assistant in the Department of Pedagogy, Faculty of Philosophy, who received a Visiting Fulbright Scholar Award to study at Florida International University in the United States, became a special friend as well. Once a soldier in the Army of the Republic of Bosnia and Herzegovina (ARBiH), Amir provided valuable insight on the defense of Sarajevo and, as an educator, valuable insight into schooling as a form of resistance to the enemy. I am especially thankful to Amir and his wife, Merjem, for the kindness they showed my daughter, Jessica, and me, escorting us around Sarajevo. I especially enjoyed the time with my three colleagues from the Department of Pedagogy and their spouses, Adila and Mirsad Kreso, Mirjana and Ranko Mavrak, and Amir and Merjem Pušina, on evenings at the Park Prinčeva, next to the Pušina family household high on Hrid, offering a striking view of Sarajevo at dusk as the sparkling of lights flashed across Baščaršija in the old quarter of the city.

During the Fulbright, I lived in the area known as *Aerodromsko naselje* (the Airport Settlement), one of the Dobrinja neighborhoods, in order to initiate research in the field. My initial hosts were Bojana Burlović, and her daughters, Maja and Sanja who, at the time, attended Skender Kulenović Elementary School. The arrangement was made possible by Ibrahim Sejfović, once a resident of Dobrinja himself where, as a young boy, he was severely wounded by an enemy mortar shell chasing a soccer ball into the street and later medically evacuated to the United States for treatment at a rehabilitation center near Pittsburgh. Ibrahim has continually assisted me with translations and, during our conversations, we would talk about drinking coffee in Baščaršija. I'm pleased to note that we did indeed drink coffee there during my first Fulbright when Ibrahim returned to Sarajevo through an internship with the United States Agency for International Development (USAID). Today Ibro is an American citizen who, after working for the United States Immigration and Naturalization Service (USINS), is now the chief executive officer of Immigration Solutions LLC, in Columbus, Ohio.

As a resident of the Airport Settlement, I visited all three elementary schools, and the one secondary school in Dobrinja, to talk with school administrators, teachers, and former students, about their memories of schooling under siege. Living in the neighborhood (*komšiluk*) provided me the opportunity to become a neighbor (*komšija*) myself and, hence, to talk with my neighbors on a regular basis, hanging out with them at "Kedaš" on the edge of the Airport Settlement talking about the times. Once an upscale townhouse complex, the settlement was in the slow process of rebuilding and, as I began this writing, the devastation that marked the fighting along the old frontline was still seen in the ghostly remains of the buildings where the walls look like sieves from the shelling and firefights. The apartments of the street on which I lived, Andreja Andrejevića today, Georgi Dimitrova at the time of the war, had been reconstructed, but a walk to the bus stop led onto Prištinska Street as it twisted its way through back alleys and the omnipresent reminders of the war.

From my initial research, I became aware of an entity referred to as the *Ratni nastavni centar Dobrinja* (Dobrinja War School Center)[1] and of a number of the educators who worked in the Center and were involved in the reconstruction of schooling during the war. I found two articles in Bosnian educational journals, both entitled "Ratni nastavni centar Dobrinja," by Smail Vesnić, who explained the reconstruction of schooling in Dobrinja in structural terms as an educational adaptation to siege conditions. The first article reviews the organization of the Center and lists nine sections (*odjela*) and the section managers (*rukovodilac*) who functioned under the administrative framework of the Center (1994). Just after the war, an updated article contained much of the same information but, given adaptations to a war situation, included a revised list of eight sections and section managers (1996). These articles led me directly to Smail Vesnić, now an expert advisor for the Ministry of Education and Science (Ministarstvo obrazovanja i nauke) of the Federation of Bosnia and Herzegovina.

In the words of Professor Vesnić, the former director of the Dobrinja War School Center, and the former director of Gimnazija Dobrinja, "When I remember those days, I think about how impossible it was to organize a school." During the summer of 1992, Smail Vesnić and his colleagues created the Dobrinja War School Center which served as the administrative framework for elementary education, with three schools and no buildings, and for secondary education, for students who had attended 27 schools/centers across the city and no building. In one of our conversations in his office over Bosnian coffee, Professor Vesnić remembered the times. "Although it was August 1993," he said, "we were told that the Americans would come and write about how we did it, how we reconstructed the schools." Today, his words offer testimony to courageous educators under siege in a struggle for the very lives of their students. "We didn't fight with guns," said the man who created schooling when nothing was there. "We fought in this way, to defend our homes, our families." In the process, "we saved those kids. We moved them from the streets to the classroom, and we saved them" (2001).

I would like to say to Professor Vesnić, who wrote the Foreword to this book, that indeed, "the Americans have come" to write about how you did it. There is perhaps no single educator who has done more for the teachers and students of besieged Sarajevo than Smail Vesnić, and there is certainly no single educator who has done more for the teachers and students of besieged Dobrinja. Indeed, I could not have written this book without his support, and I am deeply indebted to him for his support of my work which, in turn, provides me with the opportunity to tell his story to a wider audience.

Over the course of my research, Professor Vesnić assisted me in arranging interviews with five of the section managers of the Dobrinja War School Center. My interview with Halil Burić, who was manager for two of the original nine sections, the Higher Education Section and the Personnel Training Section, revealed the depth of the managers' responsibilities. I would like to thank Halil Burić and his family for their hospitality during the time I lived in the Airport Settlement. Professor Burić lives on Franca Prešerna Street and, on those dark days of 17-20 June 1992, personally witnessed the slaughter, the panic, and the fear as the enemy advanced up his street. Forced from his home at the beginning of the siege, he took me to the remains of the abandoned buildings along Prištinska where he would look through a small bullet hole in a wall back down Franca Prešerna across the frontline towards the enemy who occupied his home. Today his apartment is reconstructed, but the window frames still bear the entrance wounds of the shells that were fired upon him and his family.

Critical interviews were conducted with Seniha Bulja, manager of the Elementary Education Section, and Ilija Šobot, manager of the Secondary Education Section, of the Dobrinja War School Center, since they were the two primary figures responsible for coordinating the work of the elementary and secondary schools. In the stark words of Professor Bulja, "The children of Dobrinja can't go to school. They don't have any. These schools are dead and destroyed monuments. It is war." In response to such conditions, she organized the first "stairway school" (*haustorska škola*) in her local Dobrinja neighborhood during the summer of 1992 "in a building that was on the frontline. You will have to acknowledge," she continued, "the cheek and the courage" (1994).

These interviews led me to several document collections that provided the operational plans for the organization of schooling as well as the chronology of events during the reconstruction of the schools. Both Professor Bulja and Professor Šobot were particularly helpful providing me with invaluable documents that describe the organization and operation of both elementary and secondary education. There in her small office, Professor Bulja pulled down cardboard boxes filled with documents from closet shelves that she alone has preserved to include the "Programska osnova rada nastavnog centra u šk. 1992/93 god." (Basic Work Program of the Teaching Center in the 1992-1993 School Year). Given the articles by Smail Vesnić noting the organization of the Center, the "Basic Work Program" provides an overview of the organization of each one of the original nine Center sections.

One critical document provided by Professor Bulja was the "Almanah" (Almanac) of the Dobrinja War School Center which charts the history of the Center and the course of events from the onset of the siege in spring 1992 through to its closure in November 1993. On the one hand, the "Almanac" entries provide a firsthand account of schooling in Dobrinja as follows:

> 15 August 1992, *Saturday*: At 6:00 P.M., two shells hit the War School Center ... At that time, 40 people were inside the Center. Fortunately, nobody got killed but two boys were wounded. There was great damage to the Center building. Classes were continued after the attack ended.

On the other hand, the entries offer poignant reflections of life under siege conditions:

> 21 July 1993, *Wednesday*: What appeared to be a peaceful day for Dobrinja turned into hell around 1:30. There were new victims. The bloodthirsty beast can never get enough of human blood. It is swimming in it today too. How far does that human mind reach? (Nastavni centar, 1992-1993).

In addition to the "Almanac," the "Ljetopis" (Annals) of Gimnazija Dobrinja records the beginnings of the *gimnazija*, initially formed under the administration of the Dobrinja War School Center and, as the Center was gradually phased out, the "Annals" continued to chronicle events through the remaining years of the siege. I would like to thank Sabiha Miskin, the school director of Gimnazija Dobrinja, for her assistance during my research and, in particular, in acquiring a copy of the "Annals" as well as documents from the early years of the siege that are presently stored in the school. Director Miskin personally helped me carry, if I remember correctly, twelve large boxes of school documents out of Gimnazija Dobrinja, which we loaded into her car and then unloaded again, carrying them up a flight of stairs and into my apartment. From the pages of these documents, I came to view the experience of Dobrinja educators from the permission slips for young men to be excused from class for duty on the frontline.

At the elementary level, the collection of documents includes the annals or almanacs from two of the three Dobrinja elementary schools,[2] the "Almanah" of Simon Bolivar Elementary School (Skender Kulenović) and the "Ljetopis škole" (Annals of the School) of Dušan Pajić-Dašić Elementary School (Osman Nuri Hadžić). I would like to thank Aida Musić, director of Skender Kulenović Elementary School,[3] and Narcis Polimac, director of Osman Nuri Hadžić Elementary School, for their assistance in collecting these documents and for their continuing support of my research over the years, and I have tried to acknowledge their work in the pages of this book. I should also note that I met with Faruk Jabučar, director of Ćamil Sijarić Elementary School (Nikola Tesla), but was unable to obtain the same school documents.

I should add here that many of these documents are difficult to read, which even native Bosnian speakers readily admit, so the translation of these documents has proved especially difficult. While the directives, orders, and decisions are usually typed, many other such documents are handwritten, most notably, the annals and the almanacs, as well as the minutes of the Teacher's Council. As with any such school documents, it is rather doubtful that the writer expected much less cared about some future researcher reviewing them, and a foreign researcher at that, so minimal attention appears to have been given to whether these documents could be read, much less translated, or not. No doubt there are some mistakes here in the translations from the Bosnian, for which a later researcher may hold me accountable, and for which the ultimate responsibility is my own.

I must also thank Severin Montina, deputy minister, Ministry of Education and Science, Federation of Bosnia and Herzegovina, the former director of the Republican Fund for Secondary Education, and a member of the Teacher's Council of the Dobrinja War School Center, and Dr. Enes Kujundžić, director of the National and University Library of Bosnia and Herzegovina, and a member of the Teacher's Council of the Dobrinja War School Center, and manager of the Scientific Research Section. Both Minister Montina and Dr. Kujundžić provided me with library resources, valuable documents, and continue to assist me with my research on schooling during the postwar era.

I am especially indebted to Azra Kujundžić, an economist with OMV Istrabenz, and once the elementary and secondary coordinator for Quadrant C5 for the Dobrinja War School Center, for her assistance. Azra provided me with access to her own personal records, including her personal journal, that provided the documentary basis upon which to reconstruct the efforts of the coordinators of the war school regions and, in particular, provided a case study of the reorganization of schooling in Quadrant C5 of the Airport Settlement. The insight she offered concerning her own experience as coordinator of Quadrant C5 has proved invaluable, and I wish to acknowledge here my appreciation and my admiration for her work, which is also expressed in the pages of the "Almanah" of Simon Bolivar Elementary School.

I would like to express my heartfelt thanks to Hajriz Bećirović who, as commanding officer of Territorial Defense (TO) forces, organized ragtag groups of citizen defenders who held the lines during the early stages of the assaults on Dobrinja months before the 1st Dobrinja Brigade of the ARBiH was formed. I interviewed Hajriz on at least three occasions in his office in the Ministry for War Veterans (Ministarstvo za boračka pitanja) of Sarajevo Canton where, as minister, he is now responsible for addressing the concerns of those veterans who sacrificed so much in the defense of Sarajevo. In spite of his schedule and the demands of his workload, he was always available to me and, with courtesy and dignity, answered the most difficult of questions. It was Hajriz Bećirović who, together with Adnan Tetarić, developed the organizational framework that integrated military and civilian defense during the early months of the siege and, through Smail Vesnić, created the Dobrinja War School Center. I can only hope that I am able to do justice to the heroic efforts of these three men: Hajriz Bećirović, Adnan Tetarić, and Smail Vesnić, in the pages of this book.

I would like to thank the many former students of the Dobrinja schools for their assistance with this book as well. Schooling was difficult during these times and particularly difficult for young men of high school age since many of them also served on the frontline. Among them was Damir Hadžić, a 16-year old student, and soldier, at the time, "but I was not the youngest." The times were "unbelievable experiences for everyone," said Damir, "but especially for guys my age ... The war caught me at that age, and I came to the realization that we had to live in a different community" (2001). Today Damir is the mayor of Novi Grad Municipality who works to unite those living in Dobrinja 1 and Dobrinja 4 whom he once fought against. His written excuse to miss classes for frontline duty was one of the documents found in the files of Gimnazija Dobrinja that led me to other school administrative forms, and illustrates the importance of connecting the oral and the written lines of investigation.

Furthermore, I would like to thank all those individuals who assisted me with translations of documents and, in the process, offered me both valuable conversation and language lessons as well. Most notably, Jasmina Hadžić, a program assistant for the World Bank, and who now works at the World Bank offices in Washington, D.C., served as the primary translator of the Treća gimnazija book, and she has continued to assist me with translations of documents for the Dobrinja book as well. Jasmina has proved over time a wonderful translator and a good friend, and I have enjoyed her family barbeques and her father's green lawn at their *vikendica* in Rakovica just outside of Sarajevo. Larisa Kasumagić, coordinator of Creativus, the Youth Center for Communication and Creative Learning, based in Zenica, and who graduated from Cornell University in Ithaca, New York, helped me translate a variety of documents from the schools of Dobrinja as well. I spoke with Larisa's students at the American Corner in Zenica, and I would add that I very much appreciate my conversations with her and the insight she has offered into the mindset of students under siege.

Ema Bučan, a student of linguistics in the Faculty of Philosophy, is another primary translator of the many documents from Dobrinja schooling and has proved invaluable in a variety of ways, from introductions to arranging meetings to helping me with basic necessities. Ema has also been my language instructor during my time in Dobrinja, as has Ema's best friend, Luljeta Koshi, a student of Bosnian language and literature at the Faculty of Philosophy, who came to the University of Pittsburgh through the Bosnia-Herzegovina Undergraduate Program. I would like to thank the entire Koshi family for their wonderful courtesy and, of course, the wonderful dinner, coffee, and conversations, during my stays in Dobrinja.

I must thank Mevsud Kapetanović of the FIVA photography studio, located in Dobrinja 1, for sharing with me his incredible collection of photographs from the years of the siege. I first happened upon FIVA in my search for photos of schooling and found to my amazement that his collection of school pictures was but part of his collection of pictures of everyday life during the siege. As I offered Mevsud my business card from the University of Pittsburgh, and began to inquire about his photographs, minutes stretched into hours, only to realize that he was checking my credentials online from the University website. Once he realized that I was authentic, the atmosphere changed dramatically, and we drank *Sarajevsko pivo*, Sarajevo beer, to a business agreement which evolved into a friendship to this day. I am indebted to Mevsud Kapetanović for copies of his photographs and his permission to use these photographs in this book. I am also indebted to Miroslav Kordić for his photographs as well.

I would like to thank both Sead Hodžić, director of the Survey Institute of Bosnia and Herzegovina (JP Geodetski zavod BiH), and Smail Hodžić, the assistant director of the Property Rights Services, Survey Business and Real Estate Land Registry (Službe za imovinsko-pravne, Geodetske poslove i katastar nekretnina), Novi Grad Municipality, for providing me with maps of Novi Grad Municipality, where Dobrinja is located, and giving permission to use these maps in this book. Mirko Popović of the Federal Institute for Statistics (Federalni zavod za statistiku) provided me with invaluable statistical and census information important for understanding the demographics of the Dobrinja area. Mersa Kustura, the chief of the Section for Local Community and Local Government (Služba za mjesne zajednica i lokalnu samoupravu), and Želimir Lalić, deputy mayor, Novi Grad Municipality, provided especially valuable information on the local communities of Dobrinja and the Airport Settlement.

I must offer sincere thanks to Elizabeta Delalić, the cultural and civic affairs specialist in the Office of Public Affairs, the United States Embassy Sarajevo, as well as so many of the Bosnian staffers to include Adis Bešić and Alen Savatić in particular. It was Elizabeta who, on both Fulbrights, made the connections and set up the appointments with so many of those officials and educators mentioned above. Anyone who has worked in Bosnia knows full well the difficulty of making such connections, and I am indebted to Elizabeta, and to Adis and Alen, who made many such connections and appointments for me. Adis and Alen helped me in a variety of ways too numerous to mention whether concerns over my daughter or conversations over the Bosnian language and vocabulary. Thanks to Ivana Bušić, the librarian at the American Reference Center in the Office of Public Affairs, who assisted me with references, videotapes, and translations.

Finally, I would like to acknowledge Safia Rasidović here, the associate in what is today the Ministry of Education and Science of Sarajevo Canton, who passed away on 2 March 2006 during my second Fulbright fellowship to Bosnia and Herzegovina. As I noted in my earlier book, without Safia's support, I would still be sitting in the offices of the Ministry drinking Bosnian coffee without a clue. I owe it all to Safia who took an interest in my work, dragging me out of her office one day, pushing me onto a bus to Hrasno, leading to conversations with the teachers of Treća gimnazija, exposing me to the lives of students and teachers under siege. I very much miss drinking Bosnian coffee with Safia there in the spare offices of the Ministry, chatting about the events of the day, Safia always asking about my daughter. Doing research on the war schools of Sarajevo will simply not be the same without Safia around these days.

I am indebted to all of these wonderful people for their assistance in writing this book, for sharing something of their memories with me of a time when their world was falling apart. This book, much like the Treća gimnazija book, is difficult to write in this regard, perhaps a schizophrenic attempt at best to write an academic analysis of an intensely human experience, of a struggle for survival under the most desperate of conditions, of a struggle to save the children of Dobrinja. In academic terms, this book is a case study of the war schools of the Dobrinja set within the background of schooling throughout the besieged city of Sarajevo. In more human terms, this is the story of the teachers and students of Dobrinja, the students who asserted their right to their education and the teachers who answered their call, as did the teachers and students of Treća gimnazija, amidst the pathos of everyday life under siege.

How would we as teachers have reacted in their situation? How would we have lived our lives in besieged Dobrinja? Would we have survived? "The answers to such questions are generally feared," wrote Anna Pawłeczyńska, of life in the concentration camps of Holocaust Europe that come so vividly to mind in the aftermath of the camps of Bosnia and Herzegovina. "People today do not desire a knowledge of life which compels the asking of such questions" (1979: 4). Here I thank Barbara Burstin of the Department of History, University of Pittsburgh, for educating me on the clandestine schools of the East European ghettos during the Holocaust and the parallels to the war schools of besieged Bosnian towns, as well as to the questions that such parallels pose to us as educators today. In this regard, we can be assured that the teachers and students of Dobrinja who are portrayed in this book, like their predecessors in the ghettos of Eastern Europe, acted with courage and dignity, along with a sense of Bosnian spite, as they attempted to reconstruct schooling and, in the process, reconstruct a sense of community under siege. It is my hope that this book does justice to their stories.

Notes

[1] I have taken the liberty of translating *Ratni nastavni centar Dobrinja* as the Dobrinja War School Center. While *nastavni* translates from the Bosnian or Serbo-Croatian as teaching or instructional, *nastav/a* translates as teaching, instruction, or schooling. *Ratni nastavni centar Dobrinja* reads more easily in

English, at least in my view, as the Dobrinja War School Center, and suggests the all-encompassing meaning of the designation. *Nastavni centar*, when written alone, and *Nastavni centar Dobrinja*, which appears on many documents, are translated as the Teaching Center or the Dobrinja Teaching Centar. In the reference section, all Center documents, other than those with an author's or editors' citation, are located under the reference, Nastavni centar Dobrinja.

Throughout the text, in both citations and references, I have adhered to the traditional Serbo-Croatian orthographic style. All Serbo-Croatian or Bosnian references and terms, with the exceptions of proper names, are marked by capitalization of the first word only, as in *Ratni nastavni centar* (Dobrinja is capitalized because it is a proper name). Standard English capitalization will be used in the translations.

² The three Dobrinja elementary schools are as follows:

1. Dušan Pajić-Dašić Elementary School (Osnovna škola Dušan Pajić-Dašić) which became Osman Nuri Hadžić Elementary School, located on the military frontline and the postwar Inter-Entity Boundary Line on the eastern end of the settlement.

2. Simon Bolivar Elementary School (Osnovna škola Simon Bolivar) which became Skender Kulenović Elementary School, located in the middle of the settlement, and shelled into ruin on 15 May 1992.

3. Nikola Tesla Elementary School (Osnovna škola Nikola Tesla) which became Ćamil Sijarić Elementary School, located on the military frontline on the eastern end of the settlement.

The names of the schools were changed on 6 April 1994, two years into the war, and because the primary focus here is on the reconstruction of schooling during the early years of the war, the schools will generally be referred to by their original school names. In the reference section, the two school journals that were kept through the years of the war (1992-1995) will be referred to by their original school reference as well.

³ The poetry and essays cited in this book, to include the epigraph and chapter title pages, were written by students of Simon Bolivar/Skender Kulenović Elementary School during the war.

Several of these writings first appeared in *Putokazi* (Highways), published by the Dobrinja War School Center in March 1993 as a combined issue, numbers one and two. Gordana Pijetlovic was the main editor.

Aida Musić, the school director, also provided me with student writings when I asked her about testing conducted by the Institute for Researching Crimes Against Humanity (Institut za istraživanje zločina protiv čovječnosti) of elementary students who lost one or both parents, and those who were forced to leave their homes, to determine the manner in which they were affected by the war. According to the entry, there were multiple-choice questions as well as short essays "on how they imagine their lives to be after the war is finished, how they imagine their lives in peace," which were then submitted to the Pedagogical Institute in Sarajevo.

In the postwar era, students' poetry and essays from the war years appeared in the Skender Kulenović *Monografija: Djeca i škole rastu zajedno, 1992-1998*. (Monograph: Children and Schools Grow Together), and I have cited several of these writings as well.

The fact that the students' writings are from three different sources would explain, for example, why the stories of Lidija Ilić were written at different times. "There was an Aggressive Dog," which introduces Chapter One, was written when Lidija was in 6th grade, and published in *Putokazi* in March 1993, while "The Book," which introduces Chapter Four, was part of the collection of writings given to me by the school director, and was written when she was in 7th grade.

Čarobna Svjetiljka

Bila je jedino što je sjalo i nije se ugasila
Kad smo nestajali u boli i skrivali se od smrti …
Kad smo tražili svoje izgubljeno ja u provalijama vremena
Kad smo davali i kad nam je davano …
Kad smo gubili i kad nam je oduzimano …
Kad smo živjeli … Kad smo voljeli … Gorjela je
Kad smo pjevali i slavili, tugovali i žalili …
Kad su nam grudi pucale od čežnje, kad smo brali sumorno cvijeće svojih otetih
Proljeća i kad bi nas zameli snjegovi naših beskrajnih zima …
Kad smo gubili … Kad smo trpjeli …
Kad smo željeli bar ponekad uživati u osjećanju sreće—proste, ljudske … Gorjela je
Kad bismo oćutali pokoju nepravdu … Ili mnogo njih …
Kad bismo gledali vrijeme kako prolazi, djecu kako se rađaju, sebe kako starimo
Ili rastemo …Kad smo potiho uživali u tišini i neku, u neku jesen … ili ljeto ili zimu …
Kad smo se jutrom budili i osjećali zbog toga sreću ili strah ili možda oboje
I tad gorjela je.
I kad smo usnuli ona sja ispod naših spuštenih kapaka.
Kad se grlimo, ono sja iz naših dlanova.
Kad volimo sja nam us srcima
Kad žicvimo ona osvjetljava naš duh.
Čarobna svjetiljka njegove besmrtnosti.

—Dijala Hasanbegović, VIII razred
Osnovna škola Skender Kulenović

Magical Lantern

It was the only thing that glowed and did not die out
When we disappeared in agony and were in hiding from death …
When we looked for our missing in the depths of time
When we gave and when we were given …
When we lost and when it was taken from us …
When we lived … when we cherished … It glowed
When we sang and celebrated, grieved and mourned …
When our chests burst from longing, when we somberly picked the flowers of our spring
 and when we would be covered by the snows of our endless winters …
When we lost … When we suffered …
When we wanted at least sometimes to find pleasure in a feeling of happiness—common,
 human … It glowed
When we would suppress any injustice … Or many of them …
When we would watch how time passes, how children come into the world, how we grow
 old or how we grow …
When we secretly found pleasure in silence, in some autumn … or summer or winter …
When we would wake up in the morning and because of that feel happiness or fear or
 perhaps both
And then it glowed.
And when we fell asleep it glows in front of our sagging eyelids.
When we embrace, it glows from our palms.
When we love it glows in our hearts
When we live it illuminates our spirit.
Magical lantern of its immortality.

—Dijala Hasanbegović, 8th grade
Skender Kulenović Elementary School

8 March 1995

Journey into a State of Fear

PROLOGUE

Our Cry for a World without Fear

In peace I feared the dark, next to dogs and mathematics. We are already four years into the war. New fears came. I know, I saw, and adults are afraid the same as me. Only, now all of us are afraid of the same things. It was wonderful as long as I was afraid of the dark, next to dogs and mathematics. That lasted as long as—childhood lasted. This war is a great injustice, the greatest injustice against children who can no longer be that anymore.

My dream is a world without fear. I dream that peace returns and that not one child ever gets to know the horror.

—Dino Makarević, 7th Grade
Skender Kulenović Elementary School

From the heights of Mount Igman, where the venues of the 1984 Winter Olympics now lie in ruin, along with Olympic promises of brotherhood and unity, the view of the Sarajevo landscape beyond is breathtaking. Gazing off into the distance, one can see, at the foot of the mountain below, the Željeznica River flowing down from the mountains and into the Bosna River downstream, not far from Vrelo Bosna, the Springs of the Bosnia, pouring out onto the landscape at Ilidža. Kasindolski Stream and the Dobrinja River which, despite its name, is a channeled stream smaller than Kasindolski, flow through the valley as well, creating a sense of life and comfort there in the settlement set within the high mountain walls.

Directly across the valley lies Mojmilo brdo, Mojmilo Hill, the point of a long ridgeline that runs down from the heights of Mount Trebević, isolating the city of Sarajevo proper from the large suburb of apartment complexes together known as Dobrinja. The runways of the Sarajevo airport stretch out alongside the length of the apartment complexes that run up the valley, separating the apartments of Dobrinja from the village of Butmir resting in the shadow of Mount Igman. In fact, that portion of the apartment complex directly across from the airport entrance is called, appropriately enough, Aerodromsko naselje, or the Airport Settlement, distinctive in its amphitheater blueprint design and modest condominium appearance from the taller high-rise apartments and massive rectangular blocks of Dobrinja itself.

Yet today when I stand on the heights of Mount Igman, inhaling the beauty of the landscape, I find myself unable to escape the memories of my first trip over these mountains and down into besieged Sarajevo—questioning my sanity all the while. I observed, and then experienced these scenes, for the very first time late on a cold Wednesday afternoon, 8 March 1995, as a passenger in a Land Rover on the mountain road known as the Blue Route (*Plavi put*) on UN maps, up, over, and down Igman, and then around the airport, entering the city during the latter months of the siege. In the clarity of the cold mountain air, as the sun was setting on a late winter day, I remember the landscape exposed below Igman, and I remember the stark realization that we were on our way into the siege of Sarajevo.

I was poised there on the heights of Mount Igman, the lead faculty member of the University of Pittsburgh's Bosnia Management Team, the contract agency for the Program for Cooperation in Educational Policy, Planning, and Development in Bosnia-Herzegovina, a United Nations

Children's Fund (UNICEF) project. Other than the Team leader, Seth Spaulding, the director of the Institute for International Studies in Education (IISE) in the School of Education of the University of Pittsburgh, and the first faculty member into Bosnia, few other faculty were even interested in the Bosnia project, designed to assist in the reconstruction of schooling in the midst of the Bosnian war, much less coming to Bosnia itself.

Only four days beforehand, on Saturday, 4 March 1995, I flew into Sarajevo under siege, landing at Sarajevo Airport amidst the snow and the wind, but never actually entering the city proper that day. Instead, the following entry in my journal records my view of Sarajevo as we landed and my impressions of the situation at Sarajevo Airport:

> I saw Sarajevo off in the distance set between the snow-covered mountains. A magnificent setting!!! But the reality of Sarajevo Airport hits you immediately.
> Camis, helmets, weapons.
> Bunkers around UN vehicles.
> Sandbags around everything, piled high around bunkers which served as the terminal buildings.
> Soldiers—UN—everywhere, and moving fast.
> Soldiers helping haul baggage out of the plane onto flats. Lifts then hauled flats to the side of the runway by the exit where we picked it up.
> Sandbags and soldiers—it is all deadly serious. I had returned to a combat zone.

It would be four days after that entry before I would see Sarajevo again, however, to stand there on the heights of Mount Igman after a long and difficult journey on the Blue Route over the mountains of Middle Bosnia, and gaze off into the distance towards the besieged city, with the stark realization that I was about to enter the siege of Sarajevo.

My arrival on Igman was via a prolonged detour through the town of Zenica approximately 50 kilometers northwest of Sarajevo city. On the day that I arrived at Sarajevo Airport, I was met by a UNICEF driver who hustled me through the UNPROFOR (United Nations Protection Force) checkpoints at the airport entrance and around the outskirts of the city, bound for Zenica, located in the heart of the Republika Bosna, the Bosnian Republic. We were thinking about locating the project in Zenica, in the area known as Middle Bosnia, well within the territory controlled by the Bosnian Army, for security reasons and for easier access given the siege of Sarajevo and the difficulty of entering and leaving the capital city itself. In the words of one Bosnian Army soldier I met during my time in Zenica:

3

The people here in Zenica really don't know war. Zenica is untouched. Yes, people starved here a year ago when there was fighting outside the city and the roads were cut off. But this has ended and Zenica doesn't know the war.

During my four days in Zenica, I visited schools and talked with teachers and administrators about the immensity of the problems they had while trying to organize schooling during the war. We also travelled outside of the city into the mountains, to the villages of Arnauti and Babino, where we visited rural schools as well as schools in refugee centers for children from the Bosnian Krajina. On our way up into the mountains, my UNICEF host, Svetlana Pavelić-Durović, "asked if I was afraid of the *mujahadeen*" for there were training camps in the area, and these guys were threatening internationals since many international aid organizations were located in the Zenica area. We also visited schools in the Lašva River Valley around Vitez and Novi Travnik, travelling by the village of Ahmići where, on 16 April 1993, 116 Bosniac (Bosnian Muslim) villagers were massacred as their households were set afire with the inhabitants inside (Hedl, 2000).

Four days after flying into Sarajevo Airport, we travelled from Zenica back down to besieged Sarajevo once again. Since our UNICEF driver was carrying a load of computer equipment, we would travel the Blue Route over Mount Igman, primarily through Bosnian Army territory, into the besieged capital. The 50 kilometer trip from Zenica southeast down to Sarajevo was once a relatively straight drive on the highway but, at Visoko, we turned southwest instead, over to Kiseljak, and then on to Kreševo, where we took the mountain road over to Tarčin. Much of this portion of the trip, however, was a journey through Bosnian Croat checkpoints that defined the boundaries of the self-styled Croat statelet, the Hrvatska Republika Herceg-Bosna, the Croatian Republic of Bosnia-Herzegovina, carved out of Middle Bosnia in the midst of the Bosnian Republic, and carved out of much of Herzegovina as well. My journal for that day reads:

> From Kreševo, we took one treacherous mountain road over to Tarčin. Most of it was dirt, mud right now, one lane, but somehow trucks and tankers would squeeze by. The Kiseljak–Kreševo road was in Croatian territory; I noticed the Croatian flags in Kiseljak first. The Kreševo checkpoint was Croatian one side, Bosnian the other, UN in-between. The road to Tarčin, over high spectacular mountains, is not even on the map.
>
> At Tarčin, we hit the paved road to Pazarić, a short but another spectacular drive with Mount Bjelasnica, snow-capped, off to the right and Mount Igman dead ahead. At Pazarić, we hit a Bosnian Army

checkpoint and had to wait about 45 minutes, with traffic from Mount Igman coming this way. They wanted to hold Sarajevo traffic. They let us go around 4:00 P.M. and our ride up the Blue Route and onto Mount Igman was simply spectacular.

While much of our journey was through the Bosnian Republic, as well as through the Croat Republic of Bosnia-Herzegovina, the territory controlled by the Bosnian Serbs, the self-styled statelet known as the Republika Srpska, the Serbian Republic of Bosnia, encircled the suburbs of greater Sarajevo. This was territory controlled by the Bosnian Serb Army (BSA), and we passed through this territory with great difficulty, often with contentious struggles at BSA checkpoints, on our earlier journey from Sarajevo Airport around the city suburbs on our way to Zenica.

Our journey over the Blue Route was through territory controlled by the Bosnian Army, through both Bosnian Army and UN checkpoints controlled by French UNPROFOR troops. The Blue Route began just to the north of Pazarić, somewhere near the turnoff to Lokve from the main road towards Hadžići that, in normal times, would take you by modern highway directly into Sarajevo. The route then followed the rough mountain roads up the southwest side of Mount Igman, up onto the heights of the mountain, where it then connected with the steep and dangerous road down the other side, an extremely difficult journey, all the while exposed to enemy guns off in the distance.

> On our way up, we passed through one mountain village set on a steep slope, ravaged by war, shells through the roofs, bullet-scarred walls, many of the houses unoccupied. The village rests on a steep hillside with a spectacular view of Bjelasnica off to the right. We proceeded up Mount Igman, looking back down at the village, and across to Bjelasnica, and off in the distance the spectacular mountains that we had recently passed over from Kreševo to Tarčin. The road was dirt, mud, and snow, steep with breathtaking and frightening views over the sides. How we navigated the road, how trucks and busses did, I hardly know. To think about the *Sarajlije* who walked this mountain on their way out of Sarajevo is beyond me.
>
> The ride down Mount Igman was spectacular as well. As we descended, there were overlooks in places affording a view of the city sprawling amongst the mountains. Set out in linear fashion, one sees Mount Trebević directly above the city. The lower reaches of Trebević separate Dobrinja, with its apartment complexes, from the heart of the city. The airport lies just this side of Dobrinja on the city's southwest end. Hrasnica lies at the very foot of Mount Igman across the runway from Sarajevo.

What could be easier than to sit up in these hills and shell a defenseless city into ruin? The red confrontation line on the map shows the city surrounded, except for the route into the city through Hrasnica. "I don't know how much of the hills we hold," said one *Sarajlije* to me, "but I hope we blow them away."

Just several months later, on 19 August 1995, a French UNPROFOR armored personnel carrier (APC) transporting three members of the Richard Holbrooke's American negotiation team, Robert C. Frasure, Deputy Assistant Secretary of State and President Clinton's special representative for Bosnia, Dr. Joseph Kruzel from the Pentagon's Balkan Task Force, and Colonel S. Nelson Drew from the National Security Council, "slipped off the treacherous Mount Igman road" killing all three (Silber and Little, 1996:365). They were taking the same Blue Route into besieged Sarajevo because Ratko Mladić, the BSA commander, refused to guarantee safe passage of their flight into Sarajevo Airport suggesting that the Bosnian Army forces themselves might shoot at their airplane (Rohde, 1998: 335-336).

At the bottom of Mount Igman, a heavily-sandbagged, French UNPROFOR checkpoint controlled access at the intersection where the mountain road met the paved road at Hrasnica. French UNPROFOR checkpoints also controlled travel through no man's land between Bosnian government territory, to the north and south of the airport, and Bosnian Serb territory, at the east and west ends of the airport runway. Following the road from Hrasnica through Butmir and then around the east end of the runway, we reentered Bosnian government territory, passing through Bosnian Army checkpoints, into the Sarajevo suburb of Dobrinja on the other side of the airport.

> As we pass through Hrasnica, we see the houses destroyed by shelling, pockmarked with bullets. Some houses have been fortified with cement blocks, others have poles trimmed from trees covering them. We pass through a series of Bosnian Army checkpoints. People are out walking. Three women decked out with dangling silver earrings—where they are going or coming from I don't know. Barricades line some of the roads, some are concrete, some are overturned cars or trucks. We proceed through Hrasnica towards the east end of the airport, down small roads with sharp turns, through one demolished village [Butmir] just before the airport runway. Demolished—scenes from World War II. Bulldozed revetments, two French checkpoints. French soldiers in battle gear, APCs, sandbagged bunkers. We pass around the east end of the runway and are in the Sarajevo suburb of Dobrinja, which the Serbs have blown to smithereens.

Once through the final army checkpoint, the Blue Route became a narrow street that ran through the apartment complex known as Dobrinja 1 and further into besieged Dobrinja itself. We drove through the embattled settlement and, on the other side, passed along a single roadway around Mojmilo Hill, through barricades of cars and trucks piled high upon each other, behind huge, burlap tarps hung from buildings that served as sniper screens, into besieged Sarajevo. Our journey over the Blue Route had taken some six hours in order to travel the 120 kilometers over the mountains instead of what should have been a 50 kilometer run. Today, a short section of the old route through the village of Butmir to the south of the airport is named *Plavi put* to commemorate the lifeline. We then entered what *Sarajlije* referred to as "free Sarajevo," passing first through "the siege within a siege" of Dobrinja, "blown to smithereens," offering those of us coming in from the world outside a chilling view of the surrealistic world inside the siege.

"*Dobro Došli u Herojsko Sarajevo.*" Welcome to Heroic Sarajevo. *A banner hanging over an entrance to Dobrinja proclaims the heroism of the settlement on the frontlines of the defense of Sarajevo city. Note the frontloader used to construct the wooden barricades on the right side of the road and the barricades of cars and dumpsters on the left side which served as sniper screens for those inside the siege lines. Photo courtesy of Mevsud Kapetanović.*

Dobrinja—Otpisano Naselje

Dobrinja—Settlement Written Off
The Siege within a Siege of Dobrinja

CHAPTER ONE

There was an Aggressive Dog

Once upon a time there was an aggressive dog that bit my neighbor, Mr. Sarajevo. You're probably asking now: "What is this? Is this a joke?" No, it's not a joke. That aggressive dog is a chetnik who bites my friend, actually the city of Sarajevo. That dog shows off to the world as an innocent one, but really, it's a bloodthirsty dog which prefers ruining, burning, banishing, and killing over friendship, living in happiness, and being friends with every man on this planet. That aggressive dog is worse than a wild dog. A wild dog bites everyone, but this one only looks at nationality and religion.

And now, let's talk about my experiences. Since the first barricades were put up, hard days of sadness are beginning for children of my age and me. First, there was worry, then fear, and bullets, shells, and, at the end, a damaged apartment. Yes, these were difficult days for me. Now, I'm at my aunt's home. Mom and dad sometimes go to the old apartment to pick up what's left. And there you are now, I have a reason to worry again.

These days were somewhat quiet, but it was awful before. In the middle of the night ... BOOM! And again ... BOOM! ... Now it's really enough, I have to go to the basement. As soon as I go down—nothing. Really nothing. Even a fly can't be heard. It's like they knew we'd go down to the basement, so they stopped to get us out of it. We go back, and there it is again ... BOOM! ... BOOM! ... BOOM! ... and so on, back and forth. They are really not letting us live.

But, our time will come. Our young lilies will blossom. Bright sun will shine and blind their evil eyes, and no one will save them.

—Lidija Ilić, 6th Grade
Skender Kulenović Elementary School

A State of Fear/A State of Siege
Attack on "a Common Life"

"Dobrinja was a special place," said Behija Jakić, a sociology and philosophy teacher at Treća gimnazija, the Third Gymnasium, who was trapped in her Dobrinja residence during spring 1992 at the beginning of the siege of Sarajevo (1998). Completely cut off from the city proper during the first months of the Bosnian war, Dobrinja was the siege of Sarajevo at its most severe, referred to by many *Sarajlije* as "a siege within a siege" (*opsada u opsadi*), and by others as a "double siege" (*dvostruka opsada*). These conditions, in which Dobrinja was totally surrounded for 75 days at the onset of the siege, and "written off" by the Bosnian political leadership back in the city, served to differentiate Dobrinja from Sarajevo proper (Hromadžić, 1992). "Here we talk about Sarajevo and Dobrinja, two geographical areas that are very similar but at the same time very different," wrote Mustafa Hajrulahović-Talijan, commander of the 1ˢᵗ Corps of the Bosnian Army, one year into the war. "Even today there is something special about Dobrinja. It was like that before the war and throughout the war ... [Dobrinja] became ... a symbol for the perseverance of the Bosnian spirit" (1993: 5).

"*Dobrinja je bio čudo*," said Ismet Hadžić, the commander of the 1ˢᵗ Dobrinja Brigade, reflecting upon Dobrinja's survival on the Sarajevo frontlines. "Dobrinja was a miracle" (2001). "The organization of schools in Dobrinja was a miracle," said Hajriz Bećirović, the commander of Dobrinja's Territorial Defense forces (2006). In the words of Seniha Bulja, the manager of the Elementary Education Section of the Dobrinja War School Center, who created a war school on the very frontline:

> We were under a double siege. The plan of the enemy was "to cleanse the ground" (*čišćenje terena*) ... They thought that it would be easy to take Dobrinja. Once there was no Dobrinja, there would be no Sarajevo. No Sarajevo, no Bosnia. What happened was quite the opposite. What was incredible was the resistance shown by the population of the settlement. We were defending ourselves and our multicultural society. (2001)

The severity of siege conditions created in those who were trapped there a determined resistance to the enemy and a fierce tenacity to survive. "*Odoh i ja majko, Bosnu braniti*" they sang in defiance. "And I am leaving mother, to defend Bosnia. If I am killed, do not regret it." The scenes of besieged Dobrinjans singing in defiance of the enemy outside their gates, led by Ismet Hadžić himself, are recorded on videotape by Mevsud

Kapetanović, of FIVA Studio, and watching these scenes today with those same Dobrinjans chills the blood (n.d.).

It is this chill from the siege within a siege of Dobrinja, the chill from the heights of Mount Igman gazing down into besieged Dobrinja, "which the Serbs have blown into smithereens," that I somehow want to capture in this story of ordinary, yet extraordinary, Dobrinjans in their desperate struggle for survival. "The difficulty of putting fear and terror into words," writes Linda Green, of her own attempts to capture such violence, must be acknowledged however. The alternative is that we approach the study of those living in wartime conditions much like many academics, afraid to enter such a world in the first place, content with their theory and analysis, "from a distance, ignoring the harsh realities of people's lives" (1999: 59, 56).

"Living in a state of fear," writes Green, where "fear has become a way of life" (1999: 55). The idea of the "culture of terror"(1987: 3), writes Michael Taussig, "the notion of terror as usual" (1992: 17). My own view is that an academic analysis of schooling under siege conditions must evolve out of the appreciation of the terror of this landscape in order to understand the response and the resistance as seen here in the adaptations made by Dobrinja educators. This book is "a journey into the state of fear," where the siege of Sarajevo is the ever-present, all-consuming, and oppressive central theme, "the metanarrative of my work and experiences" in Green's words, that consumes her research on *la violencia* (the violence) wreaked upon the indigenous Maya of highland Guatemala—and my own research on Bosnia as well (1999: 59). During the course of this journey, this book will explore the adaptations of the Dobrinja community to the violence that besieged them, viewed here through the lens of the war schools of Dobrinja, amidst the extremity of the siege of Sarajevo.

The relevant questions that address those individuals and communities "living in a state of fear" are asked by Linda Green in her study of *la violencia* inflicted upon the Mayan population of highland Guatemala, *Fear as a Way of Life: Mayan Widows in Rural Guatemala* (1999). "What is the nature of the terror that pervades Guatemala society?" she asks. "How do people understand it and experience it? And what is at stake for people who live in a chronic state of fear?" In response to these questions, Green chronicles the lives of Mayan women existing in a state of fear during the counterinsurgency war in Guatemala and the effects of violence upon their everyday lives. In this context, she writes that "survival itself depends on a panoply of responses to a seemingly intractable situation" (1999: 55-56).

Green's study of the violence amongst highland Mayan communities, and the alternative forms of community constructed by the Maya in response to this violence, is one of a number of studies of the anthropology of war experience (Nordstrom and Martin, 1992; Nordstrom and Robben, 1995; and Taussig, 1992, 1987). In this image, Ivana Maček, in her monograph, *War Within: Everyday Life in Sarajevo under Siege*, writes about the anthropology of war experience, the destruction and reconstruction of community, applied to the study of the Sarajevo community under siege:

> The anthropology of war that I seek to employ in this study is meant to provide a framework for the description and interpretation of everyday life in war from the perspective of ordinary people. On that level, one of the main characteristics of war is the seemingly paradoxical co-existence of extreme destruction and creativity. I shall introduce the process and concept of the 'negotiation of normality' as a principal analytical tool, in order to capture this doubleness of socio-cultural life in war ... My aim is to give an account of war that focuses on the individual experience of war in Sarajevo which seems to have escaped most other explanatory writing. (2000: 17-23)

Maček's application of the anthropology of war framework to the siege of Sarajevo is perhaps the most detailed description of the everyday lives of ordinary people and their adaptations and "panoply of responses to a seemingly intractable situation." She describes, for example, everything from basic subsistence necessities to the importance of coffee and tobacco. She writes about the construction of tin can ovens, the acquisition of firewood, and the transportation of water in a city without water and electricity. She also writes about social relations during the siege, from the importance of the Bosnian neighborhood to familial arrangements and mixed marriages, as well as perceptions of nationhood, to include Muslim, Serb, and Croat perspectives. There is only a brief section, however, on education viewed solely within the subject of "ethno-religious traditions and innovations," an unfortunate omission, and characterization, in my view.

Maček's study evolves out of the ethnographic field experience whereby a selective group of anthropologists living in disparate communities became part of those communities which they studied. This in itself is not unusual but to become part of a community under assault, part of a community during wartime, "living in a state of fear," along with other members of the community, is no small matter. These scholars place the human experience in wartime at the center of their accounts rather than as a sidelight in pretentious attempts at some form of analysis and explanation. Linda Green notes, for example, that "anthropologists, however, have traditionally approached the study of conflict, war, and human aggression from a distance, ignoring the harsh realities of people's lives" (1999: 56). Green might as well have been writing about educators, or most academic writing about warfare, when the educator was never a participant in the war experience. "Representations of violence," she writes, "whether political or structural, that are detached from the concrete and specific experiences of people and, in particular, from the complex consequences of suffering, have tended to reduce theorizing to an autonomous, disembodied activity" (1999: 11).

In her monograph, *Une Banlieue de Sarajevo en Guerre: Les amazones de la 'kuca' ou La resistance des femmes de Dobrinja* [*A Sarajevo Neighborhood in War: The Amazons of the "Home" or the Resistance of the Women of Dobrinja*] (2000), Carol Mann also speaks to the anthropology of war experience through her focus upon Dobrinja as "a neighborhood of Sarajevo in war." More specifically, to cite Green once again, Mann speaks to the "the survival tactics" of [Dobrinja] women, their efforts to construct alternative forms of community, and how these women situated themselves during the siege (2000). Mann provides some background on the Dobrinja community and includes short sections the beginning of the war, on civil defense tactics, and "the resistance of Dobrinja."There is also a section on schooling with the emphasis upon elementary school and, most notably, Simon Bolivar Elementary School, or what is today Skender Kulenović Elementary School. In fact, the school *Monografija* (Monograph), *Djeca i škole rastu zajedno, 1992-1998* (Children and Schools Grow Together), includes a number of references to the work of Carol Mann and her assistance to the school during the years of the war (1998).

Such representations of violence that confront the harsh realities of people's lives "must acknowledge the horror of living side by side with the person responsible for the murder of your father," writes Green, "or of remaining silent and fearful in the face of half secrets of who did what to whom" (1999: 10). Such representations of violence are expressed in the shocked images of *Sarajlije*, in fear, confusion, disbelief, and disarray over the destruction of their heterogeneous local communities as paramilitary shock troops, supported by the modern military technology of regular army forces, carried out their dirty work with maniacal fury proceeding methodically through the streets of Dobrinja's neighborhoods. Thus Robert J. Donia writes that "human diversity has been Sarajevo's hallmark since it was founded in the sixteenth century. Outsiders have long marveled at its mixture of religions, peoples, and influences and have shared with its residents a certain incredulity that anyone would want to destroy it" (2006: 2).

In a larger sense, the heterogeneity of the population of the Republic of Bosnia and Herzegovina, one of the six republics that comprised the Socialist Federal Republic of Yugoslavia (SFRJ), is seen in the 1991 census, taken just before the wars of Yugoslav secession. At the time, Muslims comprised 43.7 percent of the population, Serbs 31.4 percent, and Croats 17.3 percent. Together, these three groupings comprised 92.4 percent of the population while another 5.5 percent defined themselves as Yugoslavs, with 2.2 percent classified as "others and unknown." These figures prompted Ruza Petrović to write that "the population of Bosnia and Herzegovina is exceptionally heterogeneous" (1992: 4). The words of Ekrem Baraković, a history teacher at Treća gimnazija, put these figures into historical and cultural perspective:

> My history professor was a Serb. He explained to me what Bosnia is. I accepted then and I still accept that vision of Bosnia, as my professor said. He used to say that Bosnia was like a "tiger's skin" (*tigrova koza*). Each stripe represents a people, a nation. And taken together, the stripes are interwoven into a pattern. The idea was that you cannot separate the peoples of Bosnia, that the nations of Bosnia cannot be separated.
>
> For five hundred years, the Bosnian people have lived together like this, a mixture of peoples. Bosnia has built its own culture based on three cultures, Serb, Croat, and Muslim. For years the Bosnian people (*Bosanski narod*) have always appreciated and have always celebrated the cultures of other peoples, the cultures of each other.
>
> Bosnia stands today as she has stood for centuries.
>
> My professor used to say that the one who would take a pen in his hand and divide Bosnia with the tip of that pen would slaughter hundreds of thousands of people. He used to say that you can never divide Bosnia. I learned that from him—and now he is in Belgrade. And that's how it is! (2001)

If Bosnia was like a "tiger's skin," in the words of Professor Barakovic's professor, and representative of Bosnian diversity, the diversity that has been a hallmark of Sarajevo, to Robert Donia, suggests a microcosm of a greater Bosnia. The mixture of cultures, peoples, and religions that coalesced within the mountains of central Bosnia created a profound sense of identity amongst the residents of the town as recognized by Brian Hall on his "journey through the last days of Yugoslavia":

"Zagreb is like the brain of Yugoslavia," Miroslav said. "Universities, rationality, and so on. Belgrade is the heart. Passion, anger. But Sarajevo! Sarajevo is the *soul.*" (1994: 128)

With a total of 527,049 inhabitants living in the ten municipalities (*opcina*) that comprised greater Sarajevo city, according to the 1991 census, Muslims comprised 49.2 percent of the population, Serbs 29.8 percent, Croats 6.6 percent, and 3.6 percent as others. It is noteworthy that the remaining 10.7 percent of the population of Sarajevo identified themselves as Yugoslavs, almost twice the Bosnian number, instead of signifying their identity with one of the three major ethnic groupings (Crkvenčić-Bojić, 1995). To Robert Donia, "Yugoslav identity became a refuge, a census category for those seeking an alternative to the major national identities of the twentieth century," and Sarajevo embodied this refuge which, in turn, created amongst *Sarajlije* their own unique sense of identity (2006: 3).

Donia eloquently writes that *Sarajlije* referred to the idea of "their 'common life' (*zajednički život*)" as living together amidst the human diversity of the city. As I noted in the Preface of this book, the importance of living in the "neighborhood," of living in the Airport Settlement during the course of my research, and one's identification as a "neighbor," was no small matter. In this regard, Donia explains the importance of "common life" to the *Sarajlije* in the following manner:

> They envisioned their ethnically diverse city as a "neighborhood" (*komšiluk*), spoke of those from other ethnonational groups as "neighbors" (*komšije*) and valued their association with others as "neighborly relations" (*komšijski odnosi*). These expressions more aptly capture Sarajevo's uniqueness and the traits that Sarajevans themselves value in their city's history ... Common life ... necessarily includes tolerance ... like tolerance, common life presupposes that people belong to different ethnic groups and are unlikely to assimilate into an undifferentiated homogenous whole. Sarajevans have long used the concept of neighborliness to express their respect for those of different faiths and nationalities ... Common life is neighborliness writ large. It embodies those values, experiences, institutions, and aspirations shared by Sarajevans of different identities, and it has been treasured by most Sarajevans since the city's founding. (2006: 4)

Indeed, this sense of "a common life" and "the concept of neighborliness" suggests both a cultural and cognitive orientation that provides a common thread by which to understand how the *Sarajlije* envisioned life during the prewar era, as well as their shock upon the destruction of the neighborhoods in which they lived their common life together.

TABLE 1.1
COMPOSITION OF THE POPULATION BY LOCAL COMMUNITIES
OF DOBRINJA AND THE AIRPORT SETTLEMENT

Local Community	Residents	Muslim	Croat	Serb	Yugoslav	Others
Rosa Hadživuković I	1,774	514	97	828	264	71
Rosa Hadživuković II	2,310	1,184	182	567	299	78
Rosa Hadživuković III	4,361	2,047	308	1,083	763	160
Novinarsko naselje	13,903	6,000	869	4,446	2,053	535
Dobrinja II	9,707	4,170	609	2,998	1,494	436
Dobrinja	4,940	2,020	372	1,589	685	274
Totals	36,995	15,935	2,437	11,511	5,558	1,554

Source: Opcina Novi Grad (1991).

If a heterogeneous Sarajevo was the heart of a heterogeneous Bosnia, then Dobrinja was perhaps the hallmark of Sarajevo's human diversity. Located on the western end of the city, within Novi Grad Municipality, Dobrinja was a modern apartment and townhouse complex built in the years preceding the 1984 Winter Olympic Games, the brotherhood of the

A view of the eastern half of Dobrinja and the Airport Settlement from Mojmilo Hill. Part of the apartment complex of Dobrinja 3 lies directly below Mojmilo while a part of Dobrinja 2 lies behind. To the left of the photograph in the foreground lies Dobrinja 4 while Dobrinja 1 lies behind in the background. A portion of the C5 townhouse complex of the Airport Settlement lies behind Dobrinja 2 to the right of the photograph while the runway borders the Airport Settlement. The slopes of Mount Igman lie in the background. Photo courtesy of Mevsud Kapetanović.

games symbolizing the very ideals of "brotherhood and unity" (*bratsvo i jedinstvo*) promoted by the Yugoslav state. While estimates of the population of Dobrinja often vary, a total of 36,995 residents were living in the five local communities (*mjesna zajednica* or MZ)[1], analogous to the American political ward, that comprised Dobrinja and the Airport Settlement at the outbreak of the war, seen in Table 1.1 of population by ethnic grouping (Općina Novi Grad, 1991).

The data from Novi Grad Municipality, based on the 1991 population census, indicate that in the local communities of Dobrinja and the Airport Settlement, Muslims comprised 43.7 percent of the total, Serbs 31.1 percent, Croats 6.6 percent, with others 4.2 percent. While 5.5 percent of the population of Bosnia referred to themselves as Yugoslavs, and almost twice that number or 10.7 percent of the population of Sarajevo referred to themselves as Yugoslav, 15 percent of the residents of Dobrinja and the Airport Settlement sought refuge in Yugoslav identity as "an alternative to the major national identities," or almost three times the number of an "exceptionally heterogeneous" Bosnia and Herzegovina (Opcina Novi Grad, 1991).

A view of the western half of Dobrinja and the Airport Settlement from Mojmilo Hill. Part of the apartment complex of Dobrinja 3 lies directly below Mojmilo while a part of Dobrinja 2 lies behind. The C5 townhouse complex of the Airport Settlement lies behind Dobrinja 2 while the white roofs of the C4 complex lies in the distance. The airport runway borders the Airport Settlement while the village of Butmir lies just to the other side of the runway. Mount Igman dominates the landscape in the background. Photo courtesy of Mevsud Kapetanović.

Those *Sarajlije* who found refuge in the modern apartments and townhouses of Dobrinja included a growing number of upwardly mobile young professionals of Yugoslavia, many of whom secured apartments or townhouses bought by their companies, during the decade of the 1980s. It was clear that these young professionals were the most likely strata to identify themselves other than by their ethnicity and religion and to marry outside their ethnic group or religious faith. In this regard, they were most likely to appreciate the diversity and promote the tolerance that comes with living in a heterogeneous society. Set within a broad open expanse alongside the new Sarajevo airport, in the shadow of Mount Igman, with Mount Trebević high in the background, and Mojmilo Hill directly above, contemporary Dobrinja became an attractive residential location for the new, contemporary Yugoslavia.

In the words of Behija Jakić, the Treća gimnazija teacher who remained in Dobrinja during the siege, echoing the words of Robert Donia on the common life of *Sarajlije* and of Dobrinjans:

> We lived a common life (*zajednički život*) here in Dobrinja. Dobrinja was full of mixed marriages, and my marriage was mixed. My two best friends from elementary school had mixed marriages. Our friends were of different nationalities and different religions.
>
> The young had a chance to get an apartment here after the Olympic Games. We had doctors, engineers, professors, teachers, many young intellectuals. Many young families came here. It was perfect.
>
> I loved this town. I was born here. I couldn't imagine living anywhere other than Sarajevo and anywhere other than Dobrinja. We never expected that the war would last for four years. We just never thought it would end up like this. (2004)

The fabric of "a common life together here in Dobrinja" is expressed through the lens of Dobrinja's schools as well. In the words of Narcis Polimac, the director of Osman Nuri Hadžić Elementary School today, and what was Dušan Pajić-Dašić Elementary School at the outbreak of the war, echoing the very words of Behija Jakić:

> We had a common school (*zajednička škola*) for everybody before the war. We had a common school for the whole region, for students from the east end of Dobrinja and from the area around Dobrinja, from Kasindo, from Bijelo polje. We want a common school today like we had before the war. (2006)

Viewed in these terms, the idea of ethnic warfare coming to Sarajevo was remote in the eyes of most *Sarajlije* in general and most Dobrinjans in particular. A late October 1993 entry in the "Almanac" of the Dobrinja War School Center records their bewilderment that Sarajevo is under attack by its former residents:

> 31 October 1992, *Saturday*: Today the better part of Sarajevo is under widespread attack by the chetniks on this our beautiful city. It is being attacked by yesterday's "inhabitants" who had gone to the hills, and the majority of them had just recently come down from them. They have never understood the soul of this city, of these people, of this way of living. I believe they are enjoying the air in the hills to which they are so used to, and I hope that they will be without that air. (Nastavni centar, 1992-1993)

"The war comes everywhere but Sarajevo," said Hajriz Bećirović who lived in Dobrinja 4 at the eastern end of the settlement. "How can the war come to Sarajevo?" he could only ask in astonishment while expressing the "incredulity that anyone would want to destroy it." "Everything was mixed here, mixed marriages, mixed cultures, mixed religions," he said, reiterating the words of Behija Jakić. "It was simply not possible ...The people had no idea of the possibility of this kind of war, a war in which a neighbor could kill a neighbor" (2004). Halil Burić, who lived in the C4 complex of the Airport Settlement, echoed these thoughts in the following terms: "You don't expect that your neighbor will try to kill you," he said, coming to grips with "the horror of living side by side" with the enemy, recalling the tragedy of one of his friends, that "a man's best friend would kill his friend's daughter." In the understated words of Professor Burić, waking up to tanks in the streets outside his kitchen window, "These things are not normal" (2001).

Sarajlije still speak today in daze and devastation of such unconcealed violence whereby neighbors turned upon neighbors, whose initial response was bewilderment and shock, which then created the conditions for what Green calls "the routinization of fear" and "the routinization of terror." Such "routinization" suggests an image whereby the normally abnormal conditions of fear and violence became normal or routine—in other words, creating the conditions for a state of siege. "Such routinization allows people to live in a chronic state of fear behind a facade of normalcy," she writes, "even while that terror permeates and shreds the social fabric" (1999: 60).

"Fear spread over Travnik like a bank of fog, pressing down on everything that breathed and thought," wrote Ivo Andrić of another time and place, in words that remind one of the fogbanks of Mount Igman that press down upon Dobrinja. "It was the kind of great fear, unseen, imponderable, but all-pervading, that comes over human communities from time to time, coiling itself around some heads and breaking others." Andrić was describing this state of fear in Ottoman Bosnia with the coming of the new *vizier* (governor). "The sense of extremity that gripped Travnik ... preying on the whole town but especially crushing to those individuals who happened to be the immediate victims of it, was of course localized in this mountain range which rings and hems the city" (1993: 381-382). Andrić might well have been writing of contemporary Bosnia, however, with the coming of the Bosnian war, and "the sense of extremity" that gripped Sarajevo, crushing those individuals who happened to be its first victims, the sense of extremity localized within the high mountain walls, isolating and gripping Dobrinja in its midst. From a November 1993 entry in the "Almanac" of the Dobrinja War School Center:

> 3 November 1993, *Wednesday*: It is a cold November day. Dobrinja is covered in fog and it's making that atmosphere even colder. Through the heavy fog, the heads of the students can be seen running down to the Teaching Center. They are rushing through the fog because they do not believe that it can protect them from the snipers ... It is cold at the Teaching Center, but warm as well. The students are safe there, and it is easier for them. There is no electricity, there is no water, there is no gas, there is no freedom, but there is the strength to overcome all this and there is so much will to win. The road to freedom is difficult and bloody, and so dear ... That is best known by the fighters of our Army, but also every citizen of our suffering country because the aggressor equally attacks the lines of fighters and ordinary citizens. (Nastavni centar, 1992-1993)

Talk to any *Sarajlije* about the events of the spring of 1992 and, while no one quite understood what was happening to them, everyone felt the shock of what was happening to their communities. Everyone felt a "kind of great fear, unseen, imponderable, but all-pervading" captured so well by Andrić, that came over their communities as they were being ripped apart. The writings of Sarajevo students, recorded in my first book, speak to the sense of this fear that pervaded the lives of *Sarajlije* at the time, and the fear that young students were feeling as their own worlds were shattering. Lejla Polimac, one of my students at the Faculty of Philosophy, in one of her essays, writes of this fear at the onset of the siege:

> It was the very beginning of something that is called war which can be

described with only one word—FEAR. At that time we didn't know that we would experience so many bombardments of the city, and feel fear—so many similar and worse days than the first one. Before this war, I read a lot about it but only understood what it meant when I experienced it. Nobody can understand what it means—the word "war"—until he experiences it. (1996)

Belma Huskić, then a first-year student at Treća gimnazija, in a student essay, recalls the days just preceding the fighting and the premonition of "a terrifying war":

> The television is turned on. There is electricity of course. Friends from the city are calling and saying not to leave our apartment. We are hearing from everyone that barricades have been put up on the streets. Father is nervously walking up and down in the apartment. He is sensing something that I cannot even feel a premonition of. I am pleased because I will not have a math exam. Everybody is saying that most probably war is going to "happen." In elementary school I learned about war. A couple of people defend the country, the enemy from abroad attacks, but of course honor wins in the end. Maybe this could be the picture in the world of illusions, in a world of justice. But to us, it is the best version of a terrifying war. (1995)

Jelena Andrić, a first-year student at Prva gimnazija, records in her personal diary the anxiety and confusion of 3 April 1992 just prior to the beginning of the siege:

> They let us go earlier from school today. Many parents are calling and asking if their kids will be coming home soon. I do not understand. It looks like something is happening, but mom and dad do not talk about anything. If there is something serious I know I could feel it because they would behave differently. Maybe this is one of the false alarms. Anyway, the school director came in the classroom during sociology class and asked all of us to promise that we will go straight home and not fool around after they let us out from school. (1992)

Two days later, Lejla Polimac writes of similar concerns, of the confusion and denial that was characteristic of many *Sarajlije*, especially young adolescents, on the first weekend of the war:

> It is Sunday, 5 April 1992. I am 16 years old, in the second year of secondary school. Something has changed but we cannot believe it. We don't want to believe. We don't want to accept the fact that war is here. My parents are confused. I never saw them looking like that. They don't know what to say, how to react, how to behave. The only thing they are

saying is, "Everything will be just fine in a couple of days," and they kept saying that for four years. I know now that these words helped us to stay alive—mentally. (1996)

Nevertheless, in Dobrinja, on the outskirts of the city, the situation was somehow perhaps even more difficult than back in Sarajevo itself. "This fear started around the end of 1991, early in 1992, when the first military and paramilitary units came to Lukavica Barracks nearby," said Hajriz Bećirović, on their return from the wars in Croatia and Slovenia. Surrounded on three sides by military barracks of the Yugoslav Peoples' Army (JNA), and hemmed in by the airport runways, Dobrinja was in the process of strangulation. Tanks and APCs from the wars were parked in front of Lukavica Barracks, just to the east of Dobrinja, where there was a JNA military warehouse for armored vehicles, visible for anyone to see as they passed on by. "There was not enough space for all of them" (2004). Davorin Pavelić, then an army engineer, travelling by bus from his apartment in Dobrinja 2 to an army facility in Hrasnica on the other side of the airport, remembers the barricades and checkpoints near Lukavica that began to spring up in January and February 1992.

> It was getting harder and harder to leave Dobrinja, even to go to work over to Hrasnica. We were stopped at checkpoints leaving and entering. They began asking for identification. Fewer and fewer riders rode the bus. Blockades went up around Sarajevo in March. I stopped going to work in early April. JNA vehicles were patrolling the streets. Sometimes there were soldiers, sometimes irregulars. It was strange. We didn't know what was going on. (2001)

The worst of these soldiers and paramilitaries were referred to by Dobrinjans as "drunken hordes" (*pijane horde*) or drunken mobs (*pijane rulje*). "Can you picture these drunken hordes?" asked Hajriz Bećirović. "They would come singing their chetnik songs from World War II, wearing chetnik insignia on their uniforms," harassing ordinary citizens in restaurants and on the streets (2004). "The chetniks would come into Dobrinja for beer wearing camouflage fatigues," said Ismet Hadžić. "Orgies," he called them, terrorizing the civilian population. "We have a saying, 'What the sober person thinks, the drunk says.' During this period, we learned something about what they planned. Unfortunately, we didn't have their weapons" (2001).

To Hajriz Bećirović, "the people didn't realize what was happening until they began to take our kids off the street," citing the case of a 17-year old boy whom they took away cutting off his right forefinger to send a message.

"Can you imagine these monsters would cut the finger off a 17-year old boy so he couldn't shoot a rifle?" (2004). In the words of Ismet Hadžić:

> The chetniks were acting psychologically. The idea was to instill fear into the people. Until then, the people were not really aware of the danger. The people didn't want to believe that something like this would happen. The chetniks were engaged in this "crazy euphoria." The message was, "If you stay, we will slaughter you, kill you, rape you. The idea was to terrify the population into leaving. (2001)

Eventually came the snipers. Luljeta Koshi, then a fifth-grade student at what was then Dušan Pajić-Dasić Elementary School, living in the Dobrinja 4 apartment complex on the east end of the settlement, recalls the fear that could be instilled by only one such sniper:

> I remember when a sniper in the steeple of the church above our apartment complex shot a dog in front of our building. They killed the dog to show that they could kill you too. It was so stressful. We were so scared. We didn't know what to do. Our parents wouldn't let us go out of the building. I was never so scared in my life. (2004)

The United Nations Protection Force (UNPROFOR) erects concrete barriers to serve as sniper screens across USAOJ (United Council of Anti-Fascist Youth of Yugoslavia) Boulevard, the main thoroughfare running through the heart of Dobrinja. On the left side of the photograph is the C5 townhouse complex of the Airport Settlement and on the top right side of the photograph can be seen the front of an apartment complex of Dobrinja 2. Note the wooden barricades and the barricade of cars between the boulevard and the C5 townhouse complex. Photo courtesy of Mevsud Kapetanović.

The words of these *Sarajlije* as they recall those early days at the onset of the siege suggest the state of overwhelming fear of which Ivo Andrić writes, "unseen, imponderable, but all-pervading, that comes over communities from time to time." Indeed, as the barricades went up, and the paramilitaries began their assaults, the great fear began "coiling around some heads and breaking others." In his essay, "Songs in Dobrinja," Zlatko Dizdarević writes of what many besieged *Sarajlije*, in the midst of their own desperate struggle for survival, thought about besieged Dobrinjans and the all-pervading sense of fear that came over the settlement:

> When the war started in Sarajevo, more than a few people brought up Dobrinja to evoke the worst a war can bring: hunger, death, total isolation, abandonment and injustice, tanks below your window, deportations, cigarettes made of tea used ten times over, a handful of rice to last ten days, three rifles to defend a thousand people, and continuous fear of what the next hour would bring." (1994: 157)

In her "Afterword" to the book by Dževad Karahasan, *Sarajevo, Exodus of a City* (1994), Slavenka Drakulić likens besieged Sarajevo to a concentration camp and explores the mindset of people living within such

UNPROFOR erects concrete barriers across USAOJ Boulevard to serve as sniper screens. Note the wooden barricades that extend from the boulevard to the apartment complexes of Dobrinja. Also note the open spaces in front of the apartments that have been turned into gardens. Photo courtesy of Mevsud Kapetanović.

boundaries. "Both Sarajevo under siege and Auschwitz represent a closed system, with their own set of rules and patterns of human behavior, and every closed system where people get killed and one is uncertain about the future, produces a certain kind of psychology that is not easy to understand" (1994: 114). Drakulić speaks to the manner in which people living inside a "closed system" develop their own mindset and own patterns of behavior, as adaptations to survive such extreme conditions. While Drakulić writes that "the city of Sarajevo became a sort of concentration camp, which one could enter only with the greatest difficulty, and from which one could hardly get out," she might have been writing of besieged Dobrinja in particular. Although the siege of Sarajevo began the weekend of 5-6 April 1992, the siege within a siege of Dobrinja began gradually at the beginning of 1992, eventually leading to the weekend of 2-3 May 1992, totally isolating Dobrinja and the Airport Settlement from Sarajevo for some 75 days through the first months of the war. In the words of Seniha Bulja, with the departure of the last convoy from Dobrinja on 13 May 1992, "not even a fly could get in or out" (2001).

The Illusion of Normal Life

This image of the concentration camp and the besieged community as closed systems is seen in frighteningly authentic terms in a 17 May 1992 article by Mehmed Hromadžić in *Oslobođenje*, the Sarajevo daily, entitled, "Novi Aušvić" (New Auschwitz), and datelined Dobrinja:

> Dobrinja has been under complete blockade for three weeks. Since 2 May when mines were set along the road by Mojmilo and the road by the Airport is blockaded, this settlement became a huge [concentration] camp, and its 40,000 residents are kept as hostages. If this ever ends, very few of them will cross these roads again and not have severe psychological trauma ...
>
> It's not necessary to blame the terrorists for this so-called Auschwitz, because no curse or appeal can touch their hearts; as they were told to leave the people starve and die in inhuman ways. While western countries are still mourning for Marlene Dietrich, who is as old as this century, on the doorstep of their countries, genocide against children is going on. (1992: 6)

Three days later, on 20 May 1992, another article by Hromadžić, entitled "Doktori" (Doctors), appeared in *Oslobođenje*, also datelined Dobrinja, and reiterated the concentration camp analogy:

Doctor Faust, Doctor Jekyll, Doctor Mabuse, Doctor Mengele, and Doctor Karadžić. The connection between these five doctors is their common title of unsuccessful healers.

The first three names from this list are imaginary characters from literature. The last two doctors from the same list are famous for the monstrous things that they have done in the last fifty years of this century.

Doctor Mengele used concentration camps and hundreds of thousands of people for his experiments. On the other side, Doctor Karadžić used the entire population of one country, around four and one-half million people, for his experiment.

The best example of his monstrous experiments is the settlement of Dobrinja. Forty thousand citizens of this settlement are now forced to hide inside their homes like mice inside their holes. First of all, his army was shooting at anything that was moving in Dobrinja. Then, after they completely surrounded Dobrinja, without letting anyone leave the settlement, they started the bombardment. The next stage was when the aggressors started controlling the amounts of food, medicine, electricity, natural gas and water that were getting into Dobrinja. In the last stage of this experiment, Karadžić is trying to separate families.

The thing that scares most of the citizens of Dobrinja is that they are unable to take their children to safety. The killers are very close to reaching their final goal. The settlement is almost completely empty and the remaining citizens are scared of everything. (1992: 5)

The idea of Sarajevo as a closed laboratory experiment, and the *Sarajlije* trapped within as the mice, is reiterated by Mladen Vuksanović, trapped in Pale himself, the self-styled capital of Republika Srpska. "The psychiatrist [Radovan Karadžić] and his vampires continue to lead the dance of death. They have the 'honour' to have created the largest concentration camp in the history of humanity—Sarajevo. I'm confident that the people of Sarajevo will endure all their experiments" (2004: 124). These writings suggest that conditions in Sarajevo under siege, and in Dobrinja under a siege within a siege, were similar to concentration camp conditions, and newspapers were quick to point out such analogies. In Dobrinja, with the ongoing destruction of the settlement during the spring of 1992, and the routinization of the violence inflicted upon the remaining population, along with the knowledge that "the plan of the enemy was 'to cleanse the ground'" and, in the process, take Sarajevo, conditions had reached the extreme.

While the analogy of Dobrinja to Auschwitz may be problematic, it is nevertheless clear that the situation in the besieged settlement at the outset of the war was extreme and, in the words of Tzvetan Todorov,

"We would rather not hear the accounts of these extreme situations." Yet, Todorov clarifies the relevance of such accounts:

> Concentration camps ... clearly epitomize extreme circumstances, but I am interested in them as much for themselves as for the truths they reveal about ordinary situations ... My intent is to use the extreme as an instrument, a sort of magnifying glass that can bring into better focus certain things that in the normal course of human affairs remains blurry. (1996: 27)

Indeed, extremes reveal much about the human condition and, in the case of "a closed system" such as besieged Dobrinja, they magnify decisions made by ordinary Dobrinjans in their struggle for survival. In regard to this book, such extremes magnify decisions made by Dobrinja educators concerning the reconstruction of schools for Dobrinja's children posing fundamental questions about the purposes of schooling, if not life itself. For the purposes of this study, the Holocaust analogy is perhaps most relevant here in the discussion of clandestine schooling in the ghettoes of Eastern Europe during the early days of Nazi occupation of Poland. In a recent article, "'Not Bread Alone': Clandestine Schooling and Resistance in the Warsaw Ghetto during the Holocaust" (2002), Susan M. Kardos poses the fundamental educational questions of schooling in "extreme circumstances" in the following terms:

> Central questions about the role of education emerge from the stories of the clandestine schools, which were maintained at a time when life for the Jews was shadowed by death and despair: Why have schools? What is schooling for? Should schools prepare students for the future, provide for the present, or preserve the past? For whom should schools be organized—for individuals, for communities, or even for whole cultures? ... One set of answers to the questions posed above can be found in the story of the underground schools in the Warsaw Ghetto. It is a story of organized schooling, but also of resistance. It is a story of how schools can be used for individual survival, community continuity, and cultural endurance. (2002: 33-34)

"Why Education?" Kardos asks:

> The questions remain: Given the perilous nature of the activity and the grim conditions in which it was undertaken, why did organized schooling thrive in the Ghetto? What was the purpose of the teaching and learning? (2002: 48)

The very questions asked by Kardos were once posed by an anonymous writer who was himself confined to the Warsaw Ghetto. In the writings of the *Oneg Shabbath* Archives that document life and survival in the Ghetto, compiled under the direction of Emmanuel Ringleblum, and buried for posterity's sake in 1943 upon the Ghetto's obliteration, the anonymous writer posed the same questions, in a piece, "The School System," while under threat of annihilation:

> But again, why should one study at all, when uncertain of the day and the moment, with no prospect of to-morrow, not knowing where one shall be, whether one shall eat and what?—How can one, in these circumstances, think of educating children?
>
> And yet, in spite of it all, there is a universal, primordial, unquenchable drive for learning, contrary to all logic and braving obstacles. How can this be explained? Let's try to analyze what propels youth to schools and learning, and bids parents to squeeze out the last penny in order to provide their children with some education, not bread alone. (Kermish, 1986: 501)

Indeed, the anonymous writer attempts to answer his own questions by highlighting the accomplishments of the teachers and students in the schools of the Warsaw Ghetto amidst the extremity of conditions:

> This is why one may say without exaggeration that study and learning blossom in the Ghetto. Much of this is sub-standard, adulterated, primitive and chaotic, for many unqualified and incompetent individuals exploit the demand and teach poorly and with errors, while the inexperienced, young, absorb clumsy substitutes for knowledge. Still, there is little risk in saying that, on the average, the level and standard in the Community and vocational schools, and in the elementary and high-schools, as well as the occupational "complements," is even higher than that prior to the war; and this, in spite of under-nourishment, illness, hunger, pressure of time saved from paid work, crowded space, lack of text-books and teaching aids. Students study more, learn more, know more, take more notes, do more /.../ to teachers. For indeed, study is the miraculous way of getting away from reality, of forgetting the bleak lot, the today and tomorrow, the bestiality and barbarity. (1986: 502-503)

The same anonymous writer concludes his description of ghetto schooling by noting, "The better the education provided, the more conscientious and serious its methods—the better founded might be the hope for their future *normalcy* [my emphasis], for their building a better central pillar of future society" (1986: 515).

Joseph Kermish, in an article entitled, "Origins of the Education

Problem in the Ghetto," also writes of the legacy of ghetto schools, and the creation of a documentary record, "this desire to give testimony before future generations on all that happened ... expressing *the struggle of resistance* [my emphasis] to the cruel regime" (1962: 28). Kermish cites the creation of ghetto schools; "As early as September 1941, a few teachers founded some active schools in the Wilno Ghetto. The classes were clandestine, camouflaged as nurseries." He notes that perhaps 5,000 children attended these schools although, with every action (*akzia*), the numbers decreased. These numbers, coincidentally, are analogous to Dobrinja where perhaps as many as 3,000 elementary and secondary children attended classes at the beginning of the siege. By January 1942, however, "there were only 1,097 children in the ghetto: 900 of them studied in two underground primary schools," again calling to mind the stairway schools of Dobrinja (1962: 30). Kermish writes:

> The ghetto children developed a deep awareness of the communion of their fate with that of their families. They proved eager to help them in their arduous struggle for life, notably in the smuggling of food into the ghetto. On the other hand the ghetto-child unconsciously tended to enclose himself in a faraway wonder-land to which he could escape, at least in fantasy, from the ghetto. A wonder-land of this sort was the ghetto school. There he imagined a different life, a *life of illusion* [my emphasis] which made him forget the terrible reality. (1962: 30)

Deborah Dwork addresses the illusion of normality as follows:

> All over the ghetto, students and teachers met secretly to continue the process of education. As we have seen so often before, to go to school, to persevere with one's studies, was a basic tent of childhood. It was an essential activity that embodied *the principal of normality* [my emphasis]: life would go on, there would be a future after this madness. (1991: 180)

In the midst of the realities of the struggle for survival, schooling represented "some sort of normalcy," to cite Kardos, "the principal of normality," in Dwork's terms, "a life of illusion," to cite Kermish, which made the children forget for the moment "the terrible reality" of the ghetto. In the process of reconstructing the story of the clandestine schools, scholars such as Kermish, Kardos, and Dwork, and the anonymous writer whose legacy lives on in the *Oneg Shabbath* Archives, evoke echoes of the war schools of Sarajevo in the connections traced down through history of the human spirit under conditions of extremity, of a Warsaw Ghetto, of a Wilno Ghetto, of a besieged Sarajevo, and of a besieged Dobrinja.

"*Iluzija normalnog života,*" a *Sarajlije* might say, "the illusion of normal life." In a letter to me explaining the phenomena of the war schools of Sarajevo (1998), Mujo Musagić, the editor of *Prosvjetni list* (The Educational Gazette), speaks to the desperation of people whose "life in the besieged cities was equal to that in the concentration camps" and their struggle to construct a normal life amidst siege conditions. I will cite Mujo's letter here in some detail, as I did in my previous book, in order to offer the thoughts of one Sarajevo educator on schooling under siege:

> The psychology of people in the besieged cities, in which tens of people were dying each day, and sometimes thousands of different caliber projectiles were falling, was trying to establish a "normal" life. Those people wished, at least in their illusions, to form a more ordinary environment that resembled a normal way of life because only in that way, could they have the desire to survive.
>
> Life in the besieged cities was equal to that in the concentration camps. The long-term siege was destroying in people the last spark of life, of hope for a possible solution, optimism. Stage shows were performed, art galleries were opened, poetry forums and musical shows were organized; even a "Miss Besieged Sarajevo" competition was organized.
>
> That's how we come to "war schools." They were also part of the normal illusions of life, although we can't take away their numerous functions. Children did learn, teachers did hold classes, the educational process did take place on the basis of a reduced program written by the Ministry of Education. However, my impression is, the most important value of schools during the war can't be measured by numbers and statistics but, as I would put it into words, it can be measured by *the value of the significance of life* ...
>
> There are many reasons why this aspect of "war school" research should be given special attention. For sure, the war schools in Bosnia and Herzegovina played a part in defending this country and its people. The war schools offered an additional sense of normal life to the children and adults; they offered strength and the belief that it is possible to survive the impossible conditions of hunger, thirst, wounding and dying. Even fighters with guns in their hands believed that there was a sense in fighting when they knew that their children were attending so-called classes ... Even the children concluded that peace and normal life would come because they were taught everything they would need in peacetime and normal conditions. Therefore, everyone "took advantage" ... of the belief in the possible return of peace and normal life. But sometimes during the long, war-camp life, hope and belief that peace and normal life would return, is equivalent to normal life itself. (1998)

Writing of the violence that wracked Colombia in the 1980s, if not today, Michael Taussig speaks to "the normality of the abnormal, and particularly in the normality of the state of emergency ... the notion of terror as usual" living "in a state of siege" (1992: 17). "A sad, rainy spring morning again, more like autumn," wrote Mladen Vuksanović, in his *Pale Diary*, dated 16 April 1992. "How quickly a person adapts to everything. Accepts the abnormal as normal, accepts an impossible life as the only possible kind. Bare survival acquires its full meaning" (2004: 36). "*Ovdje niko nije normalan*," reads an epitaph on the wall of a building near Skenderija in the heart of Sarajevo, "Nobody here is normal." To the date of this writing, as of the time of my last visit to Sarajevo in 2006, nobody has yet erased the epitaph.

Halil Burić, the manager of the Higher Education Section of the Dobrinja War School Center, speaks to the questions posed by Dwork, Kardos, and Kermish, in their writings on the clandestine schools of the Holocaust. As an educator, he reflects on the difficulty of the struggle for physical and psychological survival under siege since many of his own students served in the Bosnian Army in the defense of the settlement. "My students were on the frontlines," he said. "They were defending Sarajevo." Under such extreme circumstances, whereby students alternated between classrooms and trenchlines, it was very difficult to organize the teaching process, to schedule classes, and to conduct examinations with any semblance of normal conditions. Some students could only attend class in the morning, others only in the afternoon, others only on an irregular basis. For other students, it was impossible to even meet with their instructors. That is why, he suggested, it was important for professors and teachers to make every effort to accommodate their students regardless of the circumstances. For those students who found themselves on the frontlines, "it was very important for them to think about normal things, about classes and examinations, for example, as a means to forget the war, at least temporarily" (2001).

Muslija Muhović, a professor on the Faculty of Criminal Science today, then listed as a professor on the Faculty of Electrical Engineering, who taught in the Higher Education Section during the war, reiterated the words of Professor Burić:

> We were trying to work like it was normal, like there was no war. There were questions of how to organize classes and exams. *The idea was to pretend like it was normal* [my emphasis], like there was no war. In fact, the War School Center worked better than many schools today. A

normal, a moral person, can't understand what happened during the aggression anyway. (2001)

Lest we forget the circumstances, the "Almanac" of the War School Center records this entry:

> 23 September 1992, *Wednesday*: At 11:45 two shells fell behind the War School Center. Shrapnel came through to the Director's office. The following people have been lightly injured: Tahmaz M; Muhović M; Burić H; and two more women on the floor of the same building. (Nastavni centar, 1992-1993)

Both Professor Muhović and Professor Burić were wounded in the line of duty, on what teachers often refer to as "the second battle line," serving to reconstruct an educational system under siege. Today, looking out through his kitchen window with the window frame still bearing the jagged scars of high caliber shells, with his wife in tears at the terror of the memories, Professor Burić remarked on the strategy of the enemy directed towards the civilian population. "One of the major aims of the aggressor," he said, "was to try and make it impossible for students to live a normal life." In almost the very words of Mujo Musagić, at another time and place, Halil Burić then stated, "One of our major aims was to try and create the illusion of normal life" (*iluzija normalnog života*). "It was crazy," he said. "Reading, writing, one day. The next day you might be killed. Just 300 meters from our school is a bloody war" (2001).

In the same fashion, Smail Ćar, the art teacher at Simon Bolivar Elementary School, reflects on his struggle as both an elementary teacher and a soldier in the 1st Dobrinja Brigade:

> The biggest problem was to coordinate my time between the trenches on the frontline and classrooms in the schools. I would return from the frontline at 6:00 or 7:00 in the morning, shower with one or two liters of water, and go to school. I was very tired—and I was afraid for my life.
>
> The children and the classrooms were psychological therapy for me. I was able to transform myself totally. No one would know that only a few hours before, I was on the frontline and afraid for my life. Even today, I cannot understand how I did it. (2006)

On 1-2 April 1995, an article appeared in *Večernje novine* (The Evening Newspaper), "How to Carve Out a Life," which cited Smail Ćar's work and service as an artist, a teacher, and a soldier. The article notes that there were "more prominent artists" in the brigade, while Ćar notes that he was in artist (military) companies (*umjetničke čete*), in other words, military units in which artists were prominent, and that he had the support of Ismet Hadžić as the brigade commander for his teaching. "In school I learned how to give form to beauty, and look at this! Everywhere around is the wreckage of the city's beauty. The harmony of everything that is called life is disturbed. Death is at every step" (Smajlović, 1995: 14).

Indeed, schooling was viewed as a means of creating "the illusion of normal life" for Dobrinja's children within the larger struggle to create some sense of normal life amidst the wreckage and the destruction. "I was smiling all the time," said Ilija Šobot, the manager of the Secondary Education Section of the Dobrinja War School Center, as he described his efforts to organize the secondary schools:

> It was important to remain as normal as possible. Although it was not normal, you must accept it as normal if you want to survive. It was only important to stay alive. For those of us who went through all this, it is like watching a film today. It's very difficult to remember and very difficult to forget. (2001)

To Narcis Polimac, the director of Dušan Pajić-Dasić Elementary School, echoing the words of Halil Burić and Mujo Musagić, educators

Members of "the artist company" (umjetnička četa), of the 1ˢᵗ Dobrinja Brigade. General Ismet Hadžić, the brigade commander, with beret and camouflage jacket, stands in the center. Smail Ćar, the art teacher at Simon Bolivar Elementary School, stands first on the left. Mihridžan Kulenović Mimica, who organized the School of Fine Arts in besieged Dobrinja, kneels first on the left in the first row. Photo courtesy of Miroslav Kordić.

were responsible for taking the initiative to create this sense of normality rather than huddle in basements as *podrumski ljudi* (cellar people):

> It was important for the children to go to school, to not lose the school years. The alternative was to stay in a dark basement. It was important to create the conditions for children to go to school. School was an illusion of normal life. (2006)

"There was the need to keep alive," said Enes Kujundžić, a deputy minister of the Ministry of Education of the Republic and manager of the Scientific Research Section of the War School Center. To Professor Kujundžić, living there in the C5 apartment complex of the Airport Settlement on the frontline itself, Dobrinja was the siege of Sarajevo at its most severe, the place where the struggle for survival was perhaps most desperate. Today, as the director of the National Library of Bosnia and Herzegovina, he reflects upon the situation at the time and just how Dobrinja kept its spirit alive amidst the siege:

> Of course, there were the schools for the children. But we also published newspapers, newsletters, and journals. We printed self-help articles on how to survive. We had agronomists and engineers in the settlement, and we used their expertise. We planted gardens. We dug wells for water. We held art exhibitions. We wrote plays. We had a women's chorus.
>
> *The idea was to live as normally as possible* [my emphasis]. Dreaming of normality and living with reality is something else. There is no equation between them. Reality was very grim. To survive this reality, to survive four years under siege is a miracle. (2001)

Amidst the extremity of besieged Polish ghettos, or the extremity of besieged Bosnian towns, we might consider the words of Anna Pawełczyńska, writing of the Holocaust, "Conditions of extremity compel one to choose what is most important" (1979: 140). Viewed in terms of the besieged Dobrinja, the legacy of decisions made by dedicated educators under conditions of extremity is seen in the reconstruction of community schools in order to save the children. Faced with choices of what was most important in a life and death struggle for survival, Dobrinja educators made hard and courageous decisions, looking towards the future in their hope for the end of the war, creating the illusion of normality in order to survive the abnormal conditions of the siege. In this regard, the historical record of the war schools of Dobrinja recalls the historical record of the clandestine schools of the ghettos of the Holocaust, and suggests a similar struggle. To reiterate the words of Joseph Kermish, "It was this desire to give testimony before future generations ... expressing the struggle of resistance" (1962: 28) against an enemy that would annihilate them, and the very same desire of Dobrinja educators to give similar testimony, that suggests there was indeed "something special about Dobrinja."

Dobrinja was a Special Place

If "Dobrinja was a special place" to Behija Jakić, it was because educators such as her made it special as they began reconstructing the process of schooling under siege. Although a teacher at Treća gimnazija, located in Novo Sarajevo Municipality in the center of the city, Professor Jakić lived in Dobrinja 2A where she found herself trapped during the early months of the war, unable to travel outside of the settlement, even into Sarajevo proper. "Are you crazy?" her friends asked her when she refused an opportunity to leave and come into the city. "You have gone from a siege to a siege within a siege" (1998).

Among those trapped in Dobrinja and the Airport Settlement during the spring of 1992 at the onset of the siege were approximately 2,000 elementary school students, 1,000 secondary school students, and perhaps 120 teachers from schools throughout Sarajevo city, as well as approximately 400 university students who attended the many faculties of the University of Sarajevo, along with perhaps 15-20 professors. Of the three elementary schools in Dobrinja, two were located directly on either end of the settlement directly on the frontlines, and occupied by a ragtag group of citizen defenders who comprised the Territorial Defense forces and who would later be transformed into the 1st Dobrinja Brigade of the Army of the Republic of Bosnia and Herzegovina (ARBiH). On 15 May 1992, the third elementary school in the middle of the settlement was deliberately shelled and burned to the ground in full view of the bewildered residents. At the time of the siege, there was no secondary school in Dobrinja and those students of high school age who lived in the settlement traveled into the city proper to attend the 27 secondary schools located throughout the city.

In the words of Smail Vesnić, deputy director of the (Inter-Municipal) Pedagogical Institute of Sarajevo at the time of the siege, among those educators trapped in Dobrinja, "When I remember those days, I think about how impossible it was to organize a school" (2001). During the summer of 1992, however, Smail Vesnić and his colleagues from the Pedagogical Institute created the Dobrinja War School Center as the administrative framework within which to reconstruct the schools under what was then the Sarajevo City Secretariat for Education. Today, sitting in his office in what is now the Ministry of Education of the Federation of Bosnia and Herzegovina, turning the pages of the "Annals," the journal of Gimnazija Dobrinja, he reads one of his wartime entries, shaking his head at the memories of schooling under siege:

> 5 November 1993: A rainy morning, just like human souls. Blood on the sidewalk and one life less as a result of last night's shelling. How long is human blood going to flow down the streets, and the world still watch and say nothing?
> It's dangerous so the kids can't go to school, again. Classes are cancelled. Just the same, in the schools, life will go on. (Gimnazija Dobrinja, 1992-1995)

If "just 300 meters from the school is a bloody war," in the words of Halil Burić, Dobrinja was a special place because the settlement had been sacrificed to the enemy by the Bosnian political and military leadership and yet somehow found the will to survive, holding the line against impossible odds. During April, May, and June of 1992, Dobrinja existed in virtual isolation from Sarajevo and, unprepared for the assaults that threatened its integrity, struggled to survive amidst the violence and chaos. As General Ismet Hadžić noted, the total isolation of Dobrinja that lasted for 75 days began with attacks on the weekend of 2-3 May when Dobrinja found itself surrounded and abandoned. Smail Čar, then a student at the Academy of Arts, and later a teacher at Simon Bolivar Elementary School, remembers his walk from the student dormitory in Nedžarići to Dobrinja on 2 May, passing through the barricades with no problem, meeting a friend for coffee. "One hour later, Dobrinja was closed—That coffee lasted four years" (2006).

Within the week, on Friday, 8 May 1992, an article appeared in *Oslobođenje* entitled, "Dobrinja—otpisano naselje," or "Dobrinja—Settlement Written Off." Written with the bitterness and sarcasm of an observer who discerns the abandonment of the settlement, Mehmed Hromadžić writes of those early days:

> The brutality of these words is best presented by the situation in the settlement of Dobrinja. Rifle shots and machine gun bursts are heard here and there, but detonations of mines, rockets and shells are heard less often. Only, on the scene a perfidious play that not even the most monstrous Nazis could have made is playing. Simply, for six days already, tens of thousands of people can't get out of their homes. As soon as they step out on the street, sharpshooters shoot at them. Both avenues in this

settlement are blocked, all stores are demolished. People are living on the last supplies of flour. Nobody knows what's going on with his or her relatives living in the city. Everyone is going crazy ...
 That's why there is only one thing left to the residents of Dobrinja—the hope that they are all not just thrown to the wolves. (1992: 3)

If the major Sarajevo newspaper suggests that Dobrinja might be abandoned to the enemy, we might imagine the thoughts of those defenders who found a copy of *Oslobođenje*, heard the news over the radio, or received the news by word of mouth. This is precisely how Omer Musić heard the news on the C4 frontline, that the community in which he lived and was defending with his life, was being written off back in Sarajevo. Fleeing from his home on what was then 98 Georgi Dimitrova Street (today Andreja Andrejevića) in the C4 complex of the Airport Settlement during the mid-June 1992 assaults, Omer returned to the frontline along Prištinska Street, where he spent the next three months. After describing the chaos of the assaults, and how disparate groups of civilians simply defending their homes held the line on Prištinska Street, he then said, "We heard on the radio that they wrote off Dobrinja," shaking his head at the absurdity of ragtag groups with hunting rifles holding off the Bosnian Serb Army backed by the firepower of the JNA. "They couldn't believe it when Dobrinja held out" (2001).

The Dobrinjans with whom I have talked, whether an educator such as Behija Jakić or a soldier such as Hajriz Bećirović, to a man and woman, all view the defense of Dobrinja as the defense of Bosnia at its very finest. The reality that Dobrinja held out against perhaps the heaviest assaults on Sarajevo at the beginning of the war, with virtually no weapons, and with minimal support by the fledgling government, is recognized not only by every Dobrinjan, but by every *Sarajlije* as well. Everyone knows that Dobrinja was written off, that it was indefensible there on the outskirts of the city, connected to the city proper only by a single roadway. In the words of Mustafa Hajrulahović-Talijan, commander of the Bosnian Army's 1st Corps, writing of the spirit and resistance of the Dobrinja community:

> A year after Sarajevo became hell, Dobrinja became a symbol for steadfastness, courage, human strength and spite that was stronger than any force. And indeed, a powerful force had hit Dobrinja. At the same time, at the beginning of the war, the story went, "Dobrinja is sacrificed, it hasn't got a chance," but a miracle has happened ...
> So, how did we defend ourselves? Sometime even I don't know

the right answer. There is no military tactic book that can explain the way we defended ourselves, with homemade weapons, from this huge and well-equipped and organized army. The human factor was never so important on the battlefield as here in Dobrinja.

I think that we, during this time of the blockade, have won our battles with our hearts, determination, and readiness to prevent Dobrinja from becoming a new Bijelina, Višegrad, Foča ... We did everything to defend ourselves. There was no other choice—to fight meant to survive ...

Not until later did it become clear how Dobrinja survived. In the city, people felt even a little jealous that the people in Dobrinja were "privileged" to live in a society of laws and discipline. Some people just could not comprehend that a society like this one could exist in wartime ... Simply, [living in] "Dobrinja's chaos" in the most difficult times became a system, the only way of living in order to survive. People learned how to live and survive in the space they created for themselves.

With some thousands of residents, hospitals, now schools, and television, an unbreakable defense, it became a little unconquerable town, but in the human, moral, and symbolic sense much more—a symbol for the perseverance of the Bosnian spirit.

It is customary for people to say that Dobrinja is a settlement of true *Sarajlije*. (1993: 5)

Smail Ćar, as a university student from the town of Glamoč in western Bosnia, trapped in Dobrinja when the barricades were closed, remembers his personal feelings at the time:

It is important for you to know that it was a very difficult situation at the beginning. We literally did not have anything to eat. Shells were falling all over Dobrinja. Snipers were everywhere. But the lack of food and water made everything more difficult.

My personal attitude was: What am I doing here? I am not from Dobrinja. I didn't feel a part of it at first, but I became part of it. I didn't want to leave. (2006)

In this regard, the photographs of Mevsud Kapetanović capture the sense of pathos of an indefensible Dobrinja, "the harsh realities of people's lives" yet "the resiliency of the human spirit" in the banners hanging across Dobrinja roadways that proclaimed, "*Dobro Došli u Herojsko Sarajevo*," or "Welcome to Heroic Sarajevo," which greeted the international visitor passing through UNPROFOR checkpoints at the airport and entering Dobrinja before proceeding on to Sarajevo itself. The fact that an indefensible Dobrinja held out against all odds during the early months of the war created a heroic mythology around the community whereby Dobrinja became "a symbol for the perseverance of the Bosnian spirit." In the 5 May 1993 entry in the "Annals" of Gimnazija Dobrinja, the writer expressed these very thoughts:

> Our children have to understand the heroism of Dobrinja. The pride and dignity of Sarajevo are kept alive despite the worst conditions of this unfair war.
> Dobrinja is the most beautiful illustration of our life together. Like nowhere else, all the qualities and the tolerance of the Bosnian people are expressed right there.
> Anyway, I'm proud to be a resident of Dobrinja. The heart and spirit of our young country is right here. (Gimnazija Dobrinja, 1992-1995)

"Dobrinja is a Symbol for Resistance," announced an article by Hadžo Efendić, Vice-President of the Bosnian government, in *Dobrinja—Ratne novine* (Dobrinja—The War Newspaper) of the 5th Motorized Brigade, the unit that evolved out of the 1st Dobrinja Brigade, one year into the war. "I walked around Dobrinja," Efendić writes, "admiring everything I saw, everything people did. We went through the most difficult temptation [to give up] and we did not give up then and we will not give up now." The organization of the defense of the settlement is the reason for putting Dobrinjans "at the top of the list of resistance to the aggressor in this war" (1993: 5-6). Two years down the road, in September 1995, to honor the 1st Dobrinja Brigade that had now been transformed into the 155th Hill Brigade, the headlines of *Ratne novine* proclaimed, in the words of the honored guest, Premier Haris Silajdžić, "*Herojska Dobrinja: jeste vitezovi, jeste i gazije*" (Heroic Dobrinja: You are knights, you are '*gazije*'), a Bosnian word from the Turkish meaning something akin to "warriors" (Porča, 1995: 1-6).

"Unbreakable Settlement," was the title of an article by Alija Resulović in the same issue of *Ratne novine* as the Efendić article that noted "Sarajevo's opinion of Dobrinja." Resulović wrote that "occupied and surrounded Sarajevo and inside it surrounded and freedom-loving Dobrinja are both synonyms of heroism and indomitability" (1993: 17). The characterization of Dobrinja as something of a separate entity, a place separate from Sarajevo, is evident here. This idea is also seen in an article by Davor Alaupović in *Večernje novine*, entitled "No Entry for White Eagles," dated 30 June 1992, noting the resistance of Dobrinja to the Bosnian Serb paramilitary group, the "White Eagles," to be renamed "White Chickens" (*bele kokosi*) by Dobrinja's defenders during the early months of the war

(Hodžić, 1997). It is noteworthy that Alaupović refers to Dobrinja in a uniquely Bosnian way, as the *"Inat–naselje,"* or the "Spite Settlement":

Life, or at least its imitation, adapted to war conditions, however it survived. Neighbors are assisted by neighbors, civil defense headquarters are formed, hospitals are forming. Dobrinja has held its ground. On the contrary, it has become increasingly stronger.

Unfortunately, increasingly destroyed. It is difficult to hypothesize how many apartments are destroyed. The elementary school went up in flames, destroyed is what increasingly constitutes Dobrinja as a city within a city. But again, nothing is destroyed, because the people who are left, if nothing else, take actions against the aggressor every day from fists to sharp elbows.

If Miskin is called Prkosa Street, then Dobrinja merits, and we propose, that it go by the name of Spite—settlement. (1992: 8-9)

The sense of Bosnian spite that carried Dobrinja through such difficult times is a most appropriate characterization of the settlement for it provides a sense of Dobrinja as a place uniquely Bosnian and therefore representative of the Bosnian struggle. This sense of Bosnian spite is seen even in an entry, dated 29 November 1993, in the "Annals" of Gimnazija Dobrinja:

The Dobrinja 5 apartment complex under fire. The outlying apartment buildings on the western end of the settlement were known as "pancirka," or the equivalent of flak jacket or protective vest, since they served to protect the interior of the settlement from tanks, snipers, and small arms fire. Note the three young boys on the fourth floor balcony just to the right of the black smoke. Photo courtesy of Mevsud Kapetanović.

THE WAR SCHOOLS OF DOBRINJA

A closer view of the apartment building in Dobrinja 5 under fire and the three boys giving the "V" for "victory" sign on the fourth floor balcony. Note the damage to the building from shelling and small arms fire. Photo courtesy of Mevsud Kapetanović.

All of Bosnia is in waiting. The Conference at Geneva started today. Regular classes are being held although conditions are impossible. There's no water, no electricity. But we're still working. It's from spite. That's what man is like in this region, spiteful and proud, and he'll stay that way. Nothing can change him, not even this war. (Gimnazija Dobrinja, 1992-1995)

Even in educational terms, the reference continues in the years after the war: "Dobrinja Schools: The Schoolbells Rang from Spite," reads the headline of an article by Saida Mustajbegović, which summarizes the story of the Dobrinja war schools. However Dobrinja is characterized in contemporary or historical terms, it was the defense of a community that was "written off" at the very onset of the siege that proved so critical not only to its survival but to the sense of community that developed in the process. The defense of the settlement at the onset of the siege bought time for Dobrinja to construct its own unique forms of resistance to the enemy, seen here in educational terms, as it sought to reconstruct its sense of community.

Damir Hadžić, then a 16-year old student, and soldier, "but I was not the youngest," poignantly expresses the sense of the moment. The times were "unbelievable experiences for everyone," said Damir, "but especially for guys my age ... The war caught me at that age, and I came to the realization that we had to live in a different community." The community that Damir once knew was in the process of being destroyed, and what his "generation all had in common was the will to defend the country, to defend their own homes" (2001). The defense of Dobrinja during the first months of the war by "small groups of courageous men" provided the time for Dobrinjans "to construct alternative forms of community" in the process of defying the enemy. Thus the continuation of the 3 November 1993 entry, cited earlier, in the "Almanac" of the Dobrinja War School Center:

> Everything that was achieved in this Center during the difficult 1992 war year will be remembered by generations of youth of this time, but also all others because the Center, with its few denizens defied a brutal enemy and gathered the youth of Dobrinja together to give them points of freedom and light between two impacts of the shells ... That is how life went on as well as defiance. That is how there was joy and sorrow in the Center. That is how the Center was left with pride and with the richness of new knowledge. Many will be happy in the end that the difficult 1992-1993 war year found them here in Dobrinja, that they were the students of the first generation of the Gymnasium. (Nastavni centar, 1992-1993)

In the words of Zlatko Dizdarević, in his essay, "Songs in Dobrinja," writing of the role of Dobrinjans in their determined resistance in the defense of Sarajevo:

> Whatever the ultimate outcome, in Dobrinja Sarajevo has won its greatest battle. Actually, it would be more honest to come right out and say it: Dobrinja justifies all those secret hopes that while Sarajevo might be destroyed, it will never be vanquished. From the trauma brought on by days and nights of isolation and hiding from the bloodsuckers lurking at every doorstep, a resistance movement was born. (1994: 157-158)

In an analysis of his teaching experience during apartheid South Africa, Jonathan Jansen recalls the dilemma he faced in trying to write about that experience.

> First, I have told a story. In doing so I have struggled to write in such a way that I break the tension between my structuralist training and the desire to affirm the primacy of the human experience ... While some would wipe away experience an focus instead on the primacy of structural explanations for opposition in South Africa ... I have drawn on students' own experience—both the oppression they have suffered and the creativity they have shown—as a source of resistance. (1990: 68)

My intention here in this book is to tell a story, and the struggle here is my desire "to affirm the primacy of the human experience," perhaps even at the expense of structural analysis, through the voices of besieged Dobrinjans themselves. To tell this story, I have tried to draw on both the teachers' and the students' own experience set amidst the larger struggle for survival under siege.

In this regard, the stories of everyday life under siege conditions, and the adaptations made to live life under these conditions, are revealed through the documentary record compiled during these years. To be specific, the "Guidelines on Educational Activities of Preschool Institutions, Elementary and Secondary Schools During the State of War," issued by the Ministry of Education of RBiH on 25 December 1993, for the operation of schools under wartime conditions, addressed five major concerns: (1) measures of protection and safety; (2) organization of curriculum and instruction; (3) the role of teachers; (4) textbooks; and (5) evidence and documentation (Jabučar, 1997: 293-295; 1994: 4-5). "These guidelines were passed in December 1993," stated Abdulah Jabučar, deputy minister of education of RBiH at the time, "and committed every school to work, regardless of conditions—to adapt to the actual situation" (1997: 295).

Such "evidence and documentation" required for the operation of schools in Dobrinja, as an adaptation to wartime conditions, is seen today, most notably, in the "Annals" of Gimnazija Dobrinja, the "Almanac" of the Dobrinja War School Center, as well the "Basic Work Programs" (*programska osnova rada*) of the Center that organized the instructional process. Furthermore, those administrative forms that are the bane of the everyday teacher, to include special permission forms, excuses from class, and grade reports, indicate the extent to which administrators went to reconstruct the schools. In fact, each school was required to provide official documentation of student attendance and classroom performance to ensure, for example, that the section book of each class (*odjeljenska kniga*) or class book, also referred to as the class journal, was kept in accordance with legal statutes. Thus, for example, as early as 27 August 1992, an official Order (*naredba*) signed by Fuad Babić, commander of Civil Defense Headquarters for Dobrinja and the Airport Settlement, read as follows:

> I order that the Teaching Center of Dobrinja and the Airport [Settlement] insure the evidence for the 1991-1992 school year for the students of Simon Bolivar Elementary School. (Babić, 1992)

While each school was responsible for securing and protecting these documents, and the Dobrinja War School Center responsible at the outset for documents in the settlement, "to hide the school documentation in a safe place," many school documents survive to this day, many in cardboard boxes, on shelves, left for any adept educational researcher to follow (Jabućar, 1994: 5). I can only hope that such documents will embody the voices of Dobrinja's teachers and students, set within the structural analysis of academia, as portrayed here in this book. I present them in some detail, therefore, by way of establishing the historical record in order to chronicle the reconstruction of the educational system under siege conditions.

These school documents so meticulously maintained as a mundane educational task are, in turn, complemented by personal interviews as a means to enliven the historical record. These interviews serve to provide those Dobrinja educators, who gave so much of their lives to their students, a primary voice in the process of reconstructing their stories. In the image of Dobrinja as "a symbol of resistance" to the enemy who besieged Sarajevo, I have drawn on the teachers' and students' own experience under siege "as a source of resistance" as well.

In this regard, Hajrija-Šahza Jahić, of the Pedagogical Institute, asks,

"What can one say about teachers in wartime?" Her response, written during the siege, reads as follows:

> We hope that history will devote both space and time to them and to their efforts, because it is thanks to their merit that such a fundamental segment of the new state has been preserved and continues to thrive. None of this could have ever functioned without the teachers, *who were thus in the frontline in the fight against the aggressor* [my emphasis]... in the fight to preserve the schools and the educational system as a whole ... However much is written, it will never be enough, because each pupil and each teacher, each parent, represents an individual history, a drama and an inspiration. Therefore I dedicate these lines to *The Teacher*, [her emphasis] the *warrior and pedagogical patriot* [my emphasis] of our land. (1996: 27)

"Those unknown *soldiers* [her emphasis] of the classroom," writes Melita Sultanović, a colleague of Professor Jahić at the Pedagogical Institute (1996:10). In the same image, Abdulah Jabučar, deputy minister of education, writes of schooling as a form of civilian service on the Sarajevo frontlines:

> Provinces, municipalities, and particularly schools, as well as teachers, have to be maximally engaged and try to find all possible ways of successfully educating children. That is '*the second battle line*' [my emphasis], and our victory as well as the final liberation of Bosnia and Herzegovina depends on it." (1994: 5)

Indeed, the imagery of the military battle for the country is employed by teachers and students alike to describe the psychological battle for the mind and the logistical battle to reconstruct the educational system. This imagery suggests that teachers became "soldiers," in the words of Melita Sultanović, and "pedagogical patriots," in the words of Hajrija-Šahza-Jahić, and schooling became a form of "pedagogical patriotism" and, hence, a form of civilian resistance to the enemy (Bešlija, et al., 1995: 22–23). "We did this on our own," they said to me. We did this because we wanted to. It was a form of patriotism" (1998). Indeed, this imagery is seen in the very terminology used by *Sarajlije* to describe the "war schools" (*ratne škole*) that were created in order to adapt instruction to wartime conditions during the siege of the city.

In a recent interview, Smail Vesnić recalled his thoughts during the time. "Although it was August 1993," he said, "We were told that the Americans would come and write about how we did it, how we reconstructed the schools."Today, as an inquisitive and appreciative American educator, I have come to write about how they did it, how they reconstructed the schools, enabled by the documentary record they have left for any adept educational researcher to follow. In this regard, the words of Smail Vesnić offer testimony to courageous educators under siege in a struggle for the very lives of their students. "We didn't fight with guns," said the man who created schooling when nothing was there. "We fought in this way, to defend our homes, our families." In the process, "we saved those kids. We moved them from the streets to the classroom, and we saved them" (2001).

NOTES

[1] A more thorough discussion of local community (*mjesna zajednica* or MZ) organization, and the significance of local communities for this study, is found in Chapter 6, page 185.

At the beginning of the war, Dobrinja and the Airport Settlement were organized into five local communities as noted, and the population figures cited for these five local communities are from Novi Grad Municipality based on the 1991 census. However, these figures do not include the area known as Dobrinja 5, adjacent to Nedžarići on the northwest corner of the settlement, which is separated from the settlement by the main trolley line. In 1991, Dobrinja 5 was considered part of Miro Popara Local Community whose local records, to include population figures, were seized at the beginning of the siege.

Ubice u Školskim Klupama

Killers in School Benches
The War for Dobrinja and the Dobrinja War School Center

CHAPTER TWO

I Saw War Only in the Movies

I couldn't believe the war would start in Sarajevo, the war that I saw only in the movies. But, it did. The shells from the hills are mercilessly falling down on roofs of the buildings, on apartments and kindergartens. The hardest thing for me was when I was helplessly watching my school burning. Fire was destroying my three school years spent there with my friends and my teacher Jasna. Will we ever meet in the same classroom again? In a cold basement, in the middle of the night, while bullets are playing music around our building, Reuf, Dejan, Ivan, Nino, Rusmir and I are identifying what are they shooting us with. Before sunrise, I go to sleep, and by morning I always get up with the same wish for peace to come. Let this stupid war end, the war that killed many children of my age, destroyed the city, and drew worried wrinkles on the faces of my parents.

—Emir Grozdanović, 4th Grade
Skender Kulenović Elementary School

The Birds Flew Away

With the onset of the siege of Sarajevo the weekend of 5-6 April 1992, the regular school year was effectively terminated just over a month later on 15 May 1992, although teachers and administrators in selected locations attempted to continue the routine of schooling. Abdulah Jabučar, the deputy minister of education for the Republic of Bosnia and Herzegovina, offered the following explanation of the "Law on the Completion of Teaching in the 1991-1992 School Year in Elementary, Secondary, and Higher Schools," which appeared in *Službeni list* (The Official Gazette), dated 5 May 1992, and provided the legal basis for closing the schools before the end of the school year:

> The Ministry of Education, Science, Culture and Sport had been following the development of events and reacted in time. When the chetnik's euphoria gained the upper hand, we had to stop the process of teaching lest children would be killed, the Ministry then proposed, and the Presidency of Bosnia and Herzegovina issued an Executive Order with legal force concerning the end of the school year—the fifteenth of May 1992. (1994: 4)

Of particular note is the reference in *Službeni list* not only to the premature end of the 1991-1992 school year but, in Article 5, to the prospects of the 1992-1993 school year to follow:

> As a consequence of the premature termination of this school year, the subsequent 1992-1993 school year will begin when conditions are favorable for normal instruction and the work of all elementary, secondary, and higher schools, faculties and art academies in the Republic of Bosnia and Herzegovina. (Jabučar, 1997: 176)

The "Law on the Completion of Teaching" precedes by almost eight months the "Guidelines on Educational Activities of Preschool Institutions, Elementary and Secondary Schools During the State of War," issued by the Ministry of Education on 25 December 1993, for the operation of schools under wartime conditions. These Guidelines, cited in the previous chapter, addressed five major areas of concern to include evidence and documentation of schooling: (Jabučar, 1994: 4-5). As early as 5 May 1992, in the early days of the siege, the importance of ensuring school records is expressed in Article 4 of the Law which reads as follows:

> All elementary and secondary schools and higher education institu-

tions are obliged, within this framework, to make all provisions for the preservation and safety of school documentation and evidence. (Jabučar, 1997: 176)

Indeed, those school records preserved by conscientious school administrators and teachers provided the basis for the reconstruction of schooling during the years to follow. And while the reality of siege conditions resulted in the end of the 1991-1992 school year before its time, the prospects of actually finishing the school year in some sort of clandestine fashion, and reopening the schools for the 1992-1993 school year, remained in the forefront of discussions and debate. These deliberations over the purposes of education in a city under siege and a country that had just declared it independence, and in a fight for its very existence, continued through the course of the siege.

With the onset of the siege within a siege of Dobrinja, the Territorial Defense (*Territorijalni odbrani* or TO) forces had assumed responsibility for the defense of the settlement, and Hajriz Bećirović had assumed command responsibility. A legacy of military strategy and tactics of the former Yugoslavia, the TO was "inspired by the Partisan method of warfare, [a] territorially based unit ... removed from the command structure of the JNA and placed under the supervision of civilian authorities ... at the local, municipal and okrug [district] level" (Hoare, 2004: 18-19). This "localized system of territorial defence at the Republican level" meant that, here in Dobrinja, a Sarajevo suburb, the TO became "the institutional basis for the defence [of Dobrinja and] of the Bosnian state" (2004: 19-21). In addition to regular TO members, the TO for Dobrinja and the Airport Settlement included members of the Patriotic League (PL), the military wing of the Party for Democratic Action (SDA), the Muslim political party. Hoare writes:

> On 25 February [1992] the General Staff of the PL at Hrasnica drew up a 'Directive for the defence of the sovereignty of Bosnia-Herzegovina', that defined the PL's task as 'the defence of the Muslim nation and the safeguarding of the integrity and unity of Bosnia-Herzegovina, so as to safeguard the further coexistence of all the nations and nationalities on the state territory of Bosnia-Herzegovina. (2004: 31)

The PL was organized in the image of the TO command structure and Hajriz Bećirovič, initially, was the commanding officer of the PL for Dobrinja. However, "the Republican Staff of the TO formally assumed command of all units formed on the political platform of the PL on

15 April," which meant that the PL was incorporated within the TO command structure (Hoare, 2004: 57). Bećirović cites 10 April as the date when "the Ministry of Defense of the Republic of Bosnia and Herzegovina issued instructions concerning the organization and operation of the headquarters and units of the Territorial Defense" (2003: 61). Nevertheless, on 20 May 1992, Hajriz Bećirović formally assumed command of the TO *Krizni štab* (or Crisis Headquarters) for Dobrinja and the Airport Settlement, and TO forces became responsible for military defense (Bećirović, 2004).

Initially, however, with the first assaults on Dobrinja, the defenders were composed of ragtag groups of men and women who had formed small tactical units to protect their individual apartment blocks. These units were known as the "stairway guard" (*haustorska straža*), and these guards, possessing only a handful of personal and makeshift weapons, began to take on the enemy in small, pitched battles raging through the apartment complexes in defense of their homes. "Every citizen was a soldier," said Hajriz Bećirović. He estimates that, at the outset, these citizen-soldiers had, for the defense of Dobrinja against JNA tanks, APCs, self-propelled howitzers, and infantry with assault rifles, perhaps 200 weapons, to include hunting rifles, handmade pistols, Molotov cocktails made out of Coca Cola cans, and a handmade pen for women that fired but one shot (2004). In many cases, these men did not even know of the existence of organizations like the PL, and it was not until Bećirović began to integrate these guards into the TO command structure they even knew there was a central command that had assumed responsibility for defense of the settlement.

Within the background of the siege of Sarajevo that began the weekend of 5-6 April and encircled Dobrinja as well, the siege within a siege of Dobrinja is generally dated to the weekend of 2-3 May 1992 when assaults on the settlement took the form of coordinated military actions that intensified through the end of the month. Within two weeks, these assaults took most of the apartment complexes of Dobrinja 1 and all of Dobrinja 4 on the eastern end of the settlement. In his *Pale Diary*, dated 5 May 1992, Mladen Vuksanović writes, "I find out that the Serbs have 'liberated part of Dobrinja'" from the Serbian Republic News Agency (2004: 61).

Luljeta Koshi, who lived in the Dobrinja 4 complex, recalled the difficulty of the situation just prior to the evacuation of her family on 13 May 1992:

On 12 May, the chetniks were coming into Dobrinja 4 and taking people away to Kula. They were taking everyone away, men, women, and children, and separating them there. Dad was scared. He was Albanian and Muslim, so they had a double reason to hate him. The chetniks were at the entrance to our building on that day when there was some shooting. One of them was shot, so they left. We didn't know what to do. On the morning of 13 May, Dad went to get food from somewhere around Dobrinja ... A friend of Dad's living in the Airport Settlement called us around 1:00 or 2:00 and told him to take his family, his children, and get out of Dobrinja 4 immediately. We left with almost nothing, only a few bags. That night they came back and took over the entire neighborhood. (Koshi, 2004)

Sabaheta Koshi and her two young daughters, Luljeta, age 12, and Belma, age 11, and two young sons, Besnik and Bekim, age 8, got out on 13 May on one of the last convoys to leave Dobrinja organized by the Children's Embassy (*Djecija ambasada*) to evacuate women and children through the barricades. At a checkpoint below Mojmilo Hill, the passengers were told to leave the busses and walk through minefields in an area known as Soldier's Field (Vojničko polje) to get into "free Sarajevo." Duško Tomić, of the Children's Embassy, persuaded the soldiers to allow the busses through the checkpoint and, in one of the ironies of the war, as a lawyer, the advocate for children became an advocate of accused war criminals in the postwar era.

Meanwhile, the Koshi family had no idea what was happening to the father, Luan, who ended up walking over Mojmilo Hill to safety, one of approximately 4,000 people, according to Ismet Hadžić, who fled Dobrinja on foot over Mojmilo Hill into Sarajevo in the days on and around 13 May. "To Slaughter, To Scatter, To Intimidate," read the headline in *Oslobođenje*, "Ominous Ghost of Vukovar is Strolling Around Dobrinja" (Hromadžić, 1992: 5). "The message," according to Ismet Hadžić, "'If you stay, we will slaughter you, kill you, rape you'" (2001). Although the strategy to surround Dobrinja was designed to leave open an escape route into Sarajevo for those who wanted to flee at the beginning of the siege, "It was not the good will of the chetniks to allow them to go," he said. "Families fight for families" (Hadžić, 2001). However, after 13 May 1992, "We were under a double siege," said Seniha Bulja, one of those dedicated educators who remained behind. "Not even a fly could get in or out. It became a dangerous time then when you couldn't find even a bird in the sky" (2001).

In an article entitled, "The Birds Flew Away," Mehmed Hromadžić takes up the flight analogy and captures the situation in Dobrinja at the time:

> There are only people left in Dobrinja. No food, no electricity, no cigarettes. No birds either. People could tell where the gunfire was coming from by watching and listening to the birds, but no, they flew away, towards happier parts of the world. The deadly silence in Dobrinja is broken only by gunshots, fire from heavy artillery, and the sounds of rocket launchers. Now people here live in conditions worse than the living conditions of their ancestors.
>
> Silence in Dobrinja is the only answer to all the monstrous deeds that are happening here. Tens of thousands of residents of this settlement are ready to cross the minefields barehanded to leave ... No one is safe here. (1992: 5)

On 14 May, an account in *Oslobođenje* read, "Criminal bombarding of the city from early morning and attempts by chetnik-terrorists to penetrate settlements. Karadžić requested air attack from Milošević" (1992: 1). Shelling of the city intensified with the middle of May especially deadly. In an article entitled, "The War Schools of Sarajevo," Hajrija Šahza-Jahić, then of the Pedagogical Institute of Sarajevo, locates schooling within the background of siege conditions during the spring of 1992:

> April 1992, May 1992, a tale of destruction, fires, cellars, screams, sirens, the wounded and the dead, day and night fused into a gigantic hell, and in parallel, our inner compulsion to organize a school, as quickly as possible and *whatever the cost*, to normalize the lives of children living in totally impossible circumstances. (1996: 11)

Thus the Simon Bolivar Elementary School, located in the very heart of Dobrinja, "which went up in flames on 15 May 1992" on the very last day of the truncated school year, symbolized the destruction of the Dobrinja community by the obliteration of the community schools (Smajlović, 1994: 1). In an article that appeared in the very first issue of *Dobrinja—Ratne novine* of what was then the 1ˢᵗ Dobrinja Brigade, dated August 1992, this destruction of community is expressed in exceptionally bitter terms, in the title of the article, "*Ubice u školskim klupama*," or "Killers in School Benches" (Tabaković, 1992).

In the aftermath of what can only be seen as the deliberate shelling of the school, the article indicts the former school director along with many of the Serb teachers as "the criminals who perpetuated these acts." However, it should also be noted that a number of the Serb teachers stayed behind under the most difficult of conditions, including Pavka Radović, cited in the article, who worked for the school during the war. According to Muhamed Hodžić, a physical education teacher, the school director, Vojo Manojlović, was angry at her because she refused to follow him over to "the other side" and, to get back at her, left behind school documents to incriminate her (2001). Here we see in the bitterness of the article the bitterness of a community that saw the horror of its teachers turn killers (*nastavnici ubice*), and I will cite it in depth here:

Killers in School Benches

The 12 shells which the chetniks fired on the charred remnants of "Simon Bolivar" Elementary School and a few incendiary rounds to incinerate to the ground what has remained of the documentations of the criminals which prepared "a party" in the buildings, don't have any effect. There are no more secrets concerning all that happened to this school and the criminals who came out of this building. Namely, the parents whose (poor) children attended this school, together with teachers and students who have not turned traitors to the call of one

Simon Bolivar Elementary School, today Skender Kulenović Elementary School, going "*up in flames*" after being shelled on 15 May 1992 at the very beginning of the siege. Two years later, the teachers and students followed up the destruction of their school with a cultural entertainment program on the theme, "School in Flames," to commemorate the shelling. Photo courtesy of Mevsud Kapetanović.

of your own ... work on collecting pieces of information about the criminals from this school and of course, the criminals who perpetuated these acts.

We learn how the former director of this school, chetnik Vojo Manojlović, "leased out" the school building to his Serb volunteers for almost the whole school year. In the hall for physical education alongside the assistant physical education teacher, Steve Popović, "new pupils" learned to kill and murder ...

With the firing of the first bullet, Manojlović "disappeared" from the school, and his wife, otherwise the godmother of Radovan Karadžić [the political leader of the Republika Srpska], was sent first ... to Pale [the capital].

Teachers as Killers

Meanwhile, the Manojlović "people" who stayed in Sarajevo, traded school chairs [positions] for rifles, mainly sniper rifles. For now one confidently knows that this dirty work, on the bodies of small children and their relatives, was done by these Manojlović "workers: Radomir Todorović, known as King Kong, physics teacher , Mladen Telebak—school pedagogue, Momcilo Pejović—retired teacher of geography, and Pavka Radović, teacher.

The killer Mladen Telebak was eliminated, but Radomir Todorović who was known as, imagine it—King Kong, literally dropped dead of fear when members of the Territorial Defense arrested him while he aimed from a window of a rented apartment in Dobrinja at a former student. And the remaining killers whom we mention in this text are entered on the books and they will get what they deserve.

The criminals can demolish and burn at will, but that is merely the illusion they have lived, that their crime will not be revealed. (Tabaković, 1992: 15-16)

This destruction of the sense of community at the onset of the siege by the obliteration of community schools suggests there was no turning back the clock to a time before the war when neighbors lived in harmony with neighbors and children attended schools together regardless of nationality or religion. If elementary school teachers and administrators would turn enemy, and use their very own elementary school to hold planning meetings to initiate the siege, "leasing out" the building to their nationalist party members who would implement the siege, even to collect arms in the school, and then shell their school located in the very heart of the community, then this war was designed to destroy not simply lives but history and culture as well. Mladen

Vuksanović, trapped in Pale, writes of his son, trapped in Sarajevo, who "saw his teacher Radoje on the Serb television news, shelling the city from [Mount] Trebević. A teacher killing his pupils. All values have collapsed" (2004: 139).

In a 2 June 1992 article in *Večernje novine* (The Evening Newspaper), entitled "School for Crime," the plan for the ethnic cleansing of Dobrinja was revealed as follows:

> According to these witnesses, which [Slobodan] Škipina, one of the officers from the self-proclaimed [Serbian] Ministry of Internal Affairs on Vraca confirmed, [Mićo] Stanišić and [Vlastimir] Kusmuk, under the Karadžić and Krajišnik command, prepared a monstrous plan for total ethnic cleansing [*etničko čišćenje*] in Dobrinja and the Airport Settlement which was supposed to be realized in the next few days.
>
> All residents from Dobrinja and the Airport Settlement were to be driven out to the territory of Lukavica where, inside of the barracks, they would be divided into groups by nationality. The Serbs would be separated from Muslims and Croats, men from women, mothers from children. After that, the Serb men would be lined up, armed, and forced to defend chetnik bases, and their wives and children of exclusively Serbian nationality would be sent into the neighboring Muslim and Croat apartments and houses. The residents of Muslim and Croat nationality would be expelled, and most of them would fall into the arms of Šešelj's chetniks. Volunteers from Serbia and Montenegro would be settled into other apartments and houses along with their families.

The burned-out interior of Simon Bolivar Elementary School after the shelling on 15 May 1992 at the very beginning of the siege. Photo courtesy of Mevsud Kapetanović.

General Ratko Mladić is familiar with all the details of this monstrous plan. He approved it. (1992: 4)

To Hajriz Bećirović, "The enemy had a very good strategy to take Dobrinja. The strategy was to seize all the important locations around Dobrinja," to seize the waterworks on Mojmilo Hill, for example, to control the water supply, "to blockade the settlement," and to tighten the noose, terrifying the population into leaving through a single escape route over Mojmilo Hill. In his position as TO commander, he tried to negotiate with the BSA commander to ease the suffering of the civilian population:

> Their commander told me, "If there is one bullet fired from Dobrinja, we will destroy Mojmilo Hill and leave only Mojmilo." He would send me messages by phone. He would call me, and you would hear chetnik songs to the accompaniment of the *gusle* [a one-stringed folk fiddle]. "Leave if you want to stay alive," he would say. "*Vi ste slijedeći kojeg ćemo zaklati.*" [You are the next one whose throat we will cut]. He would curse me. "*Balija, vi ste Srbi. Samo ste poturčeni, balija.*" [*Balija*, You are Serb. You only turned Turk, *balija*]. (2004)

I was reminded of Brian Hall's "journey through the last days of Yugoslavia," recalling a conversation on the Bosnian identity just months before during the summer of 1991:

> "They call us *balija*," Benjamin said. "An old word for a Muslim peasant, a man with shit on his boots, an idiot. This is not in private, this is in their regular speeches."
> "They also call us half-Turks," Radina said ...
> Or just plain Turks," Benjamin's mother replied. (1994: 135)

Given the ethnic slurs endured by Hajriz Bećirović, the words of Seniha Bulja come to mind once again, "The plan of the enemy was "to cleanse the ground" [*čišćenje terena*] ... They thought that it would be easy to take Dobrinja. Once there was no Dobrinja, there would be no Sarajevo. No Sarajevo, no Bosnia (2001).

Unless besieged Dobrinjans continued to hold the line, they too would become victims of a strategy designed to cleanse Dobrinja of its non-Serb residents, seize the western half of the city, and create a Bosnian Serb capital of the Republika Srpska, the Serbian Republic of Bosnia and Herzegovina, in Sarajevo at the expense of the non-Serb population. And the inhabitants finally realized that if Dobrinja fell, the violence inflicted upon those who remained behind—"you are the next one whose throat we will cut"—soon to be witnessed in the executions on the streets of the

Airport Settlement, would be merciless. The message was sent in cold blood, on 17 May 1992, through the disappearance of Želimir Vidović Keli in the service of the Dobrinja community.

In some ways, Keli exemplified the Yugoslav ideal, a Bosnian Croat married to Bojana, a Bosnian Serb, rising to fame as a legendary football star for the Sarajevo Football Club and for Yugoslavia in international matches, living on Sefica Dorica Street in the contemporary Airport Settlement. Although "not even a fly could get in or out" of Dobrinja after 13 May 1992, Keli volunteered to take five wounded people from Dobrinja hospital through the barricades around the settlement to Koševo Hospital in the city. "He went to the Dobrinja Hospital to help out," said Mirsad Fazlagić, his former football coach. "That's the kind of guy he was. Everyone liked him. He knew everybody. Everyone knew him" (2006). In the words of Hajriz Bećirović, "The popular Keli was a volunteer on whose courage the lives of the wounded depended."

He cleared the checkpoints into the city and reached the hospital with the wounded patients. However, on his return, "Keli did not listen to his friends, nor his commander, perhaps for the first time, and set out on a one-way trip perhaps having believed in the fortunes of war and the possibility that to him, without any reason whatsoever, the chetniks will do nothing" (2003:180). He was seized at the Serb checkpoint on Kasindolska cesta where he fell into the hands of the Arkanovci, Željko Ražnjatović Arkan's paramilitary thugs, and was "liquidated" (2003). According to Bećirović, there was a witness to the treatment of Keli who was imprisoned in the military barracks in Nedžarići later to be repatriated to the Bosnian side in a prisoner exchange, and it serves no purpose here to relate the inhuman torture Keli suffered. However, at the very end, he was killed in the same manner they had threatened to kill Hajriz Bećirović—Keli was "the next one whose throat we will cut." Today the Minister of the Ministry for War Veterans of Sarajevo Canton, Hajriz Bećirović remembers it this way: "They tortured and killed Keli to send us a message," he said. "Keli was a VIP. Their strategy was to kill all VIPs and, in that way, to destroy the idea that we could still live together. Their message was, 'There was no turning back'" (2006).

"There were no rules to this war," said Halil Burić, citing the slaughter, the overt executions, and the deliberate shelling of the civilian population (2001). If someone like Keli, "a sports idol," whose popularity extended across the former Yugoslavia, who was known and liked by everyone, could disappear, then anyone could suffer the same consequences. "We didn't know what happened to him," remembers Dajana, his daughter, 14 years of age at the time. "No one knew what happened to him." In silence, the family waited 13 years until his remains, found in 1995 at the end of the war, were identified through DNA samples from his two daughters. Bojana, his wife, remembers that she went to identify his remains and refused to let her daughters go with her, but Dajana went anyway (2006). Today there is a street leading from Dobrinja through Nedžarići named after Želimir Vidović Keli in recognition of his service but hardly compensation to a family who, on 5 July 2005, was finally able to hold funeral services. As a 14-year old girl, Dajana remembers with stark clarity the last time she saw her father:

> I remember we were playing cards that day, and he decided he needed to go out. He was wearing a track suit. He never wore a complete track suit. He always wore the top and blue jeans. He gave me his watch and his sunglasses. He said he didn't need them. He gave my Mom his gold necklace. I remember watching him through the window. He turned and waved at me and blew me a kiss. He never did that before. (Vidović, 2006)

At least 42 men and boys taken off to Kula prison in Lukavica from the neighborhoods along Kasindolska cesta about the time of Keli's disappearance simply disappeared as well and are still listed as missing. "It's much sorrow and pain every 14 May," read a recent headline in *Oslobođenje*. "How long will the residents of Kasindolska cesta in Sarajevo wait for justice?" (Dučić, 2006: 18).

With no rules to this war, it was clear that as long as the siege of Dobrinja would last, such unconcealed violence directed against the civilian population would become the routine, "the routinization of fear" and "the routinization of terror," to repeat the words of Linda Green. "Such routinization allows people to live in a chronic state of fear behind a facade of normalcy, even while that terror permeates and shreds the social fabric" (1999: 60). To this day, the remembrance of those times and the shredding of the social fabric lives on in the words of those Dobrinjans who have shared the trauma of their experience with me and who, to this day, continue to commemorate those who are still missing.

A Few Good Men
The Coordination Board for Dobrinja and the Airport Settlement and the Dobrinja War School Center

"The educational system was a function of defense," said Ismet Hadžić, commander of the 1st Dobrinja Brigade. "In order to survive the specific conditions of the siege, I got a copy of Churchill's book of the defense of London during World War II. I remembered Churchill's words that everything was a function of defense." General Hadžić recalled how he integrated the educational structures, initially developed under the direction of Smail Vesnić, with civil defense operations. "I called Fuad Babić, the coordinator of civil defense for Dobrinja. I told him that my idea was to gather all the intellectuals in Dobrinja to organize all the schools—preschool, elementary, secondary—to give people a purpose for living" (2001).

Dated 3 August 1992, one month after Ismet Hadžić took command of the 1st Dobrinja Brigade, the "Order concerning the Establishment of a Teaching Center," signed by Fuad Babić, the commander of Civil Defense Headquarters for Dobrinja and the Airport Settlement, officially created the parameters of the Dobrinja War School Center, here referred to as the Teaching Center. The Order read as follows:

> On the basis of the indicated emergency, and in the aim of organizing education and socialization in Dobrinja and the Airport settlements, I ORDER
>
> 1. the organization of the Teaching Center of Dobrinja and Airport settlements.
>
> 2. I designate the premises of the Games Club for the Teaching Center.
>
> 3. The Teaching Center will operate according to the curriculum which the Teaching Center Council will enact.
>
> 4. I designate SMAIL VESNIĆ, deputy director of the Pedagogical Institute of Sarajevo, as manager of the Teaching Center.
>
> 5. The Teaching Center will work with the Inter-Municipal Pedagogical Institute of Sarajevo in this process.
>
> 6. The order takes effective IMMEDIATELY. (Babić, 1992)

Copies of the Order went to the Ministry of Education of RBiH and the Pedagogical Institute back in Sarajevo, Novi Grad Municipality, and the

Teaching Center. The Order (*naredba*) signed by Fuad Babić is reiterated almost verbatim by the Directive (*odluka*) signed by Adila Muhamedagić, director of the Pedagogical Institute, on the very same day (1992). Consistent with the Babić Order, the Directive reinforces the working relationship between the Pedagogical Institute and the Teaching Center under the direction of Smail Vesnić, a deputy director of the Institute himself (1992).

The integration of educational administration in Dobrinja under Civil Defense Headquarters and, in particular, the integration of military operations and civilian services such as education under a central command, was seen by General Hadžić as a necessity to ensure the psychological survival of the community, at least if education was viewed as a function of defense. Given its isolation from military headquarters and civilian government offices in Sarajevo, General Hadžić viewed Dobrinja as an entity unto itself and, for all practical purposes, on its own in a struggle for survival. In this regard, "Dobrinja was like a small state during the war, and everything was under control. Dobrinja was the most beautiful place during the war," General Hadžić said to me, given the purity of the common goal of resistance against the enemy, and in contrast to the infighting, the criminal gangs, and the black market back in Sarajevo. "It was much more beautiful in wartime than it is now," he said a bit wistfully. "'*Zemlja Dobrinja.*' Dobrinja je bio čudo. '"The Land of Dobrinja.' Dobrinja was a miracle" (2001).

"Every House the Frontline," read the headline of an article about Ismet Hadžić that appeared in the European edition of *Oslobođenje*, dated 5 December 1995, at the end of the war. The article refers to General Hadžić as "a man who created a myth out of Sarajevo's Dobrinja," and who is "surely one of the most interesting, and yet controversial personalities that grew out of the war" (Kurtović, 1956: 6). Indeed, by the end of the war, General Hadžić had become something of a mythic figure, considered a hero of Bosnia by some, and cited in books and film, and a gun-slinging cowboy by others. Thus one of the section headings of the article is entitled, "Iron Hand," for the manner in which he organized Dobrinja's defense, leading Steven L. Burg and Paul S. Shoup to refer to "his iron-fisted control of the district and of his independence from the Bosnian government" (2000: 139).

If education was a function of defense, and the organization of schools was a priority of General Hadžić, it is nevertheless clear that even before General Hadžić took command, planning was underway for the reconstruction of education as noted in the 20 May "Almanac" entry citing the proposal by Smail Vesnić for the creation of the Dobrinja War

School Center (Nastavni centar, 1992-1993). And while Ismet Hadžić may be the most prominent military figure associated with Dobrinja, it was Hajriz Bećirović, at the outset of the siege, and Adnan Tetarić, who together forged the connection between military and civilian government and, with Smail Vesnić, created the organizational framework in order to establish "the educational system [as] a function of defense." It was Hajriz Bećirović who, as commanding officer of TO forces, organized the defense of Dobrinja during spring 1992 several months prior to the formation of the 1st Dobrinja Brigade and the appointment of General Hadžić as brigade commander, and who recognized the necessity of a civilian government in support of military operations:

> Since Dobrinja was chopped off, not only from its own municipality of residence [Novi Grad] but from the rest of Sarajevo and BiH, we had to step forward forming an organ of civil government, which was called a popular and civilian government ...
>
> It was imperative to organize the Dobrinja territory in a new, wartime manner [and] that I form a new popular government ... But the actual organ of popular government in which direct participation of the endangered people was not formed in the war until the month of May 1992.
>
> The first organ of the new popular government, which only Dobrinjans formed, was the Provisional Self-Help Board which consisted of all structures of military and civilian life. The first president of this organ was Adnan Tetarić. (Bećirović, 2003: 96)

With the formation of the Provisional Self-Help Board that developed in response to the chaotic conditions of the siege, an unofficial and interim "organ of popular government," the mechanism was set in place for the development of an official, civilian government structure as an extension of the extant municipal government. The intent was also to develop a civilian governmental structure to complement military operations in defense of the community. A 28 May 1992 letter from Adnan Tetarić, who signed the letter as president of the Provisional Self-Help Board, to the War Presidency of Novi Grad Municipality, proposes the formation of a Coordination Board "as an organ of the municipality" and outlines the spectrum of civilian services required, to include school services, for a community under siege:

> We are appealing to you that in the framework of our authority, a ruling is in effect concerning the formation of a Coordination Board for Dobrinja and the Airport Settlement which will take effect as an organ

of the municipality as long as the circumstances of the war encirclement of this settlement lasts.

The Provisional Self-Help Board nominates to the Coordination Board:
1. Hajriz Bećirović, Commander, Territorial Defense
2. Adnan Tetarić, Vice-President
3. Dževdet Radončić, Member for Health Services
4. Rasim Tahirović, Member for Ministry of Internal Affairs Services
5. Smail Vesnić, Member for School Services
6. Rabija Bajraktarević, Member for Housing and Public Utility Services
7. Fuad Babić, Member for Civil Defense and Well-Being of Residents
8. Kemal Aljičević, Member for General Financial and Economic Services
9. Dževad Džiho, Member for Citizens' Information Services.
(Bećirović, 2003: 96-97)

Just three days later, dated 1 June 1992, Ismet Čengić, president of the War Presidency of Novi Grad Muncipality, answered that a Ruling (*zaključak*) was enacted in response to the official letter (*dopis*) of the Coordination Board:

1. The formation of the Coordination Board for Dobrinja and the Airport Settlement, completely in its entirety, is in accordance with the order of the War Presidency of the Municipality concerning the formation of the crisis headquarters in the local communities in the territory of the municipality.

2. As long as the complete encirclement of Dobrinja and the Airport Settlement lasts, the Coordination Board has united authority for the organization of life in the conditions in which it is situated. It is fair to say that services of defense and domestic services must be performed by information and coordination with the Municipal TO Headquarters and Novi Grad Sarajevo Public Security Stations.

3. The War Presidency approves the proposal of the members of the Coordination Board. (Bećirović, 2003: 97)

The Coordination Board provided the structural framework for the organization of civilian services as conceived by Hajriz Bećirović, the military commander, and Adnan Tetarić, whom he personally chose as his civilian counterpart. In his own words, reflecting upon those days, and in very emotional terms, Hajriz Bećirović reflected back on the difficulty of the times:

> Dobrinja was in bad shape. It was totally surrounded. I was aware of how difficult everything was, and I had no experience in this. I was looking for important people who would try to help out. I was looking

for important people who could be helpful. I contacted everyone who could help. Adnan Tetarić offered his assistance, and Smail Vesnić also. Adnan told me he was a psychologist, and I knew a psychologist could be helpful. It was war. People were dying all around.

We had a military command, but we were thinking about how to create a civilian government. Each citizen had to be put into a position to function as a citizen. I needed to give them something to do, to be useful—so we started to establish the institutions of government.

I wanted to establish the institutions of a civilian government. We discussed whether the civilian government should be placed under the military command. This was upside down, but it was war. It was Adnan's initiative to form the Coordination Board, but he wanted to name me as the president. I disagreed. I rejected that. I said that I am the military commander, and we have to respect civilian authority.

Together, we had the power to command. We were trying to establish the same model based on the same principles as a small state within the siege within a siege of Dobrinja. The Coordination Board looked like a mini-presidency, like the mini-presidency of a small state, and Adnan Tetarić was the president. (2004; 2006)

Hajriz Bećirović notes that "later," with authorization from Novi Grad Municipality, Command Headquarters ... "in place of the Provisional Self-Help Board, formed the Coordination Board for Dobrinja and the Airport Settlement." The same nine individuals cited in the 28 May letter comprised the membership of the Coordination Board but Adnan Tetarić, consistent with his signature on the letter, became the president of the Coordination Board and Hajriz Bećirović was listed as the commander of the Territorial Defense (2003: 98). Adnan Tetarić, a psychologist with the Pedagogical Institute, then designated Smail Vesnić, a colleague who was a deputy director of the Pedagogical Institute, as the person-in-charge (*povjerenik za prosvjetu*) for "school services." In the very same manner in which he recognized the initiative of Adnan Tetarić in the formation of the Coordination Board, Hajriz Bećirović also recognized the initiative of Smail Vesnić in the formation of the Dobrinja War School Center:

> While it was my idea to organize the schools, I put Smail together with Adnan on the Coordination Board with responsibility for school services. Each member of the Coordination Board had his own responsibilities. Smail had responsibility for the schools.
>
> His task was to organize the schools, to contact the teachers, the professors, to locate premises for schooling, to organize the stairway schools for elementary students. And we had no secondary school in Do-

brinja. One of the most important reasons to establish Gimnazija Dobrinja was to give students the opportunity to finish secondary school.

One of the most important reasons to establish education was so students could complete their education. It was important for students not to lose their school years. I have to say that almost all the teachers from Dobrinja answered the call.

Having in mind his experience, it was Smail's idea to form the Dobrinja War School Center. Smail Vesnić created the Dobrinja War School Center. It was his idea to form this Center. (2004; 2006).

On 20 May 1992, five days after the official closure of the 1991–1992 school year, and with no functional schools whatsoever, and Dobrinja totally cut off from Sarajevo city, the very first entry appeared in the "Almanac" of the Dobrinja War School Center, several weeks before the Center was even officially created. The entry read:

> At the meeting of the Coordination Board for Dobrinja and Airport settlements, which was appointed by the War Presidency of Novi Grad Municipality [one of ten municipalities that comprised prewar Sarajevo city], the proposal of Smail Vesnić, representative for the school system and a Coordination Board member, concerning the formation of a Teaching Center was considered. (Nastavni centar, 1992-1993)

Although the 20 May entry notes that Smail Vesnić was a representative for the schools as well as a Coordination Board member, and that "the formation of a Teaching Center was considered" at the Coordination Board meeting, this entry might more properly refer to the Provisional Board, or simply be a reference after the fact, considering the 28 May letter from Adnan Tetarić as president of the Provisional Self-Help Board proposing formation of the Coordination Board. Nevertheless, the 10 June 1992 entry, almost two months prior to the official Order of 3 August, indicates that the formation of the Dobrinja War School Center, as proposed by Smail Vesnić, was approved by the Coordination Board operating under the authority of the War Presidency of Novi Grad Municipality of Sarajevo City:

> At the meeting of the Coordination Board, the decision concerning the formation of a Teaching Center was approved. Smail Vesnić, deputy director of the Inter-Municipal Pedagogical Institute Sarajevo, is in charge for its organization and work. (Nastavni centar, 1992-1993)

The work of Smail Vesnić and his colleagues in the creation of the Dobrinja War School Center and the reconstruction of schooling in Dobrinja is cited by Hajrija-Šahza Jahić and her colleagues in an article,

10 April 1993 (Saturday): In the early morning, consultations with students, taking exams, and daily activities. At 11:00, the promotion of the gazette, Putokazi [Highways], began. Smail Vesnić [the director] spoke about the work of the Dobrinja War School Center. The promotion of the gazette, Putokazi, was carried out by the well-known writer, sculptor, and fighter from Dobrinja, N. Ibrišimović. The program was lead by Gordana Pijetlović, Mediha Pašić, and Safet Ovčina. "Senči," a likeable group, and "The Little Guys from Dobrinja," performed in the program. It was humble and nice. It was short, but it will be remembered for a long time (from the "Almanac" of the Dobrinja War School Center). Photo courtesy of Miroslav Kordić.

"Pedagogical Patriotism," three years into the war (1995). Here the importance of the Pedagogical Institute of Sarajevo was cited in the reorganization of the educational system during the war. The article begins in the same fashion as the article by Professor Jahić noted in the previous section, but specifically cites those educators involved in the reconstruction of schooling at the outset of the siege:

> April 1992, May 1992, destruction, burning ... days and nights blending into one and our mutual feeling within of creating the Institute no matter what the cost, as soon as possible. A great number of us came from all over the city ... During those first war days, the connection with the Institute was restored by Smail Vesnić, then manager of the Section for Promoting Educational Work, who was situated in Dobrinja and who, as a worker of the Institute, immediately was involved in the organization of the socialization-education process in Dobrinja. Zlatan Pravidur, professional advisor, was in Dobrinja too, and was also involved in the work as much as he was able taking into consideration that he was a member of the Army of the Republic of Bosnia and Herzegovina. A worker of the Institute, Adnan Tetarić, deceased, tragically lost his life together with his son, a young psychologist. (1995: 22)

Adnan Tetarić and his son, Samir, lost their lives early on a Wednesday morning, 17 June 1992, during the most intensive assaults on the settlement yet as the enemy sought to close the noose. Around 6:00 A.M., Halil Burić, who lived at 28 Franca Prešerna Street in the C4 complex of the Airport Settlement, and who would become the manager of the Higher Education Section of the War School Center, woke up to tanks and paramilitaries in the streets outside his kitchen window where the window frames still bear the scars of their bullets. Cited in the previous chapter, Professor Burić recalled that "everything happened so fast. I remember the first words out of my mouth: 'Tanks!' I realized at that moment what was happening for the very first time," as women and children from further up Franca Prešerna sought refuge from the gunfire echoing through the narrow streets in the garage below his apartment. The stories came echoing up the streets with them, of "a friend whose best friend killed his daughter," of a colleague who, "with a gun to the chin," had the choice of giving up his ring or his finger. As for Professor Burić, "After 25 years, I left with a ring on my finger and a watch," along with his family, fleeing for their very lives (2001).

The assault began in the narrow streets of the Airport Settlement, the apartment complexes known as C4 and C5 alongside the airport, as tanks, howitzers, and mortars pounded the apartments into ruin and paramilitaries terrorized the civilian population. Bewildered families emerged from their apartments only to escape further within besieged Dobrinja. Damir Hadžić, a 16-year old student at the time, who lived in C5, rushed to the frontlines along with his friends in efforts to defend his neighborhood. John F. Burns wrote in the *New York Times* of "a local volunteer defense force consisting of boys as young as 16 and men as old as 65 that had been holding off tank and infantry assaults by Serbian forces with firebombs and weapons that included World War II tommy-guns and hunting rifles" (1992: A16).

There along what was then Prištinska Street, Damir witnessed the executions in the streets of C4 of those who were caught by the enemy and cut into pieces by "cold steel" weapons (*hladno oruzje*) in a message to those who would stay behind (2001). We may remember here the words of the BSA commander to Hajriz Bečirović, "*Vi ste slijedeći kojeg ćemo zaklati,*" or, "You are the next one whose throat we will cut." Among those executed with cold steel weapons in front of their families were Adnan Tetarić, the vice-president of the Coordination Board for Dobrinja and the Airport Settlement, along with his son, Samir, a psychologist himself. The last hours of Adnan Tetarić are related by Alija Dacić in his "Narration of a Fighter":

> In the late evening hours, 16 June 1992, I was getting ready to go to the Airport Settlement. Professor Adnan Tetarić set out a few moments before me, but came right back to Headquarters all flustered and pale: "Alija, I was nearly killed, a bullet passed by my ear, I think it grazed me a little." For this professor, this exceptional man, that bullet, which to him passed by his ear a little before, was not sufficient warning to abandon his departure for his family in the Airport Settlement. I changed an order and stayed behind at the Headquarters that evening.
>
> In the early morning hours, 17 June 1992, strong aggressor forces from the direction of the Airport and Nedžarići with tanks, transporters, and other equipment, fortified by "Niš commandos," entered the perimeter to divide the Airport Settlement.
>
> Our underarmed defenses were unable to halt the advance of the enemy and retreated together with the residents towards C5 settlement. Some of the residents of the Airport Settlement were taken prisoner.
>
> In the time of the morning hours, I was at Headquarters in Dobrinja. The Airport Settlement was covered all over in smoke and couldn't be seen, but from the force of the tank and artillery shells, piecemeal running fire couldn't be recognized. Everything appeared as a terrible thunderstorm.
>
> The professor did not come to Headquarters that morning. Hajriz

Bećirović, the commander, said in passing, "Alija, call the professor to see what is up with him." I called the professor and he answered. I said to him: "Professor, pull back towards C5." His answer was: "Alija, my son was murdered, in the middle of the heart, send Doctor Radončić to me," and he dropped the headset. This was uttered through tears and deathbed death rattles. That morning he was murdered in the street on the doorstep to his building. I believe that I am the last man in his life, who heard his voice over the telephone, and that he was murdered after his son's death. (Dacić, 2003: 177-178)

"They almost tore him apart," said Smail Vesnić of his colleague, "a good man," to whom he dedicated the first issue of *Putokazi: List Nastovnog centra Dobrinja* (Highways: The Gazette of the Dobrinja Teaching Center) (Pijetlović, 1993), and to whom I dedicated the occasional paper that was the forerunner to this book (2005). "In Dobrinja and Nedžarići, where we too once lived," writes Mladen Vuksanović, in his *Pale Diary*, dated 19 June 1992, "the chetniks cut the throats of some fifteen people. I can't believe it, but anything is possible. Crime has become our everyday reality" (2004: 128).

Somewhere between 2,000-3,000 residents were expelled from their homes during this assault. Perhaps 80 people were killed, about 40 on the first day, and an unknown number were incarcerated in the Kula prison camp in Lukavica. On 18 June, in the midst of the assault, perhaps 12,000 shells of various types, from tanks, howitzers, rockets, and mortars, fell on Dobrinja within a four-hour period that morning (Hadžić, 2001). I had to ask General Hadzić twice to be sure of the number. Burns wrote:

> In the two months that Sarajevo has been under siege by Serbian nationalist troops, a still more pressing drama has been developing, mostly unwitnessed by outsiders ... Dobrinja, less than four miles from the city center, has been the site of a siege within a siege, a suburb of about 35,000 people that has been surrounded by Serbian troops, tanks, and artillery for more than 10 weeks ... Serbian commanders appeared to be aiming at taking complete control of an arc of territory on the western edge of the city, including Dobrinja, which has been one of the last strongholds of Bosnian Government loyalists on the city's periphery. (1992: A1)

These attacks took most of the C5 complex of the Airport Settlement, further reducing the size of besieged Dobrinja, establishing a Bosnian Serb salient and hence the frontline for the rest of the war, yet "small groups of courageous men" like Omer Musić, one of those men, in the absence of a Bosnian Army still in the process of formation, held the line against impossible odds. "That line held through Dayton," he recalls, and along with his small group, he "remained on that line, in front of my own building [from 17 June 1992] until March 1993" (2001). Today, a small memorial at the end of Habibe Stočević Street behind the C4 complex looks across to the airport in honor of the sacrifice of 27 men of C4 and C5 who died while holding the line, including Adnan and Samir Tetarić. Thus Hajriz Bećirović pointed to the assaults on the Airport Settlement as "the crown of the battles" for Dobrinja (2004). And in the words of Ismet Hadžić, who would soon assume command, "People really didn't believe that something like this would happen. Only then, with the heavy attacks on the Airport Settlement, did people begin to understand" (2001).

On 6 July 1992, the 1ˢᵗ Dobrinja Brigade of the Army of the Republic of Bosnia and Herzegovina (ARBiH) was officially formed out of the Territorial Defense forces to organize the defense of the settlement, and Ismet Hadžić was appointed brigade commander. Datelined 12 July, Burns wrote the following:

The frontline along Prištinska Street that runs through the eastern edge of the C4 Quadrant of the Airport Settlement. During the early days of the siege, valiant groups of citizen-soldiers, "small groups of courageous men," prior to the formation of the Bosnian Army, armed with hunting rifles and pistols, held the line along Prištinska, defending their homes and their neighborhoods from enemy assaults. Much of the Airport Settlement was taken during the assaults that began on 17 June 1992, but the line was held on Prištinska, and the street remained the frontline through the remainder of the siege. Photo courtesy of Mevsud Kapetanović.

The anxieties and hopes of 35,000 people poured forth today as a convoy of United Nations relief trucks crept across no man's land and into the devastated landscape of Dobrinja, penetrating a siege-with-a-siege that has turned the Sarajevo suburb into a ghetto of hunger and death.

For 71 days, Dobrinja has been the hardest-hit area of this besieged city, cut off from the rest of the Bosnian capital by Serbian troops who have attacked it with artillery, antiaircraft guns and sniper fire.

The high-rise suburb was built to serve as the athletes' village for the 1984 Winter Olympics, and its plight has transfixed the rest of the city's 400,000 inhabitants, who have found inspiration in accounts of the residents' endurance under fire. (1992: A6)

With the arrival of the UN convoy on 12 July, the first humanitarian aid arrived in Dobrinja after 71 days under total blockade. The arrival of the convoy was precipitated by the arrival of Canadian UNPROFOR troops on 29 June who took control of the airport from JNA forces who had occupied the runway, and who served as BSA operatives, while blasting the Airport Settlement into ruin. On the same day, Bosnian Army troops assaulted the enemy on Mojmilo Hill, taking control of the ridgeline overlooking much of Dobrinja, and forcing the enemy back to the ridgeline above Dobrinja 4. With the airport in the hands of the UN, and Bosnian Army troops establishing a defense line on Mojmilo, the siege within a siege of Dobrinja that began the weekend of 2-3 May was partially broken.

Several weeks before the official Order of Civil Defense Headquarters signed by Fuad Babić, dated 3 August, the 12 July 1992 entry in the "Almanac" notes that "the premises of the former Games Club are given to the Teaching Center" (Nastavni centar, 1992-1993). The Games Club was located in a shopping area on what was then called USAOJ (United Council of Anti-Fascist Youth of Yugoslavia) or AVNOJ (Anti-Fascist Council of the National Liberation of Yugoslavia) Boulevard that ran through the heart of Dobrinja just behind Simon Bolivar Elementary School, and the task of converting it into a Teaching Center for the administration and operation of schooling in the settlement was immense.

Indeed, throughout July, there are a series of entries in the "Almanac" that provide an indication of the both the workload and the work that was underway well before publication of the official 3 August Order. On 19 July, for example, the entry records that "members of the Teacher's Council were appointed," along with a secretary, and that "the first meeting of the Teacher's Council was held." Entries over the next several days record that registers (*knige evidencije*) for students were established as well as registers for all those who entered the Center. Mirsada Miraščija was hired as a typist and by 31 July, "daily consultations of professors [teachers] with students are being conducted" (Nastavni centar, 1992-1993).

Perhaps the most important work of those early days is seen in a planning document, dated July 1992, entitled, "The Basic Work Program of the Teaching Center in 1992," developed in concert with the Pedagogical Institute of Sarajevo, and leading to the eventual adoption of the "Basic Work Program" (*Programska osnova rada*) on 6 August 1992. This document provides an overview of the work and organization of the Teaching Center, information on educational personnel, and includes the documentation that established the Center as well. It also provides the basic objectives and tasks that would guide the work of the Center listed here as follows:

* to plan, program, and realize all activities in the field of education which will contribute to faster normalization of life and work in the settlement with the aim of increasing the total defense capabilities.

* to collect and analyze the necessary data on possible users of the Teaching Center and to plan and program its activities.

* to initiate, direct, and offer assistance for completion of remaining work in the 1991–1992 school year in the schools of Dobrinja.

* to assist and direct activities for their appropriate application based on regulations with legal power, to determine conditions on temporary internal organization, systematization and allocation of employees in institutions in the fields of education, science, culture, and sports, during war or immediate war danger.

* to offer appropriate professional services to the users in an instructive and consultative manner for successful continuation of schooling on the basis of the program of work for elementary and secondary schools.

* to register, program, and organize examinations in the Teaching Center in cooperation with the Rectorate of the University of Sarajevo, based on the Guidelines concerning the examination schedule, the time and place where examinations will take place in the higher education institutions of the Ministry of Education, Science, Culture, and Sport of the Republic of Bosnia and Herzegovina.

* to program, prepare, and realize in an instructive and consultative manner other educational activities for students and for the population of Dobrinja in general.

The Teacher's Council of the Center shall discuss in detail current problems in the education and socialization of students and shall undertake concrete measures in this regard. (Nastavni centar, 1992: 5-6)

Of particular note is that, along with these objectives, the "Basic Work Program" also makes specific reference to the conditions of elementary and secondary education:

> Along with other things, all aspects and possibilities shall be analyzed for repair of existing [elementary] school buildings, as well as further developments, especially secondary education and socialization and, in that sense, to generate worthy proposals to appropriate institutions for the establishment of a secondary school in Dobrinja. (Nastavni centar, 1992: 6)

The basic objectives and tasks are followed by what translates as "Programs of Instructive Teaching" (*Programi instruktivne nastave*) which are analogous to curricular guidelines for the organization of instruction. These "Programs" provide an outline for the range of school subjects in the curriculum at the preschool, elementary and secondary school, and university levels, and were compiled by representative groups of instructors from all such levels. The fact that these "Programs" appear as early as July 1992 indicates the amount of thought and work on the part of the teachers who were in the process of adapting a regular school curriculum for students without schools and regular classrooms under siege conditions.

Given the chaotic conditions of Dobrinja under siege, with residents fleeing the settlement, and others killed or living in basement shelters, one objective specifically noted the importance of collecting and analyzing information in order to plan and program Center activities. Thus the "Basic Work Program" notes the assignment of Asad Nuhanović to gather the appropriate demographic data from the settlement in order to determine educational needs with a deadline of 20 August 1992 for completion of his assignment.

> Before everything else, it will be necessary to determine the exact number of students who will receive an education in the stated period. For that purpose, a survey will be organized to collect relevant data on the users of services, mainly secondary school students and "future" secondary school students. (Nastavni centar, 1992: 9)

To implement this task, the Program contains two survey forms designed for both elementary and secondary school students. The specific reference to secondary education is, no doubt, because no secondary school was located in Dobrinja prior to the war, so all secondary students who lived in Dobrinja attended the 27 secondary schools throughout Sarajevo. The emphasis on numbers of secondary students was to develop the administrative framework for secondary schooling, to include both gimnazija and vocational emphases, and to determine the need for creating a secondary school as the center for secondary education. There was also the necessity of determining precise numbers of elementary students but, in regard to elementary education, the administrative framework remained in place from the prewar era since three elementary schools were located in Dobrinja at the outbreak of the war. In regard to the results of these student surveys, they are noted in the discussion of the "Basic Work Program of the Teaching Center, 1992-1993," dated November 1992, that was based on work accomplished by Asad Nuhanović during the interim months.

In regard to the survey instruments, in addition to the usual requests for information, we should note one question in particular asked of both elementary and secondary students—"Are you a member of the Armed Forces of BiH?" (Nastavni centar, 1992: 11-12). This question is obviously designed to determine how many Dobrinja students served in the military in order to provide a better sense of how the schools might accommodate their situation. In regard to this question, the very first objective of the "Basic Work Program" cites the need "to plan, program, and realize all activities in the field of education which will contribute to the faster normalization of life and work in the settlement with the aim of increasing the total defense capabilities" (1992: 5). This educational objective makes clear that "the educational system was a function of defense" and the idea of integrating "the structures of military and civilian life," with a civilian government placed under military command, although it was upside down, in the words of Hajriz Bećirović, was a military reality. "It was war" (2004).

Thus the "Basic Work Program" closes with a brief section on "Activities of the Teaching Center in cooperation with the Armed Forces of the Republic of Bosnia and Herzegovina." It reads, "In cooperation with the Command of the First Dobrinja Brigade, the Teaching Center will realize all necessary professional military training of members of the Armed Forces of the Republic of Bosnia and Herzegovina by special programs" (Nastavni centar, 1992: 76-77). The significance of the Center and the role played by Smail Vesnić in this regard is noted by Hajriz Bećirović who writes simply:

> Special measures (on "the government-level") were undertaken to or-

ganize the work of schools. These dealings were considered as special assignments. Smajo Vesnić, who is responsible for schools, worked in the best possible manner so that students completed the 1992-1993 school year successfully (like all other war years). That had an exceptional effect on strengthening the fighters' and the peoples' morale. (2003: 100)

In addition to the objectives and programs, the document also identifies 17 members of the Teacher's Council (*Nastavničko vijeće*) of the Center, established 19 July 1992 as noted in the "Almanac" entry of that date, that included representatives from the university faculties, teachers from Sarajevo schools, two directors of Dobrinja elementary schools, Enes Kujundžić, deputy minister of education of the Republic, Severin Montina, director of the Republican Fund for Secondary Education, and Smail Vesnić. Eight members of the Teacher's Council were appointed as section managers (*rukovodilac*) with responsibilities for the Center's eight educational sections to include preschool education, elementary education, secondary education, and higher education. There was also a coordinator for culture and public activities and a manager for information. Asad Nuhanović, who was manager for the programming and development section and responsible for the survey of students, was also in charge of coordination with civil defense agencies.

While section managers would change over the years of the war, there are several important names for the purposes of this study to include Smajo Halilović and then most notably, Seniha Bulja, managers of the Elementary Education Section, and Zlatun Pravidur and most notably, Ilija Šobot, managers of the Secondary Education Section. Gordana Pijetlović and Subhija Čehić, managers of the Preschool Education Section, and Halil Burić, manager of the Higher Education Section, should also be noted here. These individuals, working under the administrative framework of the Center, were given the initial responsibilities of meeting the objectives outlined in the "Basic Work Program" for the reconstruction of preschool, elementary, secondary, and higher education within Dobrinja during the long summer of 1992.

The significance of the July "Basic Work Program" as a framework for schooling in Dobrinja, and as a forerunner for a more comprehensive program developed during the fall and dated November 1992, is belied by the simple notation that closed the document: "The Teacher's Council of the Center adopted this Program at the meeting of 6 August 1992." The notation was signed by Smail Vesnić (Nastavni centar, 1992). A simple notation in the "Almanac" on 6 August, although underlined, read almost as an afterthought as well: "At this session, the Work Program of the Teaching Center was adopted," followed by a brief sentence that stated simply, "The day was tumultuous with heavy firing" (Nastavni centar, 1992-1993).

A Model of Educational Work

The entries in the "Almanac" during those August days in preparation for the 1992-1993 school year point to the complexity of tasks and the intensity of the workload. These entries clearly indicate that the Dobrinja War School Center was up and running but, periodically, descriptions of the workload and responsibilities are interspersed with notations of the siege outside that intrudes into the daily flow of events. A selection of these entries is presented here as follows:

- 8 August 1992, *Saturday*: The Center did not work because of the danger of shelling and heavy firing.

- 9 August 1992, *Sunday*: The commander of the Armed Forces of the RBiH for Dobrinja, Ismet Hadžić, visited the Teaching Center. He was accompanied by Fuad Babić and others ... After their departure, three shells fell in front of the Center and caused great panic. Four people from the Teaching Center were injured, two slightly and two heavily. Paintings were damaged, the entrance door was destroyed, mirrors were broken.

- 15 August 1992, *Saturday*: Every day we are accepting and registering students for exams. At 6:00, two shells fell in front of the Teaching Center, and one onto "Solid" [a business]. At that time, 40 people were in the Center. Fortunately, only two young men were slightly injured. Great material damage was done. After that the training continued.

- 21 August 1992, *Friday*: Regular training for members of the Armed Forces of RBiH continues. Consultations with teachers from the "Stairway Schools" [*Haustorske škole*] from Dobrinja 3. It was suggested that the "Work Program" be developed and a work journal [*dnevnik rada*] of teachers be maintained. Consultations of teachers with students continue.

- 22 August 1992, *Saturday*: Increased activities concerning the selection of directors of the elementary schools in Dobrinja, through contact with the director of the Center with the municipal organs of Novi Grad Municipality. Creation of materials for the initiative for the opening of a *gimnazija* in Dobrinja. (Nastavni centar, 1992-1993)

On 28 August 1992, just prior to the regular beginning of the new school year, the headline of an article in *Oslobođenje* posed the question: "Gimnazija opens in Dobrinja?" (1992: 6). The subheading noted: "Directors of the majority of elementary schools in the region of Novi Grad Municipality are appointed; Gimnazija in Dobrinja [is created] with four sections." The article updates the reader on the educational situation in Novi Grad Municipality, which includes Dobrinja, and cites the situation in regard to the three Dobrinja elementary schools and the status of the proposed secondary gimnazija:

> The arrival of September always signified the beginning of the new school year. Will that be in this wartime, it is difficult to say, although it is evident that all competent organs pursue maximum efforts so the work of schools will be normalized and the functioning administrative organs restored. So it is the War Presidency of Novi Grad Municipal Assembly brought about a decision abolishing past administrative organs in the elementary schools. Then instead of school boards, councils, and directors of the schools, steering and supervisory boards were formed and the directors of the schools appointed ...
>
> During these days the decision on appointing directors in the majority of elementary schools in the region of Novi Grad Municipal Assembly was passed ... in Nikola Tesla Elementary School, Faruk Jabučar ... in Dušan Pajić-Dašić Elementary School, Narcis Polimac, in Simon Bolivar Elementary School, Senadin Topić ...
>
> The War Presidency of Novi Grad Municipal Assembly supported the initiative of the Teaching Center in Dobrinja concerning the formation of four sections of the gimnazija with 160 students, in view of the fact that currently in Dobrinja the teaching staff has permission for the work of one secondary school institution ... Although only a small portion of the secondary school students of Dobrinja will attend this gimnazija, this initiative that came about in wartime deserves the attention and support of all authorized authorities. (*Oslobođenje*, 1992: 6)

Although Dobrinja had three elementary schools prior to the war, and now had three elementary school directors, but no school buildings, the elementary school administration remained in place. It is clear, however, that this framework had changed in response to wartime conditions with the creation of the Dobrinja War School Center. At the secondary level, with no secondary school in Dobrinja prior to the war, there was now a proposed gimnazija on the table that would serve not only as an academic secondary school to prepare students for the university but also as the administrative framework for all secondary schools under the direction of the Center. It is also clear that the severity of siege conditions forced

Dobrinja educators trapped in the besieged settlement to confront the educational realities of the siege much earlier than in most areas of the city. If for no other reason, these realities would confront the safety of the students as well as provide them with the basics of an education, especially at the elementary level, in the absence of the opportunity to attend school on a regular basis.

Against the background of the siege of Dobrinja, the work of education continued for Dobrinja educators as seen in the August entries in the "Almanac" of the Dobrinja War School Center. At the same time, against the background of the siege of Sarajevo, alongside the regular entries in the "School Annals" of Treća gimnazija, the academic secondary school in Novo Sarajevo, contemporary newspaper accounts record the official pronouncements of the Ministry of Education of the Bosnian Republic directed towards schools throughout the country. Dated 8 September 1992, for example, an article in *Oslobođenje* entitled, "War Determines the Term: Maximum care will insure that children and their parents are not exposed to danger." This article is cited in some detail here, as it was in my previous book, for the background it provides about the beginning of the new school year in a country at war and a city under siege:

> The preparation of plans for registration in the secondary schools in the Republic is in progress. The authorized ministry states that the date of the beginning of the school year will be given later because it highly depends on war operations and the situation at the front.
>
> Therefore, it can be spoken about some kind of "slippery" beginning of the school year. Municipalities will individually decide about the beginning of the school year depending on the circumstances. In the Ministry of Education, Science, Culture and Sport, four different school program proposals are prepared which will determine the length and duration of classes. Because of the war, however, they are likely to be changed.
>
> According to the Decision on Conditions and Temporary Criteria for Registration of Students in the First Class of Secondary School, the secondary school registration requirements will be announced through the media, and will be based on the grades of the last four years of elementary school ...
>
> The registration plan is based upon the estimates of last year's statistics and the actual number of students. Considering the war in the region, ethnic cleansing and the large migration, the actual number and classes of students today is disastrous, even though the there is a certain optimism in the Ministry that, in spite of everything, instruction will be given as planned.

In the Ministry they want to deny rumors about the possibility of creating ethnic schools or classes. The unified plan and program of schooling does not mention that possibility nor consider it a good solution.

When it comes to elementary schools, the conditions are similar to secondary schools. Maximum care will be taken that children and their parents do not expose themselves to any kind of danger when they go to schools or while they are in schools, which will be taken care of by the municipalities in which the schools are located ...

In the end, there is still a question of how instruction will be implemented in practice. Many schools have been demolished, some serve as shelters, and parents fear letting their children go farther than the yard of the house. Possibly this will be yet another problem that will be attract the interest of officials. (*Oslobođenje*, 1992: 4)

On the following day, 9 September 1992, the Government of the Republic of Bosnia and Herzegovina, "on the recommendation" of the Ministry of Education, made a "Decision on the Registration of Students in Elementary and Secondary Schools and the Beginning of Instruction in the 1992-1993 School Year." The Decision reads as follows:

I

The executive organ of the municipality and/or city community, in cooperation with the jurisdictional, district secretariat for social work, is responsible, taking into account the safety of students and teachers and securing the conditions for normal instructional procedures in elementary and secondary schools, to bring about:

1. A Decision on the beginning, duration, and place where the registration of students for the first class of elementary school and the first class of secondary school;

2. A Decision on the beginning and place where instruction is to be conducted for the 1992-1993 school year in elementary and secondary schools.

II

The registration of students for the first class of elementary school shall be done for those student who will by 1 September of this year be seven years of age.

In exceptions, in elementary schools that have the space and the teaching staff, it is permitted to register children who will, by 1 September of this year be six years of age.

The registration of children, as described above, will proceed according to the lists of children in the school-age group, of the municipality administrative organ responsible for education, or on the basis of applications submitted by the parents of the children from the territory of the municipality, as well as on the basis of applications submitted by the parents or legal guardians of the refugee children or displaced persons residing in the respective municipality.

III

The registration of students in secondary schools will proceed on the basis of open competition for student admission into the first class of secondary school for the 1992-1993 school year, a decision on equal criteria and evaluation for admission of students into secondary institutions, and the Plan for registration of students in the first class of secondary school in the Republic of Bosnia and Herzegovina in the 1992-1993 school year, which will be decided upon by the Republican Public Fund for Secondary Education and Upbringing, in agreement with the Minister of Education, Science, Culture and Sport. (*Službeni list RBiH*, 1992)

On the next day, 10 September 1992, another article entitled, "Instruction to be Adapted to Wartime Conditions," appeared in the pages of *Oslobođenje* reviewing the Decision enacted the previous day. The article reiterates the Decision on the registration of elementary and secondary school students for the new school year and reads in detail here as follows:

> The Government of the Republic of Bosnia and Herzegovina yesterday adopted a Decision on the Registration of Students in Elementary and Secondary Schools and the Beginning of Instruction in the 1992/93 School Year.
>
> With this Decision, the Government of the Republic of Bosnia and Herzegovina ordered municipality and city community executive organs, that are responsible for the safety of students and teachers, to insure conditions for conducting normal instructional procedures in elementary and secondary schools.
>
> In harmony with this, municipalities, with regards to city communities, will decide about the beginning, the length, and the place for holding the registration of students in the first class of elementary and secondary school, and the decision about the beginning and the place for holding instruction in the 1992/93 school year ...
>
> Instruction in elementary schools and secondary schools will be carried out according to the program that was designed by Educational-Pedagogical Institute of the Republic of Bosnia and Herzegovina, and the organization and supervision of instruction in harmony with the Decision of the Government of the Republic of Bosnia and Herzegovina will be

executed by the appropriate secretariat that works in wartime conditions—it was said in the report from yesterday's meeting of Government of the Republic of Bosnia and Herzegovina. (*Oslobodenje*, 1992: 8)

It is clear that the Ministry of Education allocated responsibility to school administrators at the municipal and local community levels to implement the decision to initiate the 1992-1993 school year "depending on the circumstances." These school administrative units were to decide not only upon the registration of new students at the elementary and secondary levels, but upon the appropriate places for instruction, and upon the duration of the new school year as well. In Sarajevo, the responsibility for these decisions rested with the City Secretariat for Education, along with the Pedagogical Institute, the school administrators in the four remaining municipalities of "free Sarajevo," and the local communities of each of these four municipalities. The beginning of the new school year in Sarajevo would be decided whenever "the question of how instruction will be implemented in practice" would be resolved. In Dobrinja, it was clear that these responsibilities rested in the hands of Smail Vesnić as director of the Dobrinja War School Center, the 17 members of the Teacher's Council of the Center, and the respective section managers, in cooperation with the Coordination Board for Dobrinja and the Airport Settlement operating under the War Presidency of Novi Grad Municipality.

At the very same time, dated September 1992, the Pedagogical Institute of Sarajevo adopted a "Work Program in War Conditions for 1992." The typed copy of the document provided me by Melita Sultanović, an Institute advisor, was significantly revised in longhand, with sections crossed out and statements added. Here I will refer to the original document which provides an overview of Institute operations and personnel during wartime and presents those tasks at hand "insuring conditions for the work of the schools up to the beginning of the new school year" which had yet to get underway. Nevertheless, as of September 1992, in accordance with "some kind of 'slippery' beginning" to the 1992-1993 school year, the Institute document specifically refers to the extremity of the situation in Dobrinja, the relationship of the Pedagogical Institute to the Dobrinja War School Center, and the "Basic Work Program" of July 1992:

> During war actions, special activities were underway in the territory of encircled Dobrinja. The Institute, in cooperation with the Command of the Armed Forces of Bosnia and Herzegovina which was stationed in Dobrinja, established a Teaching Center with the task to initiate, direct, and organize all activities in the areas of education, science, and culture.

The Work Program of the Center was delivered earlier and the achieved results are known to the general public. (Pedagoški zavod, 1992)

The Institute document reiterates the statements of Institute advisors, cited earlier, concerning the relationship between advisors of the Pedagogical Institute back in Sarajevo and Institute advisors such as Adnan Tetarić and Smail Vesnić trapped in Dobrinja who were responsible for creating the War School Center. In the words of Hajrija-Šahza Jahić, one of those advisors, "Dobrinja was an example of education in complete isolation, but our advisors were there" (1998). In the words of Melita Sultanović, another one of those advisors, noting to me the role of the Institute in the reconstruction of schooling, "Everything was an improvisation ... The idea was to normalize the situation for the children, to start first with programs in one location [Dobrinja] and then implement these programs throughout other parts of the city ... but we were the cell of the organization" (1998).

In this regard, the Institute document sets forth operational plans for the forthcoming school year citing the work of the Dobrinja War School Center as "a model of educational work," to reiterate Seniha Bulja, for schooling throughout Sarajevo city:

> The advisors of the Institute will take an active part in the compilation of instructional programs under war conditions for elementary and secondary education which means compilation of operational plans for individual subjects, compilation of technical guidelines for stated programs, and repeating programs and processing missed instruction from the previous school year.
>
> To this end, the experience gained in the operation of the Dobrinja Teaching Center, which links all segments of education, culture, and information, and represents a novelty in our educational system, should be used in view of the efficient and successful organization of all activities ...
>
> The new situation requires, on the part of school institutions, a swift and efficient restructuring and a different organization at the internal and external levels. The experience gained in the operation of the Dobrinja Teaching Center should be used here. (Pedagoški zavod, 1992: 4)

Drsko i Hrabrost

Cheek and Courage
The Stairway Schools of Dobrinja and Elementary Education

CHAPTER THREE

She did not understand anything. The sharp "no" echoed like thunder. All she wished for was just an ordinary pair of shoes. What happened all of a sudden? She always had everything and now they did not even let her go out. Everything had changed since they had emigrated from their apartment. Her favorite dolls, bicycle, computer all remained there. This pushed her further to make the decision:

"I know, I will run away, just as did many children in the movies. But first, I will write a goodbye letter." She sat by the writing desk and with neat and legible handwriting started writing:

> Dear mother, dear father,
> I can not live like this any longer, I am leaving and going to my aunt's and uncle's house. They will not yell at me! But know, that I love you both very much.
> Yours, Adisa

She left the letter on the table and tiptoed out of the room. The house was filled with silence. Her sister was in school, her father on the war front. This she knew very well. But her mother, where was she? She searched all the rooms of the small emigrant flat but her mother was no where to be found. She came to the kitchen from where she could hear the clapping of the plates and glasses and the splashing of water. The door was half open. That is when Adisa saw her mother washing the dishes in cold water. She noticed her freezing and stiff hands. She also noticed her tired and exhausted face. Her heart suddenly crumpled and she moved away from the door. She thought how selfish and unthoughtful she was, not thinking even once about her mother's and father's struggle for the family to survive. Her dark eyes filled with tears and she started to cry. She sprang to her room and took the letter. She read it once again and threw it into the smoky fire. Then she ran to the kitchen, took away a glass that her mother was holding and put it on the table. With all her strength, she hugged the stunned woman and whispered: "I love you mummy!"

—Amra Kujundžić, 6th grade
Skender Kulenović Elementary School

A Few Good Women
The Stairway Schools of Dobrinja

"The children of Dobrinja can't go to school," wrote Seniha Bulja, the manager of the Elementary Education Section of the Dobrinja War School Center. "They don't have any. These schools are dead and destroyed monuments. It is war" (1993: 1). Although there were three elementary schools in the settlement, there were no longer any school buildings for students to attend within a month after the start of the siege. Dušan Pajić-Dašić Elementary School, on the eastern end of the settlement, was directly on the frontline, "full of bullet holes," since it was now occupied by the defenders of Dobrinja, "and now it looks like an old, empty castle." Seniha Bulja continues, "Until yesterday this school was alive, happy, and its doors were wide open for the little ones ... Its doors are still wide open but now that school is empty. One can easily get killed just by being next to it." Nikola Tesla Elementary School, on the western end of the settlement, just across the street from the C4 complex of the Airport Settlement, was directly on the frontline as well and "also in ruins" (1993: 1). "We put up barracades at Nikola Tesla Elementary School," said Hajriz Bećirović, but the defenders of Dobrinja who now occupied the school held the line there during the mid-June assaults on the Airport Settlement (1993: 55).

As for Simon Bolivar Elementary School, located in the very middle of the settlement, Seniha Bulja writes, "Simon Bolivar School, even though being burned to charcoal, again is an everyday enemy target" (1993: 2). A notation from the *Monografia* of Skender Kulenović Elementary School, the new name of Simon Bolivar from April 1994, reads, "They set fire to education, socialization, children's wishes and dreams. Everything burned, but everything remained" (1998: 8). And the previous chapter noted the bitterness of the article from *Dobrinja—Ratne novine* entitled, "Killers in School Benches," that blamed former teachers and administrators for "the 12 shells which the chetniks fired on the charred remnants of Simon Bolivar Elementary School, and a few incendiary rounds, to incinerate to the ground" what remained (Tabaković, 1992: 15).

With three elementary schools and no school buildings in May 1992, and the siege lines tightening around the settlement, Seniha Bulja organized "the first 'stairway school' [*haustorska škola*] in this part of Dobrinja," in the local community known as Dobrinja 2B, which began classes on a Friday, 19 June 1992, "in a building that was on the frontline. You will have to acknowledge," she wrote at the time, "the cheek and the courage" (1993: 1). Although perhaps a more literal translation is "corridor school," the common reference is to "stairway school(s)" that were located in the hallways and stairways of apartment buildings as well as in basements, shelters, utility rooms, and private apartments. Bulja also notes that "'little schools' were formed on the quadrants of Dobrinja which will in the first phase work in stairways and shelters ... henceforth the name 'stairway schools'" (2001). And Hajrija-Šahza Jahić of the Pedagogical Institute writes:

> We knew too that school has a comforting and healing effect on all children and in particular represents a rich source of psycho-social support for the child who has suffered severe emotional wounding. Many teachers, educationalists, nurses, doctors and artists began spontaneously to gather children round them in cellars, stairways, and safe flats. This is the origin of the first so-called *war schools*, often called *stairway schools*, *mobile schools* or *resistance and defiance schools* ...
>
> The location of *war schools* was dependent on the number of children who could come to them, and on the buildings and even individual stairways, in which the so-called *stairway schools* were opened. These schools were particularly characteristic of the settlement of Dobrinja, in which nearly every stairway had an organized school initiative as part of the so-called *war schools*. (1996: 11-12)

Located in the shelter (*sklonište*) of an apartment complex along a narrow lane known then as Salvador Allende Street, in stairway numbers 5, 9, and 11, the Dobrinja 2B stairway school was a stone's throw from the frontline at the end of the street where Bosnian defenders occupied Dušan Pajić-Dašić Elementary School. Class sessions met everyday for two hours, between 10:00–12:00 A.M., because "that time period was the safest." Two groups of students, organized by grade level, rotated around a regular class schedule that included mathematics, Bosnian language, art, physics, chemistry, and music. The students in Section A, grades 1-4, were listed as follows:

- Adel Salihović   grade 3
- Haris Hasanagić   grade 3
- Mensur Sejfović   grade 4
- Reuf Džinović   grade 4
- Adrijana Radić   grade 2

The five students in Section B, organized by grade levels 5-8, were listed as follows:

- Samir Demirović   grade 5

- ✦ Nedim Hasanagić,   grade 5
- ✦ Safet Šatara,   grade 5
    (student discontinued regular classes and now does not come)
- ✦ Badrudin Banjanović   grade 8
- ✦ Ibrahim Sejfović   grade 8 (Bulja, 1992).

Today, one of the former students in Section A of the 2B stairway school, Ibrahim Sejfovič remembers: "I attended stairway school in Dobrinja between 1992 and 1993. The stairway school was exactly as it sounds, a makeshift academic environment located in stairways of our apartment building" (2005). Ibrahim's brother, Mensur, who attended Section 2B, vividly remembers his time in the stairway school as well with the sound of shelling and firefights outside the school (2005). Yet these young students, with the consent of their parents, continued to attend classes on a regular basis in their stairway school classrooms. "Above the names of the students written on the wall," writes Seniha Bulja, "it says: 'First Stairway School 'Dobrinja 2B'" (1994: 1).

In a paper entitled, "The Stairway School: A Model of Socialization–Education Work in Dobrinja," presented at an educational conference, *Školstvo u Ratnim Uslovima* [The School System in War Conditions], on 18 April 1994 in wartime Sarajevo, Bulja writes:

> The children of this street, these nine little kids, sat bravely at their desks which were not standard, they were not for students, made out of canvas, but as long as they could sit, the desks and chairs were OK. The student classroom is small. Nine of them could barely fit together ... The classroom has three walls. The fourth is a hallway and it leads outside of the stairway onto the street in front of the building ...
>
> The source of light for the classroom is a student-made candlelight. The way it's made is by filling half a glass with oil and half with water. Then two thin cotton lines are taken through the cork of a wine bottle and placed in the glass. When those cotton lines are soaked in oil, they are lit and they stay lit as long as there is oil. (1994: 3)

As the stairway schools often took their names from the streets and stairways where classes were held, the Dobrinja 2B Stairway School took on the name of the Salvador Allende Stairway School #9. Hence, from the "Work Journal" (*Dnevnik rada*) of the Salvador Allende Stairway School, it is clear that a regular class schedule was organized around specific topics and learning objectives for each class and developed from a regular although abbreviated curriculum that included the sciences and mathematics. Bulja notes that teachers also attempted to talk with students about contemporary events, introducing classes on first aid and civil defense, in order to confront the reality of a war that was occurring just down the street from their modified classroom. Furthermore, teachers made an attempt to adapt the regular subject matter to address the implications of such a dangerous situation. Thus themes for art classes included such topics as "War in My Street," "War in Dobrinja," "War in Sarajevo," and "War in Bosnia and Herzegovina," while instructional units (*nastavne jedinice*) for music included "Patriotic Songs of Bosnia and Herzegovina, and "socialization" objectives for literature (what we might call affective objectives) included "the development of patriotism towards Bosnia and Herzegovina" (1992). Bulja writes about schooling during wartime conditions:

> Before the realization of the program, it was necessary to talk with the kids and, in a way, explain what was happening around us. These kids did not understand where this sudden hatred and evil come from. You will admit to yourself that even after all these things that we have lived through, it still is not quite clear ...
>
> The students in higher grades who took chemistry were also educated about poisonous gasses, nerve agents, and means of protection. It sounds impossible but it happened. Most of this information obtained by the students came in useful, not just for them, but also for their parents.
>
> The Teaching Center supported such work with a warning on the very dangerous situations being present in this part of Dobrinja. (1994: 3)

The Salvador Allende Stairway School could not have existed without the support of the Dobrinja War School Center and the parents of the children who attended the school, not to mention civil defense, local government, and military authorities. Bulja specifically mentions the parents' contribution in the first parent-teacher meeting at the War School Center on 17 June 1992 during the height of the enemy assault on the C4 complex of the Airport Settlement. It was at this meeting that "we decided that classes would be held in the area of the shelter at [stairway] number nine" (1994: 4). Yet, just two days later, amidst the continuation of those assaults, the first classes for students in a stairway school in the extreme western end of the settlement began just off the frontline. Ten students, one more than the regular nine, from grades two through five as well as grade eight, attended the first class session where they were even given a homework assignment that consisted of three questions, one each on biology, chemistry, and physics. The theme for the art class that day: "War in Dobrinja" (1992).

In fact, much of the work of organizing the stairway schools of Dobrinja during those early days, especially for preschool and elementary students, was accomplished by individuals who simply had no experience as teachers. The listing of the 14 teachers from the Emile Zola Stairway School, for example, located at Emile Zola Street numbers 3 and 5, running perpendicular to Salvador Allende Street in Dobrinja 2B, included the following individuals: one student in the Music Secondary School, one undergraduate student at the Fine Arts Academy, one Master's student in economics, two economists, two engineers, one retired teacher, one retired professor, one political science professor, one preschool teacher, two elementary school teachers, and one whose occupation is not listed.

These 14 teachers taught 45 students organized into six different class levels: preschool (7 students), grades one and two (9 students), grades four and five (12 students), grade six (7 students), grade seven (4 students), and grade eight (6 students). They taught on a regular, weekly class schedule, Monday through Saturday, and taught a regular although abbreviated offering of subjects. Nevertheless, the concerns over the safety of these young students is seen in a brief notation entered by the War School Center on one of the school documents of the Emile Zola Stairway School:

> If and when parents believe that on a determined day children cannot be sure of coming to the street in which certain instruction is held, they are not to trifle to bring the children to school. (Nastavni centar Dobrinja, 1992)

In another paper presented at the 18 April 1994 conference on schooling in wartime Sarajevo, "Reporting on the Theme of the 'War School' (on the Basis of Partial Experience from the Work of the 'KRIN' [Lily] Stairway 'War' School on M. Oreškovića Street #9—Dobrinja)," Faiza Kapetanović writes about her experience as "an amateur in this line of work" noting that she had no experience as a teacher. Nevertheless, she organized a stairway school in "a dark basement area" of Marka Oreškovića Street #9, just behind Simon Bolivar Elementary School in the middle of the settlement, in the area known as Dobrinja 2A, "which was the safest place for our gatherings." That dark basement "became something of an oasis, a world that did not have a place for hatred and death."

With a total of 26 children ranging in age from 4 to 16 at the outset, and 9 preschool children who "came to join us from neighboring stairways," the Lily Stairway School included students from preschool through eighth grade. "Personally I am not a qualified educator," Kapetanović writes, "but the need for preserving the mental health of these kids grew stronger and stronger. We gathered around and that is how the 'Lily' War School began.

Forgive me for being personal, but you will understand that this school is a part of me, a wonderful experience and a memory for the rest of my life" (1994: 1). The Lily Stairway School began work on 15 May 1992, the very day that the 1991-1992 school year officially ended, and the very day that Simon Bolivar Elementary School was shelled, with classes "in a dark basement area" on a narrow lane located just behind the burned-out elementary school.

With the official end of the school year, and amidst the intense assaults on the settlement during May and June, there was mass confusion on the part of teachers and students alike along with the uncertainty of whether there would even be a school year to follow. In Dobrinja, with three elementary schools but no school buildings, and no secondary schools in the settlement, and with students and teachers virtually unable to leave their buildings amidst the shelling and the snipers, the uncertainties over the future, not to mention the future of schooling, were overwhelming. Within this background, it is clear that in the minds of those educators and volunteers who took responsibility for organizing the stairway schools, these schools had, at the very least, two specific objectives.

First, the early formation of the stairway schools of Dobrinja appears to be in direct response to the concerns of both parents and educators to somehow complete the 1991-1992 school year without the loss of class time. Seniha Bulja writes, for example, in regard to the Salvador Allende Stairway School, that "the teaching contents which were planned for April, May, and June of that school year are being repeated in classes" (1994: 3). As noted in the "Basic Work Program of the Teaching Center in 1992" of July 1992 and formally adopted on 6 August 1992, one of the primary objectives of the Center was "to initiate, direct, and offer assistance for completion of the remaining work in the 1991-1992 school year in the schools of Dobrinja" (Nastavni centar, 1992: 5).

Second, the formation of the stairway schools was also a direct response to concerns for the safety and sanity of the children, particularly the elementary school students, and an attempt to keep them off the streets where they were fair game for shells and snipers. Faiza Kapetanović writes of the traumatic effects of the war on the children:

> Wartime situations have a deep psychological impact on people. They cause regular life habits to change and continuous intense feelings. Fear and uncertainty knock down the walls of composure and rationality. War and the horror it causes have the greatest effect on children. Personally, I realized that while spending long hours in basement shelters, seeking

shelter from the deadly mortar shells falling nearby. I have observed those kids and almost felt the change that was happening to them. Overnight they grew older. Their happy eyes, those mirrors of pure and innocent souls, lost their light, which was replaced by some terrible darkness. On the other hand, the older kids were concerned with safety for their very lives. That is what inspired me to gather these kids from our stairway. (1994: 1)

Kapetanović writes of the priorities of the Lily Stairway School. "The basic one was companionship and developing a whole sense of the collective [or team]. Stimulating, developing, and testifying to the creative capabilities of each child was the second priority" (1994: 1). Thus she developed activities designed to promote relationships between children who would otherwise be isolated in their apartments, basements, or shelters, as well as activities to stimulate the creative capacities of the children who lived under the oppressive nature of wartime conditions. The fact that the Lily Stairway School functioned in the shadow of the burned-out Simon Bolivar Elementary School was an image which she, the teachers, and the children had to confront on an everyday basis.

So professional educators such as Seniha Bulja, and concerned volunteers

A group of elementary students standing in line outside their war school classroom in Dobrinja 2 in the middle of the settlement. Note the vertical concrete barriers that protect the entrance to the classroom and the sandbags on either side of the entrance to the apartment building. Photo courtesy of Mevsud Kapetanović.

such as Faiza Kapetanović, and the hundreds of others who, unfortunately, remain nameless here, constructed a stairway school system throughout the settlement under siege conditions designed to ensure the safety and the sanity of their students. In the process, they educated students about the dangers around them and the response to such dangers through classes in first aid and civil defense and integrated themes such as "War in My Street" and "War in Dobrinja" into the regular curriculum. Nonetheless, a closing notation in the "Work Journal" for the Salvador Allende Stairway School, dated 15 July 1992, reveals just how close these dangers were and how they affected the operation of the stairway schools. The notation reads:

> Because of the dangers to which the children of this street are exposed (on the frontline), work with this group of students is brought to an end on 15 July (Wednesday) 1992 ... However, it is expected that the start of work of stairway schooling at Franca Rozmana Street will be instruction for the subjects of physics and chemistry to be developed according to the same curriculum which was turned in earlier to the archives of the Dobrinja Teaching Center. (Bulja, 1992: 24)

With the dangers surrounding the Salvador Allende Stairway School located almost on the frontline itself, it is clear that safety considerations were foremost in the minds of those who organized the school. Yet, under these conditions, provisions for the continuation of classes were made at another location nearby which suggests the importance of schooling for teachers, students, and parents alike. Faiza Kapetanović explains the significance of such classes and the significance of the stairway schools in this manner. "Luckily, on the initiative of faculty and us amateurs, a generation of little ones was saved who, in fact, represent the future of the country" (1994: 2). To reiterate the words of Smail Vesnić, reflecting back upon the struggles of reconstructing schooling during these early days of the war, "We saved those kids. We moved them from the streets to the classroom, and we saved them" (2001).

During the period from June through October 1992, according to Seniha Bulja, "about 900 students attended [at least 28] stairway schools, and 89 teachers carried on instruction" (1994: 4). With the Dobrinja War School Center up and running as summer 1992 progressed, the Center, through the Section for Elementary Education, with Seniha Bulja as the section manager, began to take on the responsibility of both supporting the individual stairway schools in various ways as well as organizing these schools uner the administrative framework of the Center. Bulja notes the importance of this connection:

The Teaching Center made available all necessary professional assistance around the entire organization of work not only to this school [Salvador Allende Stairway School], but to all other stairway schools which from June to October 1992 operated on abbreviated intervals on every street ... All stairway schools in Dobrinja were organized by the same principles and worked by the same completed programs which were modeled in the Section for Elementary Education within the framework of the Teaching Center. (1994: 4)

Entries in the "Almanac" of the Dobrinja War School Center also make specific reference to the operation of the stairway schools and the support of the Center for the initiatives taken by the teachers of these individual schools during summer and early fall 1992: Three such entries, for example, read as follows:

31 July 1992, *Friday*: An exhibition of works done by children from the "Stairway Schools" was organized (A. Nuhanović, S. Halilović, S. Ovćina).

24 August 1992, *Monday*: Preparations for publishing the Teaching Center's journal titled *Putokazi* began. Tasks within the editorial office were assigned. An initiative and activities providing the "Stairway Schools" with necessary supplies began.

25 October 1992, *Sunday*: Office supplies for the "Stairway Schools" were provided. Notebooks, paper, etc. (Nastavni centar, 1992-1993)

In the "Almanac," dated 31 October 1992, Smail Vesnić writes a particularly poignant entry concerning the hopes and dreams for the children of the "stairway schools" of besieged Dobrinja, which also suggests something of the relationship between the Center and the stairway schools that were organized on the initiative of individual teachers and volunteers:

A lot of work is expected today at the Center. I arrived to work at 7:00 A.M. As usual, we are late. The equipment was brought in at 11:00. At 12:00 the stage was arranged. Some of the desks and chairs for the "stairway schools" were taken to Dobrinja 4 and 5. At 3:00, general rehearsal began for tomorrow's show, "Children Singing the Hits." The room was full as if there was a show. Hopefully everything will go well and in peace. The children had wished more than the adults for something like this to happen. Looking at their faces in their performance, it is easy to see that they could easily forget the damn war. I hope that their little smart eyes will see days of freedom. (Nastavni centar, 1992-1993)

On the following day, the performance of "Children Singing the Hits" was held in the War School Center and included a number of prominent

Sarajevo artists as guests. It followed a Catholic mass in the presence of French UNPROFOR priests as well as the Croatian priest from the area of Stup nearby. The entry reads:

> At 2:00 the children began to arrive at the Center. It was so crowded. The event itself was fantastic. The children greeted every performer with applause. It was not important to them who the winner would be. Everyone was a winner today because they managed at least on this afternoon a victory over the war with the width of one's own soul and the size of one's children's heart. The flame of peace could be seen in their eyes. (Nastavni centar, 1992-1993)

THE SYNCHRONIZATION OF WORK
THE STAIRWAY SCHOOLS, THE THREE ELEMENTARY SCHOOLS,
AND THE ELEMENTARY EDUCATION SECTION
OF THE DOBRINJA WAR SCHOOL CENTER

With at least 28 stairway schools in operation across Dobrinja during summer 1992, according to Seniha Bulja, the individual stairway schools were integrated under the administrative framework of the three Dobrinja elementary schools during fall 1992 in preparation for the official beginning of the 1992-1993 school year to be determined by the Ministry of Education of RBiH. In her role as manager of the Elementary Education Section of the Dobrinja War School Center, Professor Bulja notes the administrative assignments for each of the three elementary schools for those stairway schools located within the elementary "school regions." In her "Notice Concerning School Regions," dated 1 January 1993, sent to "All Local Communities of Dobrinja and the Airport Settlement," Professor Bulja writes, "From 10 November 1992, in accordance with the directive of professional advice of the Teaching Center, we are notifying you concerning the provisional war school regions of Dobrinja and the Airport Settlement" (1993). This was a work in progress, however, and, in this regard, Seniha Bulja addresses the developing relationship through fall 1992 between the Dobrinja War School Center, the three Dobrinja elementary schools that existed prior to the war, and the 28 stairway schools scattered throughout the settlement:

> The Teaching Center rendered all necessary professional assistance concerning the entire work organization, not only to this school [Salvador Allende], but to all other stairway schools which operated with abbreviations and interruptions in the time from June to October 1992 on every street . . . on the streets of Jawaharlal Nehru, Emile Zola, Nikola Demonja, Omladinskih Radnih Brigada [Youth Work

Brigade], October Revolution, Sulejman Filipović, and Petra Drapšina and many others.

All stairway schools in Dobrinja were organized by the same principles and operated in accordance with the same programs which were modeled in the Section for Elementary Education within the framework of the Teaching Center.

According to the data from the mentioned Section, stairway schools during this period were attended by around 900 students, and 89 teachers carried out instruction.... Among the teachers, some of them were engineers, doctors, lawyers, and economists. All of them wanted to help those kids through school and to get away from the reality of war.

The experiences in the operation of the stairway schools were possibly and perhaps certainly a reliable professional foundation for programming the shape of socialization-education work in the coming school year. It is carried out on the war district regions of Dobrinja in the three existing elementary schools.

Dušan Pajić-Dašić covers the territory of Dobrinja 1, Dobrinja 2B, and Dobrinja 3B. Simon Bolivar covers the territory of Dobrinja 2A and Quadrant C5, whereas Dobrinja 3A and Dobrinja 5 are part of Nikola Tesla School. (1994: 4)

Although elements of this document were cited previously, it is cited in depth here to provide a sense of the developing organizational framework for elementary schooling in Dobrinja.

With the development of an administrative framework for the organization of elementary education, Bulja writes of the initial administrative responsibilities, as noted previously in the "Basic Work Program of the Teaching Center in 1992," dated July 1992, that recorded the appointments of the eight section managers:

> As early as the month of July in the Teaching Center, special duties were defined and managers of all [eight] Sections were appointed. Smajo Halilović was in charge of the Section of Elementary Education and Socialization for a brief time, but after that Seniha Bulja was left with the task of organizing, directing, and supervising the realization of program assignments. (1994: 4)

By the end of summer 1992, with Seniha Bulja assuming the role of manager of the Elementary Education Section, seven regional coordinators (*koordinator*) were selected during fall 1992 to organize the individual stairway schools within their respective regions to eventually be integrated within the administration of the three elementary schools:

For that purpose, the coordinators of elementary education over the regions of Dobrinja were appointed. For Dobrinja 1, Elvir Ćosić; Dobrinja 2A, Fata Trle and Fehim Adžanela; Dobrinja 2B, Mirsada Balić and Huso Peco; Dobrinja 3A, Azra Tahmaz; Dobrinja 3B, Marija Čalija; Dobrinja 5, Hatidža Rašić and Binasa Adrović and for Quadrant C5, Azra Kujundžić.

The task of the coordinators was to take care of all planned activities associated with *the synchronization of work of the stairway schools in specific regions* [my emphasis], to continuously update data which are relevant for socialization-education work, and to carry out all necessary preparations for beginning the new school year. (1994: 4)

It is quite clear that the coordinators at the "regional" level were operating well in advance of their official appointments that came down from the Elementary Education Section of the Dobrinja War School Center. Thus Azra Kujundžić, as elementary education coordinator for Quadrant C5 of the Airport Settlement, dates her first official correspondence to 13 September 1992, when she prepared and delivered "the first official list of students of elementary and secondary education for the region of Quadrant C5 to the Dobrinja Teaching Center." She also prepared a list of teaching staff "which at this moment are available" that included students attending the Pedagogical Academy and the Faculty of Philosophy "who are willing to work with children in war conditions" (Kujundžić, 1993). However, in her own personal journal, a series of entries indicate that Azra was involved with the Center operations at least a month before the official correspondence. The 3 August 1992 entry, for example, reads as follows:

They officially authorized me to be the future coordinator for elementary and secondary education for Quadrant C5 of the Dobrinja Teaching Center.

Today was an exceptionally difficult and bloody day. Shells from chetnik positions fell from early morning.

However, I am spiteful enough that I am trying to answer new problems all by myself these days. (Kujundžić, 1992)

Azra's journal entry for 23 August 1992 reads:

Since Quadrant C5 belongs to Simon Bolivar Elementary School, I received the assignment to coordinate the work of this school in our region. The new director is set but I do not know yet who he is. (Kujundžić, 1992)

Thus, it is clear that, by the end of summer 1992, what Azra Kujundžić refers to as "the summer war period," the "synchronization of work" of the elementary schools, in Seniha Bulja's terms, was well underway. In other words, the integration of the 28 stairway schools organized during the summer months of the war, under the administration of the three elementary schools that existed prior to the war, was a work in progress taking place under the direction of Seniha Bulja as manager of the Elementary Education Section of the Dobrinja War School Center.

Azra Kujundžić's 13 September listing of teaching staff is a "working list" of 27 individuals who were employed in a variety of educational settings, from elementary school to secondary school to university, teachers, professors, and administrators, past and present. Several individuals worked in various capacities in other fields reflecting Azra herself who was an economist at Energoinvest, the state energy company, but who brought skills from outside the teaching field, and perhaps most important, the commitment that the situation demanded. As a working list, a number of names are crossed out and a number added.

Another list of ten students "able to work with children" includes three from the Pedagogical Academy, four from various University of Sarajevo faculties, and two unidentified names. One individual is a "veterinary technician [who] is able to teach civil defense and first aid." There is an attached list of the first four grades of elementary students along with their addresses to include: 18 first grade students, 17 second grade, 27 third grade, and 30 in fourth grade, a total of 93 elementary students in grades one through four who, at that time, lived in the "provisional war school region" of Quadrant C5 (Kujundžić, 1992).

A second listing contains the names of all elementary students, grades one through eight, organized by street address, ten different listings with the names of 228 students, their parents, date and place of birth, and grade level. "They asked me to do even more," Azra said, "to make more precise lists. I was obligated to do what they asked me to do" (2004). It is also noteworthy that two addresses are listed if needed, one for the original residence, and one for the temporary or current residence, an indication of the instability of the situation. The listing of the 23 students of one group, whose immediate residence is Louis Pasteur Street, indicates that only nine of these students were living at their original home residence in Quadrant C5 while the home addresses of the other 14 students are locations in Quadrant C4 of the Airport Settlement, overrun during the mid-June assaults and under control of the enemy. The listing of the 18 students on several narrow streets in the middle of C5 notes that 14 of these students were living at a location different than their original residence.

The Kujundžić family itself illustrates these unsettled conditions. For the purposes of the elementary listing, the immediate residence of Emina and Amra Kujundžić, ages twelve and eight, the two daughters of Enes and Azra Kujundžić, is listed as Bitka za ranjenike Street #2, while their former residence is listed as Koste Abraševića Street #1. With the fall of Quadrant C4, the outlying row of townhouses along Koste Abraševića Street on the western side of C5 was exposed to enemy fire, so the Kujundžić family moved to Bitka za ranjenike Street further within C5 of the Airport Settlement (1992).

We can, of course, only imagine the work of constructing these lists of students, organized by grade levels, by street residence, by neighborhood and by school region, and the ongoing listing of teachers as well. As a volunteer, who originally only wanted to offer her assistance to the children in a time of great need, Azra Kujundžić found herself taking on more and more responsibility for schooling as the need increased until she found herself as one of the primary figures who assumed responsibility for organizing education within the settlement.

Azra told me that there were more than 700 families living in Quadrant C5 at the time, many of whom were refugees from Quadrant C4 next door, and she made more than 700 visits to individual residences around the quadrant to locate and register both elementary and secondary students for school during those early months of the siege. Given the reference above to the immediate and previous student residences, we should remember the setting in which she accomplished this work, that C5 was one of the outer war school regions, and Azra assumed responsibility for schooling with the frontlines approximately 50 meters away (2004).

From the initial assault on Quadrants C4 and C5 of the Airport Settlement on 17-18 June 1992, almost all of C4 was in enemy hands, and the frontline was across an open grass field to the west of C5. To the south across the roadway was the airport, in JNA hands at the beginning of the war, which lined up tanks and self-propelled howitzers on the airport runway and blasted the outlying rows of C5 townhouses into ruin. Azra recalls the tank gunners deliberately going townhouse by townhouse down the outlying rows, as if townhouses were but target practice, pounding the once upscale outer complex into ruin. Indeed, I heard this same story from any number of Dobrinjans who simply could not believe that their homes in the once thriving Airport Settlement were being destroyed in such a blatant and inhuman fashion. Those of us who viewed the obliterated landscape of Quadrants C4 and C5 either during or just after the war could only wonder how anyone could have even lived there much less walk the streets to locate and register students for school. It should be noted that Azra Kujundžić during those dark days of 1992, along with many others who remain nameless here, did just that.

In recognition of her dedication to the children and her service to the school, the "Almanac" of Simon Bolivar Elementary School, following the entry of 17 April 1993 entry, records the following notation:

> Until 17 April 1993, the entries in the "Almanac" were recorded by Azra Kujundžić, and this is only a small part of the rich war experience and difficult and dangerous work which was invested in establishing and starting the school.
>
> Great enthusiasm, energy, and love for the children characterized Ms. Kujundžić, who inspired and motivated all others by her passion, and even though she is not an educator by her professional background, she succeeded in completing her work in such a way as if she had years of experience in teaching and educational work.
>
> It was not important for Azra Kujundžić if the city was under shelling, because her priorities were arranging a new school playground, organizing meetings, and fixing schedules. Azra did not know the expressions, "I do not know," or "I cannot"—because she was managing everything (and still does) in the spirit of, "We have to do this." All the children from Quadrant C5 know Ms. Azra and they also know that whenever they meet her she will be open to answer all of their questions. Thanks to Ms. Azra Kujundžić, the students from Simon Bolivar Elementary School, as well as the secondary school students, are back in their school benches, and they can study and socialize once again. (1992-1995)

As coordinator of elementary education for Quadrant C5, Azra Kujundžić was one of ten coordinators for the seven elementary regions for Dobrinja and the Airport Settlement. In this regard, four regions each had one coordinator while three regions had two coordinators, although it should be noted that coordinators changed over time given the circumstances. The organization of these regions, and the role of the coordinators, is seen in a November 1992 document entitled, "Basic Work Program of the Teaching Center in the 1992-1993 School Year," to be discussed in detail in the following section. Here it should be mentioned that the "Work Program of the Section for Elementary Education and Socialization" of the "Basic Work Program" indicates the formation of Teacher's Councils (*nastavničko vijeće*) at the elementary level for each of the seven regions, the number of teachers who comprise each Council, and the role of the Council in the organization of schooling.

Throughout November 1992, Seniha Bulja, the manager for the Elementary Education Section, "on behalf of the War School Center," was meeting with each of the regional Teacher's Councils, with the exception of Dobrinja 3B, to discuss with all interested parties the ongoing developments concerning the reorganization of schooling. In fact, at least six meetings were held over the course of the month with six of the seven Teacher's Councils, and the coordinators of each region, with a seventh meeting attended by six of the regional coordinators excluding Dobrinja 3B. The discussions, the problems, the questions, and the responses are seen in the "Minutes" (*zapisnici*) of each of the meetings usually recorded by the region coordinator and verified by Seniha Bulja herself (Bulja, 1992).

The initial Teacher's Council meeting, dated 2 November 1992, for example, was held for Quadrants C4 and C5 at 11:00 AM at Civil Defense Headquarters. It included Seniha Bulja, representing the War School Center as Elementary Education Section manager, Azra Kujundžić, the regional coordinator for C5, "all teachers who live in these two quadrants," as well as Smail Vesnić, director of the Center, and the three elementary school directors at that time: Faruk Jabučar, director of Nikola Tesla, Narcis Polimac, director of Dušan Pajić-Dašić, and Senadin Topić, director of Simon Bolivar. The minutes note an introduction and discussion of curricular tasks by Seniha Bulja, a series of questions from the teachers who attended along with Bulja's responses, and a series of conclusions accepted by the Council. The questions included concerns over textbooks, lack of available space, concerns over heating the classrooms, problems with parents, and the concern over children from Dobrinja 1, adjacent to C5, which "is exposed to aggression more than the other regions." The conclusions noted the responsibilities of the regional coordinator to locate premises for classes and who was "to deliver a list of teaching staff from this region and a list of students by grades" to the War School Center (Bulja, 1992).

With six meetings of the Teacher's Councils at the regional level, a seventh meeting of all the regional coordinators from across Dobrinja was held on 28 November 1992 at 9:00 A.M. in the War School Center. The agenda of this meeting: "Activities to date of the coordinators of elementary education and socialization and the next assignments." At this session, the data compiled on numbers of students, teachers, class sections, and school locations by region were reviewed—and will be discussed in some detail in the following section. The problems identified were many to include notations that there are not enough teachers in general, enough qualified teachers in particular subjects, and enough locations for classrooms.

The difficulty of finding and acquiring both secure and adequate classroom locations, for example, is seen in a series of early fall memos from Smail Vesnić to Civil Defense Headquarters. In a 29 September 1992 memo, for example, to Civil Defense Headquarters of Dobrinja and the Airport Settlement, and to Civil Defense Headquarters of Dobrinja 2A, "Securing student space for the needs of elementary and secondary education," he writes, "We request that you secure space for the needs of elementary and secondary education on the following streets: October Revolution 12, October Revolution 15, and Danka Mitrova 11." Three weeks later, in a 22 October follow-up memo, "Securing space (classrooms) for students of secondary and elementary schools in Dobrinja 2A," he writes the following:

> On the basis of memo number 02-SŠ 15/92 on 29 September 1992, the DOBRINJA TEACHING CENTER is committed to hold out for spaces (classrooms) and specifically:
>
> 1. October Revolution Street 15 (*3 classrooms*)
> 2. October Revolution Street 12 (*1 classroom*)
> 3. Danka Mitrova Street 11 (*1 classroom*)
>
> Not one of these spaces today is secured and set to function for instruction.
>
> Instruction in Dobrinja 2A proceeds only in Youth Work Brigade Street 9 (1 classroom) which ought to be in order (to function) for instruction on the basis of the established criteria for classrooms (in accordance with Civil Defense Headquarters of all settlements in Dobrinja, memo number 02-SS 14/92 on 25 September 1992.
>
> Needed supplies and repairs included:
>
> ♦ Sandbags
> ♦ Repair of wet joints
> ♦ Repair of entrance doors to classrooms
> ♦ Securing lighting
> ♦ Securing clean space. (Vesnić, 1992)

In a 15 November memo to Civil Defense Headquarters of Dobrinja and the Airport Settlement, "Request for securing student premises for carrying out instruction in elementary education," Director Vesnić identifies 14 spaces at ten locations on four streets in Dobrinja 3A to use for elementary classrooms. He concludes the memo with the notation, "It is repeatedly pointed out that we are talking about basement premises" (Vesnić, 1992).

Amidst the problems of finding adequate space for classrooms, it is clear that the meeting of regional coordinators on 28 November was designed to ensure "the synchronization of work" of the stairway schools of Dobrinja with the elementary schools in accordance with instructional plans for the official beginning of the 1992-1993 school year. Thus from the minutes of this meeting, Azra Kujundžić, C5 coordinator, notes while there are teachers for all subjects except the English language, there is only one location available for classes. Nevertheless, she indicates, "The conclusion is that instruction may also begin in this region." Binasa Adrović, the regional coordinator for Dobrinja 5, also speaks to the beginning of the new school year but offers serious concerns as well:

> Based on the introductory remarks and the reports submitted from the field, it can be concluded that organized instruction may begin, but it is also necessary at this time to receive consent of the parents in writing that his/her child go to school. The proposal is to collect the approval of parents, at the parent's meetings which need to be held before the start of the school year, at that meeting. (Bulja, 1992)

Mirsada Balić, coordinator for Dobrinja 2B, offers this statement: "The conclusion is that all activities concerning the organization for the beginning of the school year are completed in this region." She also offers the recommendation that "from now on all these activities [the work of the stairway schools] be taken on by the director of Dušan Pajić-Dašić or someone from that school," citing the elementary school that has responsibility for the Dobrinja 2B school region (Bulja, 1992).

Consistent with Seniha Bulja's "Notice Concerning School Regions," dated 10 January 1993, these seven regions, each with a coordinator for elementary education, were placed under the administrative framework of one of the three elementary schools. To repeat the "Notice," "From 10 November 1992, in accordance with the directive of professional advice of the Teaching Center, we are notifying you about the provisional war school regions of Dobrinja and the Airport Settlement" (Bulja, 1993). Here the "Notice" refers to the creation of the "provisional war school region" (*privremena ratna rejonizacija skolskog*) for each of the three elementary schools (1993), or what is referred to as the war district region (*ratna rejonizacija područja*) in another Bulja document (1994). In other words, three "provisional war school regions," or "war district regions," were created consistent with the three elementary schools, and the seven "school regions," depending upon their location, each with a region coordinator, were organized within their respective elementary "provisional war school region" under the administration of the elementary school director with responsibility for that region. To repeat the words of Azra Kujundžić, "Since Quadrant C5 belongs to Simon Bolivar Elementary School, I received the assignment to coordinate the work of this school in our region."

Thus Dušan Pajić-Dašić Elementary School, whose building was occupied by soldiers, was responsible for the educational administration of the stairway schools located in the local communities of Dobrinja 1, Dobrinja 2B, and Dobrinja 3B, on the eastern end of the settlement. Nikola Tesla Elementary School, whose building was also occupied by soldiers, was responsible for the educational administration of the stairway schools in the apartment complexes of Dobrinja 3A and Dobrinja 5 on the western end of the settlement. And Simon Bolivar Elementary School, whose building was shelled into ruin, was responsible for the educational administration of the stairway schools of Dobrinja 2A and Quadrant C5 of the Airport Settlement in the middle of Dobrinja.

The administrative responsibility of the three elementary schools for their respective neighborhoods within their "war school regions" is seen clearly in their relationship with the regional Teacher's Councils. The "Basic Work Program," dated November 1992, states that "the work of the Teacher's Council is managed by the directors of the parent elementary schools in Dobrinja, by regional basis, pertaining to the designated local community in the school region" (Nastavni centar, 1992: 35). By November 1992, it is now clear that the elementary school directors have assumed the responsibility for schooling within their respective war school regions that had previously been assumed by the elementary coordinators for school regions at the local community level.

In concluding remarks to the 28 November 1992 meeting of all regional coordinators for the local school regions, Smail Vesnić notes that "from now on, [for] everything concerning instruction (schedule of classes, testing of children, securing of premises, etc.), the coordinators will make arrangements with the school directors" (1992). In other words, the administrative framework for elementary education that existed prior to the war was resurrected in the absence of actual school buildings and physical locations, in order to recreate the operations of the elementary schools and, hence, "the illusion of normal life," under siege conditions. These school documents clarify the nature of the transitional process as the stairway schools within their respective local school regions were integrated into more expansive "provisional war school regions" under the administration of the three existing elementary schools, upon the direction of the Dobrinja War School Center, in preparation for the official start of the 1992-1993 school year.

The Basic Work Program for Elementary Education (November 1992)

The "synchronization of work" of the stairway schools with the three elementary schools, and the incredible amount of data compiled by the regional coordinators to support the work of the schools, is presented in systematic detail in the "Basic Work Program of the Teaching Center in the 1992-1993 School Year," dated November 1992. In the larger sense, the November "Basic Work Program" provides a clear and comprehensive picture of the administration and operation of each of the eight sections of the War School Center through individual "Work Programs" for each section. In regard to the "Work Program of the Section for Elementary Education and Socialization" (*Odjela za osnovno obrazovanje i vaspitanje*), in particular, the document provides systematic detail concerning the organizational framework for elementary education and the operational plan for each of the seven elementary school regions under the administration of the three Dobrinja elementary schools.

Furthermore, these data provided by the "Basic Work Program" clearly reveal that the Elementary Education Section of the Dobrinja War School Center established educational policy and created educational programs for Dobrinja schools. The Center thus provided the direction for reorganization of both elementary and secondary schooling consistent with the administrative framework that existed prior to the siege. While the "Almanac" of the War School Center clearly indicates the ongoing support provided for the stairway schools, the Center was responsible for standardizing, to a degree, the work of these schools consistent with traditional educational standards that existed prior to the war. To reiterate the words of Senija Bulja here: "All stairway schools in Dobrinja were organized by the same principles and operated in accordance with the same programs which were modeled in the Section for Elementary Education within the framework of the Teaching Center" (1994: 4).

As noted previously, the "Basic Work Program of the Teaching Center in 1992," developed during July, set forth the Center's educational objectives and clarified the many tasks at hand and the specific problems to be addressed. As the initial "Basic Work Program," this document established the organizational framework of the eight administrative sections of the Center, but also included a "Basic Work Program" for each of these eight sections to include curricular outlines for each subject area for both elementary and secondary education. Furthermore, the July "Basic Work Program" provided the substantive basis for developing the November 1992 "Basic Work Program" designed to address the implementation of programs for each of the sections during the 1992-1993 School Year.

In the "Introduction" to the November "Work Program of the Section for Elementary Education and Socialization," a caveat is offered concerning the wartime conditions under which the elementary schools will operate:

> Programming activities of the Section for Elementary Education and others that are participating in the realization of tasks set forth in the 1992-1993 school year will be conducted in very difficult conditions. That is why it is the responsibility and obligation of every participant (individually) . . . to offer his/her best knowledge and skill in order to ease and overcome the current situation ...

A group of elementary school students making their way to a war school classroom behind a row of garbage dumpsters piled high with sandbags for protection from snipers. Photo courtesy of Mevsud Kapetanović.

Taking all this into consideration, the efforts of the Section for Elementary Education will be directed first of all at creating physical and other conditions for secure operation of all possible forms of educational activity. In that regard, the whole organization of the teaching process will be programmed in such a way to completely avoid possible crossing of streets, squares, and other insecure spaces in order to have the security of teachers and students at the highest level possible. In cooperation with the ARBiH, civil authorities, and civil defense, the remaining premises to be used for educational activities should be secured and equipped in accordance with the objectives and tasks of the teaching process. (Nastavni centar, 1992: 19)

The "Work Program" for elementary education sets forth the following objectives:

♦ to work on gathering and processing new data on the number of students who attend classes in elementary school and the number of engaged teachers in the aim of better planning of programming activities;

♦ to work on coordinating activities with the appropriate people or institutions on securing school space with the aim of preparing for the start of the 1992-1993 school year;

♦ to conduct all necessary preparations (medical examinations, psychological tests, etc.) for the enrollment of first grade pupils;

♦ to implement the reduced curriculum for elementary schools which was passed by the Ministry of Education, Science, Culture, and Sport in BiH in all organizational forms of educational activities;

♦ to cooperate with the Armed Forces of BiH, civil defense, and local communities in the region of Dobrinja in the aim of realizing the objectives and tasks and with all other relevant subjects which can offer their contribution in that direction;

♦ to cooperate with the Ministry of Education, Science, Culture, and Sport, the Republican Fund for Elementary Education, the Inter-Municipal Pedagogical Institute, and with other relevant institutions for the efficiency of all activities which are undertaken in the Section for Elementary Education. (Nastavni centar, 1992: 20)

The initial task was to gather accurate information on the numbers of students and teachers in order to provide the basis for organizing the schools within the administrative framework developed by the Elementary Education Section. The greater objective here was develop this administrative framework with the intent of initiating classes for the official beginning of the 1992-1993 school year. The task of gathering data on students and teachers, as seen in the work of Azra Kujundžić in Quadrant C5, was placed squarely upon the shoulders of the coordinators of each of the seven Dobrinja school regions. The data these coordinators compiled from the local regions during summer and fall 1992, with coordinators like Azra visiting 700 C5 households, becomes an integral feature of the Elementary "Work Program."

Whereas Seniha Bulja cites numbers of approximately 900 elementary students and 89 teachers in the stairway schools (1993), the November 1992 document updates those numbers citing a precise total of 1392 elementary students in grades one through eight, and 92 teachers in six of the seven Dobrinja regions as noted in Table 3.1. Only the data for Dobrinja 3B is lacking with one citation noting that the "data are not final" (*podaci nisu konačni*) while another notes "formation in progress" (*formiranje u toku*). The total number of teachers is broken down according to membership on the Teacher's Councils of each local region with a brief discussion of the organization and operation of the Councils. Teacher numbers range from lows of 10–11 teachers in Dobrinja 5 and Dobrinja 1, to 20-23 teachers in Dobrinja 2A and Dobrinja 3A, with a total of 92 teachers in the six regions. A narrative explanation notes that "there are around 1,500 elementary school students living in Dobrinja and over 100 teachers," which is perhaps a general reference since the data had yet to be compiled from Dobrinja 3B (1992: 20-21).

TABLE 3.1
NUMBER OF ELEMENTARY SCHOOL STUDENTS IN GRADES 1-4 AND GRADES 5-8 IN THE STAIRWAY SCHOOLS BY REGIONS OF DOBRINJA AND THE AIRPORT SETTLEMENT, AND REGIONAL COORDINATORS, PRIOR TO THE OFFICIAL BEGINNING OF THE 1992-1993 SCHOOL YEAR (NOVEMBER 1992)

Region	Coordinator	Numbers of Students		Totals
		Grades 1–4	Grades 5–8	
Dobrinja 1	Elvira Ćosić	51	55	106
Dobrinja 2A	Fehim Adžanela	135	243	426
Dobrinja 2B	Mirsada Balić	86	149	235
Dobrinja 3A	Azra Tahmaz	123	163	286
Dobrinja 3B				
Dobrinja 5	Binasa Advrović	87	55	142
Quadrant C5	Azra Kujundžić	80	127	207
Totals		610	782	1,392

There are data on the number of classes for each grade level and for each individual stairway school to include the number of students who attended each of the classes. Excluding Dobrinja 3B, there are 26 classroom locations, or *punkts* (points, from the German, or *punktovi*), throughout the six regions for the 1392 Dobrinja elementary students as of November 1992, a number consistent with the 28 stairway schools cited by Seniha Bulja in her later paper. Each of these classrooms is listed according to the local community region in which it is located and broken down, first by the number of students by grade levels 1-4 and grade levels 5-8, and then by classroom location and the number of students in each grade.

Thus, in Quadrant C5, as seen in Table 3.2, there are 80 elementary students in grades 1-4 attending 6 classes taught by 5 teachers at 3 primary classroom locations or *punkts*: Ivica Marušića Ratka Street numbers 5-7, Louis Pasteur Street number 3, and Vase Butozana Street numbers 5-9. For grade levels 5-8, there are 127 students attending 7 classes taught by 5 teachers at the same 3 classroom locations. These figures indicate that there are a total of 207 elementary school students grades 1-8 who attend classes in Quadrant C5 taught by 13 teachers responsible for their instruction and safety. It was these very numbers gathered by coordinators such as Azra Kujundžić across Dobrinja and the Airport Settlement, as they walked the streets of their local communities, "in the aim of better

TABLE 3.2
NUMBER OF ELEMENTARY STUDENTS, TEACHERS, AND CLASSES IN THE STAIRWAY SCHOOLS OF QUADRANT C5 OF THE AIRPORT SETTLEMENT (NOVEMBER 1992)

Grades	Students	Teachers	Classes
Grade 1	17		1
Grade 2	16		1
Grade 3	24		2
Grade 4	23		2
Totals (Grades 1–4)	80	5	6
Grade 5	18		1
Grade 6	36		2
Grade 7	39		2
Grade 8	34		2
Totals (Grades 5–8)	127	5	7
Totals (Grades 1–8)	207	10	13

Source: Nastavni centar (1992:27,34).

planning of programming activities," that provided the basis for the reorganization of elementary education under the administration of the three elementary schools of Dobrinja in preparation for the official beginning of the 1992-1993 school year.

The importance of the Pedagogical Institute is also noted in the "Basic Work Program." As noted previously, the relationship between the Pedagogical Institute and the Teaching Center that was established at the outbreak of the war provided the opportunity for the involvement of the Institute in the work of the Center through both Smail Vesnić and Adnan Tetarić who were Institute advisors. This relationship is seen particularly in regard to both the training of teachers and in the development of curricular programs. In the "Minutes" of the 2 November Teacher's Council meeting of Quadrant C5, for example, one of the conclusions reads simply, "The Pedagogical Institute and the Center are the authors of all abbreviated

An elementary art class in their makeshift, war school classroom of Simon Bolivar Elementary School, with their teacher, Smail Ćar. Ćar was a teacher and a soldier, spending his days teaching students in war school classrooms and his nights defending the settlement on the frontlines. In his words, "the children and the classrooms were psychological therapy for me." Photo courtesy of Mevsud Kapetanović.

curricula." In the "Minutes" of the 9 November Teacher's Council meeting for Dobrinja 3A, one of the conclusions reads:

> All teachers are obliged to be engaged ... for the realization of the abbreviated curriculum which was created by the Republic's Pedagogical Institute. The MPZ [local communities] and the Dobrinja Teaching Center will deliver orientation work plans for all subjects for which the programs have been completed. (Bulja, 1992)

With the Pedagogical Institute in the forefront of reorganizing the curriculum in order to adapt instruction for wartime conditions, the Elementary "Work Program," in a section on "Training of Teachers and Associates," clearly states that "advisors and associates of the Pedagogical Institute will hold regular sessions of professional groups at which methodological and didactical guidance will be given for the realization of the reduced curriculum" (Nastavni centar, 1992: 20). In other words, the school curriculum was in the process of being restructured across all grade levels and across all subject areas, and for a Ministry of Education, Science, Culture, and Sport of a new and independent Republic of Bosnia and Herzegovina.

Furthermore, with the new school year yet to get underway across Bosnia and Herzegovina, pending official announcement by the Ministry of Education, the curriculum had to be restructured for what was becoming an abbreviated school year and for class sessions of reduced class time. It was the responsibility of both the Pedagogical Institute and the Teaching Center to train both experienced and volunteer teachers to meet these new teaching conditions. According to the Elementary "Work Program," "Special attention will be given to individual professional development of every teacher and associate appropriate to the conditions of work in every school" (Nastavni centar, 1992: 20).

In the concluding section of the "Minutes" of the 28 November 1992 meeting of the regional coordinators that culminated the regional Teacher's Council meetings of November, a summary of the organizational issues is presented along with a number of questions and concerns expressed by the teachers. Based upon consultations with grade 1-4 teachers, a series of "methodological and didactical guidelines" are also offered directed towards "the realization of elementary-socialization work" for the beginning of the new school year:

> The concept of the "little schools" [stairway schools] has been accepted at the city level and when the security situation is assessed, the 1992-1993 school year may begin.

However, as it is war, and as the society needs to be built in the postwar period, a great burden will again fall on educators. That is why we need to prepare and to adapt our work to the conditions ... The Director [Smail Vesnić] has warned that now the responsibilities of the teachers are huge and that the same teachers can provide a great contribution to normalization of the existing situation. The Manager for Elementary Education and Socialization [Seniha Bulja] is to provide all anticipated documentation connected with work in the schools. (Bulja, 1992)

In a concluding question, Fata Trle, one of the coordinators for Dobrinja 2A, expresses a fundamental concern for educators, parents, and students alike. "I would like to ask whether this school year will be recognized because this needs to be said to the parents." In response, Smail Vesnić offers this answer, "If all this is well-organized, this school year will probably be recognized" (Bulja, 1992). It was this very concern, that the invaluable work of those Dobrinja educators who organized the stairway schools of the settlement during the early days of the siege, given the inability of the three existing elementary schools to function in traditional fashion, would not be wasted, that the school year would not be lost to the enemy who besieged the schools. And it was this very concern, that the invaluable work of those Dobrinja educators who gathered the fundamental data necessary for the three elementary schools to organize the instructional process would not be wasted as well.

Thus, to repeat Seniha Bulja, writing of the Dobrinja 2B Stairway School on Salvador Allende Street, "the teaching contents which were planned for April, May, and June of that school year are being repeated in classes" (1994: 3). And the July 1992 "Basic Work Program" noted that one of the primary objectives of the Center was "to initiate, direct, and offer assistance for completion of the remaining work in the 1991-1992 school year in the schools of Dobrinja" (Nastavni centar, 1992: 5).

The ultimate recognition of this work of untold numbers of dedicated educators, that "the concept of the 'little schools' has been accepted," provides the underlying structural basis for the reorganization of elementary education in besieged Dobrinja and the Airport Settlement. These stairway schools were first organized by local neighborhoods as school regions, and then organized within provisional war school regions under the administration of the elementary schools, providing the basis for the three extant Dobrinja elementary schools to function as administrative entities in the absence of their prewar physical locations.

With "the concept of the 'little schools'" or the "stairway schools" accepted by the Sarajevo City Secretariat for Education, these "little schools" scattered all across Dobrinja provided the organizational basis by which to adapt instruction to wartime conditions—consistent with the message of Abdulah Jabučar, deputy minister, Ministry of Education of the Republic itself. "It is necessary to adapt to conditions and organize the work of schools," he wrote (1994: 5). And later, the "Guidelines on Educational Activities" set forth by Minister Jabučar, and eventually passed in December 1993, "committed every school to work, regardless of conditions—to adapt to the actual situation" (1997: 295).

To repeat the words of Seniha Bulja in anticipation of Minister Jabučar, "As it is war, and as the society needs to be built in the postwar period, a great burden will again fall on educators. That is why we need to prepare and to adapt our work to the conditions" (1992). In other words, the adaptation of the "little schools" of Dobrinja to siege conditions, and hence the acceptance of the concept of these schools, meant that "this school year will probably be recognized" by the Sarajevo City Secretariat for Education. The recognition of the school year serves to validate both the formation and the operation of the Dobrinja War School Center which assumed responsibility from the Coordination Board for Dobrinja and the Airport Settlement for the work of schools in besieged Dobrinja.

As noted in these documents, all this work to compile all this information on schooling in Dobrinja was with "the aim of preparing for the start of the 1992-1993 school year." In this regard, the "Basic Work Program of the Teaching Center in the 1992-1993 School Year" provided the critical documentation in systematic detail for "the synchronization of work" necessary for schooling to function under siege conditions. In this regard, although the "little schools" were in operation all across Dobrinja during the fall months of 1992, the official beginning of the 1992-1993 school year was on hold pending decisions by the Ministry of Education of the new Republic, in a country in a struggle for its own survival and, in particular, by the Sarajevo City Secretariat for Education, in the capital of the country under siege. The "Basic Work Program" reads as follows:

> Taking into account the security situation and assessing the possibilities of the realization of educational work during the last school year, we started forming "small" stairway schools that began in stairways, shelters, and other safe spaces. In this way, the last school year, with instructive education during July, August, and September, was brought to an end. Such a concept offered very good results, and on the safety plan as well,

and not one student had been injured during instructions in any way. On the contrary, this way of organizing instruction was also of a preventive character, so in terms of percentage, the number of children killed or injured in Dobrinja, compared to the number of killed or injured civilians, is far less than the number in the city region.

That is why we decided, in this school year and based on the experience gained, and in cooperation with the elementary schools in this region, to offer a possible concept and themes for the organization of socialization-education work for all of us, especially for students and their parents, and we are bringing about the new school year with certainty. (Nastavni centar, 1992: 19-21)

The reconstruction of the educational system in general, and the reconstruction of elementary education in particular, offered a new conceptual framework for educational organization, administration, and operation under siege conditions. In besieged Dobrinja and the Airport Settlement, the development of this conceptual framework began almost with the beginning of the siege itself and was implemented through the early months of the siege. A variety of agencies provided the necessary assistance to Dobrinja educators during this time to include the Pedagogical Institute of Sarajevo, Territorial Defense headquarters, local civil defense authorities, the command headquarters of the 1st Dobrinja Brigade, and the local Dobrinja communities. Of course, the primary agency responsible for conceptualiziation of this framework and then developing and implementing these initiatives was the Dobrinja War School Center itself, through the initiative of the director, Smail Vesnić and, for elementary education, the Section for Elementary Education, and its manager, Seniha Bulja. In this regard, the dedicated work of the many professional educators and the many educational volunteers should not go unrecognized. Indeed, by the end of the 1992 calendar year, the work of these dedicated people had set the stage for the official beginning of the 1992-1993 school year for Dobrinja's elementary school students.

Rođena je u toku Rata

Born During the War
Gimnazija Dobrinja and Secondary Education

CHAPTER FOUR

The Book

Through the fog I can see my mother's hands taking a book from the bookshelf and slowly bringing it towards the fire which has just been built. The flame slowly embraces the pages of this beloved book ... and all of my dreams are going away with those pages and in the fire of this flame. I am not crying. What do those books mean when people are dying? It is difficult to see how the flame swallows all of my happy moments which I spent with that book not having the time to read it till the end.

My thoughts are wandering somewhere far away, to a place where migratory birds move, even further ... to a place where things written on the pages of the books occur ...

My thoughts came back again to a little room with the woodstove. Through the fire and dust I can still see the cover page of the book with the boat painted on it. The fire suffocates the boat ... and the black scarf made of smoke covers the boat, and the boat is trying hard to use its last atoms of strength to grasp the ruins and like a person drowning in the sea, works hard to stay alive, defies the fire while looking through the woodstove in search of help ...

All of a sudden ... one little flame slowly sneaks away to the cover page, jumps on it, and puts the boat on fire. The boat, which has been sailing on the endless sea until that moment, was now lost in flame and transformed into the black site of a fire ... and in that moment a flood of suppressed tears came out ...

When I raised my head and dried my tears, I looked at the book next to the stove ... no, no, it was not the book, it was something that remained of the book. It is still like that ... Whenever I remember that scene, I am moved with the same feeling ... As if I was still looking at the same gray dust in the stove ... as gray as that day was gray.

—Lidija Ilić, 7th Grade
Skender Kulenović Elementary School

The Basic Work Programs

In the absence of a secondary school in the settlement, Smail Vesnić and his colleagues created one, Gimnazija Dobrinja, which began instruction on 25 January 1993, nine months into the siege. The significance of the new gimnazija[1] in Dobrinja was not simply the creation of a new secondary school itself, but that the new gimnazija served as the administrative center for students trapped within the settlement who attended secondary schools across the city. In fact, the managers of the Section for Secondary Education and Socialization of the Dobrinja War School Center, Zlatan Pravidur, and then, Ilija Šobot, would supervise seven regional coordinators for the seven secondary regions of Dobrinja, 22 secondary school coordinators representing 27 secondary schools throughout the city, and one coordinator specifically for the four city gimnazija, the academic secondary schools that prepared students for the university. However, the story of the reconstruction of secondary schooling in Dobrinja begins well before the opening of Gimnazija Dobrinja on 25 January 1993.

As noted in previous chapters, the July "Basic Work Program of the Teaching Center in 1992" set forth a series of objectives and tasks at hand to include specific reference to the work of both elementary and secondary education as follows:

> to offer appropriate professional services to the users in an instructive and consultative manner for successful continuation of schooling on the basis of the program of work for elementary and secondary schools. (Nastavni centar, 1992: 6)

Of course, there were no secondary schools in Dobrinja at the time, but with the construction of a "Work Program" for secondary education, the proposal for a secondary school to complement the elementary schools that previously existed is reiterated here:

> Along with other things, all aspects and possibilities shall be analyzed for repair of existing [elementary] school buildings, as well as further developments, especially secondary education and socialization and, in that sense, to generate worthy proposals to appropriate institutions for the establishment of a secondary school in Dobrinja. (Nastavni centar, 1992: 6)

The July "Basic Work Program" includes a secondary "Work Program" analogous to the "Work Program" for elementary education. In this early document, a particular emphasis is placed upon the development of "Programs of Instructive Education" (*Programi instruktivne nastave*) at the secondary level. Such "programs" encompass the curricular organization and subject area classes for only four of the secondary subject areas: the mother language, mathematics, physics, and history. There were no programs at the time for biology, chemistry, geography, foreign languages, or the multitude of specialized courses offered for students who attended the many vocational-technical schools in the city. Nevertheless, the description from the mother language section provides the rationale and the direction for programs to be developed for secondary instruction:

> To realize the instruction of a [curriculum] unit of planning for the months of April, May, and June, with students of secondary school, [directed] towards the importance of the instructional plan and program, with special emphasis on literacy and cultural expression ...
>
> Realization of the program, dependent on the safety situation, will take place in the premises of the Teaching Center or at shelters and other suitable spaces.
>
> Instruction will be performed in the settlements: Dobrinja 2, Dobrinja 3, Dobrinja 5, Quadrant C5, and the Airport Settlement. (Nastavni centar, 1992: 39)

Given the special emphasis to be placed on literacy and cultural expression, it should be noted that the history curriculum (*istorija* or *povijest*), for example, includes one objective designed for instruction and one for socialization. The instructional objective reads:

> Giving new knowledge to students and to prepare candidates for the qualification (entrance) examination at the Faculty of Philosophy in the Department of History and at the Pedagogical Academy. (1992: 47)

The socialization objective reads:

> Realizing critical relationships by students concerning thematic units and developing patriotism towards the homeland of Bosnian and Herzegovina, especially through the history of Bosnia and Herzegovina. (Nastavni centar, 1992: 47)

The history curriculum, compiled by Smajo Halilović, a secondary history teacher, encompasses 18 instructional weeks, beginning with the prehistory of Europe, citing Greek and Rome, and continuing through medieval Europe. It should also be noted that the instructional units of the curriculum include: "Development of the Croatian State," "The Croatian Homeland in the Early Feudal Era from the 7th to the 12th Century," and "The Serbian Homeland in the Early Feudal Era to the

12th Century." In a new country shredded by nationalist politics in the process of breaking into self-proclaimed Serbian, Croatian, and Bosnian statelets, the inclusion of units on both Croatian and Serbian historical homelands is no small matter.

Beginning with the 15th unit, "The Bosnian Feudal State from the 7th to the 15th Century," the remaining units emphasize the Bosnian historical experience. The units that follow include "The Cultural History of Bosnia and Herzegovina," and "Bosnia and Herzegovina during the Time of Turkish Rule." The concluding unit is entitled, "Bosnia and Herzegovina from the Congress of Berlin, 1878 to 1903," where there is no further citation to chronicle the Bosnian experience into the 20th century. Of further note, given the emphasis upon the development of patriotism towards the Bosnian homeland, is the absence of any curriculum unit that addresses contemporary Bosnian history to include recent historical events and the wars of Yugoslav secession that began in 1991.

However, it should also be noted that while the July "Basic Work Program" included "Programs of Instructive Education" for virtually every elementary subject area, the development of similar curricula for the secondary level, however, was still a work in progress. It is, therefore, highly understandable that the history curriculum was lacking in the initial stage of development, not to mention that the history curriculum and the history textbooks would eventually be rewritten at the Ministry of Education itself. The Center documents make quite clear that the reorganization of secondary education in Dobrinja, as seen in the curriculum development of only four of the secondary subject areas, for example, with no secondary school at the time and, therefore, no organized cadre of secondary teachers and administrators, lagged well behind the development of elementary education, with a cadre of teachers from the three elementary schools, and a cadre of concerned volunteers for younger children, where "stairway schools" seemed to spring up in corridors, basements, and shelters across the local communities.

In addition to curriculum development, another indication of this developmental disparity is the organization of secondary school regions. Indeed, there were only five secondary regions cited in the July "Basic Work Program," as noted above, in contrast to the seven elementary school regions at the time. These five secondary regions included Dobrinja 2 and Dobrinja 3, neither subdivided into A and B regions, Dobrinja 5, and Quadrant C5, along with the Airport Settlement as a separate region which would appear to include what remained of Quadrant C4 or perhaps the refugee children from C4. There is no reference to Dobrinja 1, located adjacent to C5, as a school region. As noted in the "Minutes" of the elementary Teacher's Council meeting of Quadrants C4 and C5, dated 2 November 1992, perhaps this is due to the fact that Dobrinja 1 "is exposed to aggression more than the other regions."

Whereas the July "Basic Work Program" was a preliminary document for secondary education in particular, the November "Basic Work Program of the Teaching Center in the 1992-1993 School Year" indicates that Zlatan Pravidur, who first assumed the role of manager of the Section for Secondary Education and Socialization, and Ilija Sobot, who later assumed the role of manager in November, along with their secondary school colleagues, had accomplished an enormous amount of work during the intervening months. Much like the comprehensive "Work Program" for the Elementary Education Section, a comprehensive "Work Program" for the Secondary Education Section had been constructed, in contrast to rough curricular outlines for selected subject areas of the July document. The introduction to the "Work Program" indicates the setting in which this work took place and the tasks at hand:

> The months-long isolation and blockade of Dobrinja and the war developments in their entirety have put forward another plan of life and work for the students and teachers of secondary schools.
>
> The truth is, today in Dobrinja, you need to survive first, and then figure out a life outline. One of the elementary needs of a young person is the need for learning and education, so the planning of these activities is of special importance.
>
> In order for this situation to change, we started collecting data on students and teachers of secondary schools who remained in Dobrinja in this difficult time. On the basis of the proposal of the Dobrinja Teaching Center, we started organizing forms of instruction in almost all parts of Dobrinja. (Nastavni centar, 1992: 39)

In addition to a general background on the educational situation, this November "Work Program" contains an operational plan for secondary schooling and includes a curricular framework by which to organize instructional plans for individual subject areas. Although the July secondary curriculum addressed only four subject areas, the November secondary curriculum includes the scope, sequence, and content of instruction in virtually all the major academic subjects as well as in a variety of vocational classes, not to mention civil defense as well. In the words of the elementary education objectives, the "Work Program" for secondary education was developed "with the aim of better planning of programming activities." The basic objectives for secondary education programs include the following:

- that students gather in organized school premises and in that way protect themselves from injury in these difficult times;

- that students prepare and complete class in order not to break the continuity of education;

- that students form and develop as healthy, physically, and mentally capable, independent, and culturally enriched persons. (Nastavni centar, 1992: 42)

The basic tasks for secondary education are to enable the students to:

- gain knowledge based on the achievements of modern science, technique, technology, and social development as well as enabling one for work;

- adopt cultural, social-economical, natural-mathematical, productive-technical, and other socialization-education content which enable inclusion in social life and work;

- develop a responsible relationship toward work as a source of values and measures of the social and economic status of a person;

- rear the independent personality of a human being, the critical spirit for work, moral and cultural habits and characteristics;

- prepare and train for the defense of the country and community self-defense;

- develop healthy and human relationships towards people;

- make an orderly choice of profession. (Nastavni centar, 1992: 42)

In addition to a clear sense of purpose, these goals and objectives place secondary schooling within the larger context of adolescent socialization and the wartime situation. It is also clear that the managers of the Secondary Education Section were aware of the difficulty of the situation for adolescents who were trapped within the settlement. Prior to the war, all of these adolescents had left their residences within Dobrinja to attend their respective secondary schools which were scattered across the city. To be trapped within their neighborhoods, unable to travel to the city, much less to attend their schools, was an extremely difficult situation for these students, and it is noteworthy that their situation was recognized by their teachers.

It is also clear that the educators of the Secondary Education Section had gathered comprehensive data on secondary students and teachers in the local Dobrinja communities. "We had started collecting data on students and teachers of secondary schools in Dobrinja," the document reads, and this was no small task since there was simply no existing data available since there were no secondary schools located in Dobrinja prior to the war. Whereas no quantitative data was cited on the numbers of students and teachers in Dobrinja and the Airport Settlement in the July "Work Program," and no indications of the possibility of classroom locations other than some general references, there was no concrete basis upon which to construct instructional programs for secondary students. However, the November data compiled by the Secondary Education Section provided this basis.

Furthermore, the document reveals the continuing development of secondary school organization at the level of the local school region in a fashion analogous to elementary school organization. Whereas five secondary education regions were listed in July 1992, with no listing of Dobrinja 1, and with the Airport Settlement included, the November 1992 document indicates there are now seven secondary coordinators for the secondary regions listed, analogous to the seven elementary regions, to include: Dobrinja 1, Dobrinja 2A and Dobrinja 2B, Dobrinja 3A and Dobrinja 3B, Dobrinja 5, and Quadrant C5. There are also Teacher's Councils organized by the Secondary Education Section in each of the seven regions, analogous to the Teacher's Councils for the Elementary Education Section, with meetings to

TABLE 4.1
NUMBER OF SECONDARY SCHOOL STUDENTS BY REGIONS OF DOBRINJA AND THE AIRPORT SETTLEMENT, AND REGIONAL COORDINATORS, PRIOR TO THE OFFICIAL BEGINNING OF THE 1992-1993 SCHOOL YEAR (NOVEMBER 1992)

Region	Coordinator	Class				Totals
		I	II	III	IV	
Quadrant C5	Rade Soko	25	31	28	10	94
Dobrinja 1	Ahmed Plečić	13	14	24	13	64
Dobrinja 2A	Mahira Krivošić-Tanasić	63	67	50	40	220
Dobrinja 2B	Mirsada Balić	32	42	46	33	153
Dobrinja 3A	Nisveta Jamak	32	39	29	17	117
Dobrinja 3B	Husein Prcić	20	31	25	11	87
Dobrinja 5	Ilija Šobot	17	15	13	10	55
Totals		202	239	215	134	790

Source: Nastavni centar (1992: 60, 66).

be held at least once a month when "issues related to the work of the section of a particular region will be discussed," along with a Teacher's Council for the Secondary Education Section "for all divisions of Dobrinja."

These data compiled for the "Work Program" of the Secondary Education Section indicate there were a total of 790 secondary students from the first-year class of secondary school through the fourth-year class, (grades nine through twelve), who registered for the 1992-1993 school year across the seven secondary school regions as seen in Table 4.1. There were a total of 89 teachers to teach 44 individual class sections in 14 available spaces that were converted into classrooms throughout all of Dobrinja and the Airport Settlement. However, in regard to the students, "this number changes very often, because students leave, and more often return," given the instability of the situation in the settlement:

> When looking at the divisions of Dobrinja, the majority of students come from the central region of Dobrinja: Dobrinja 2A, Dobrinja 2B, and Dobrinja 3A. There are students from all types of schools. The fewest number of students in classes II, III, and IV are from the gimnazija. However, in accordance with the wishes expressed by the students of class I, a great number of them are interested in enrolling in a gimnazija, and that is, of course, the reason for opening the gimnazija in Dobrinja. (Nastavni centar, 1992: 43)

At the time this data was collected, by November 1992, there is a clear sense of the numbers and locations of students and the secondary classes they planned to attend. In this regard, the "Work Program" provides the quantitative basis to determine the number of teachers needed, the number of classroom locations required in the local communities, and a better sense of curriculum and instructional needs as well, although the distinction between gimnazija and vocational-technical schools is critical for determining these needs, as well as for an understanding of the organization and operation of the secondary school system.

All of the basic secondary subject areas, to include the class level and number of sections, and class periods required, along with the number of teachers organized by each subject area, are now listed. The listing of subjects and teachers available include: the mother language (8 teachers); mathematics (8 teachers); foreign language [English (6), German (1), French (2), and Russian (2)]; physics (5); chemistry (5); biology (7); history (3); geography (3); computer and information science (4); sociology, psychology and philosophy (6); the arts to include visual arts and music (4); civil defense (3); vocational subjects and professional subjects (not listed).

There are a total of 67 teachers available for all of the secondary subject areas noted above with the exception of the more specialized vocational and professional subjects.

Given the number and variety of vocational-technical schools in Sarajevo, it is interesting to note that the number of teachers for vocational and professional subjects is not listed, but the narrative also indicates that a large number of "experts" with diverse profiles were living in Dobrinja at the time. "Some of these experts (around 20) will be involved as external associates for the realization of the teaching material for the subjects from the professions and subjects from the field of professional education" (Nastavni centar, 1992:44). This number is consistent with the difference between the total of 67 subject area teachers and the total number of 89 teachers and associates listed for instruction. The secondary "Work Program" states:

> Classes will begin to be realized with a condensed teaching plan and program which will be produced by the teachers of the respective subjects. These teaching plans and programs may apply until the completion and acquisition of innovated teaching plans and programs. The teaching material is programmed for 18 working weeks for 50 percent of the regular teaching material.
>
> The Dobrinja Teaching Center will be engaged to provide innovative plans and programs as soon as possible, especially with subjects where great changes are expected, for example: the mother language, history, and geography. Until these plans and programs are produced, the teachers of the respective subjects are at liberty to create and realize the teaching plan and program on their own in which the elements of the Constitution of the Republic of Bosnia and Herzegovina will be fully emphasized. (Nastavni centar, 1992: 51)

The July "Basic Work Program" noted the need to begin instruction in order to makeup those classes missed during April, May, and June when the regular school year ended 15 May. In this regard, the November "Basic Work Program" notes that 14 available classrooms "are used for conducting instructive education in September, October, and November for the teaching material which was not realized in the last school year" (Nastavni centar, 1992: 45). It is clear, therefore, that any secondary schooling which occurred in these 14 classrooms during the fall months of 1992 was directed towards the completion of classes for the 1991-1992 school year. Whereas the stairway schools that operated during spring and summer 1992 served the purpose of completing the 1991-1992 school year for elementary students, there was no organized system of counterpart "stairway schools" for secondary students during that time. Instruction that did take place was on an individualized and specialized basis.

In regard to classroom locations, a series of memos were sent to Civil Defense Headquarters in the Dobrinja regions during mid-September by Zlatan Pravidur, then the manager for the Secondary Education Section, requesting additional spaces. In one such memo to Civil Defense Headquarters in Dobrinja 2A, dated 16 September, "Securing spaces for carrying out instructive teaching for students who have completed the first and second class of secondary school," the memo requests two spaces for classrooms in order to teach the following subjects: mathematics, the mother language, the English language, history, and physics, "but pertaining to program content which students did not take in April, May, and June," in order to "prepare the student for the next school year," consistent with the November "Basic Work Program" (Pravidur, 1992).

However, with only 14 rooms available for classroom instruction for approximately 790 secondary students, and only one location each in Dobrinja 1, Dobrinja 3B, and Dobrinja 5, the "Basic Work Program" notes the concern over classroom locations and the severe adaptations that will have to be made in order for instruction to occur in these circumstances:

> The classrooms are secured by unique measures and criteria which were established by the Dobrinja Teaching Center in cooperation with Civil Defense. Preparations are in progress to paint these rooms and provide heating. The average floor area of these rooms is around 30 meters square. That can be adequate for work with a group of 10–25 students or 18 students on average.
>
> Lack of space, until a final solution, will be made up by working in three shifts, working 6 or 7 days a week, joint use of premises intended for preschool or elementary education, and other appropriate premises.
>
> Sometimes the premises of the Dobrinja Teaching Center will be used. (Nastavni centar, 1992: 45)

The document clarifies the adaptations of instruction that must be made in order for classroom instruction to occur at the secondary level:

> The teaching material is being programmed by subjects to 18 working weeks or 50% of the teaching material.
>
> Because of the difficult conditions of work and lack of space, these instructions will not be realized in all parts of Dobrinja at the same time, and the school year will vary from 18 to 24 weeks.
>
> So the school year begins mid-December 1992 and ends mid-June 1993.

In the regions of Dobrinja which have the necessary number of classrooms, instruction will be organized in two shifts with a normal number of 6 classes daily, and the school year in those regions will last only 18 weeks.

In the Dobrinja regions which do not have a sufficient number of classrooms, instruction may be organized in three shifts and can work 6 or 7 days a week.

In winter periods, for security reasons, lights and heating, classes will be made shorter, and instruction will be organized daily between 9:00 A.M. and 4:00 P.M., and will be in two shifts for 5 classes and three shifts up to 4 classes daily, with 5 minute breaks between classes and 15 minute breaks between shifts.

In spring, when it gets warmer, and if there is peace, we will be moving toward normalization of instruction, that is, classroom instruction will last 45 minutes and 6 classes will be held daily. (Nastavni centar, 1992: 47)

However, in spite of the concerns over classroom locations, the November "Basic Work Program" clearly suggests a "reduced teaching plan and program" of 18 weeks to be offered "in the planned time, from mid-December 1992 to mid-June 1993," which provides a clear indication of planning for the next school year (Nastavni centar, 1992: 45). Given the difficulty of wartime conditions, the security situation, and the lack of classroom space, the school year would vary in length from 18 to 24 weeks, but the critical element here is that the work and plans of the Secondary Education Section had resulted in the adaptation of curriculum and instruction to allow the new school year to get underway. In this regard, the November "Basic Work Program" was intended to serve "the aim of better planning of programming activities" designed for the forthcoming 1992-1993 school year whenever it would begin.

In other words, the "Basic Work Program" indicates that, by November 1992, the administrative framework for the organization of secondary schooling, based upon the collection of data "on students and teachers of secondary schools who remained in Dobrinja in this difficult time," was well under construction. Furthermore, the emphasis placed upon the adaptation of the secondary school curriculum across the secondary subject areas for reduced course offerings provides the teachers a basis to plan the instructional process accordingly. Nevertheless, in spite of plans to begin the new school year in mid-December 1992, the beginning of the 1992-1993 school year would be decided by the Ministry of Education and the City Secretariat for Education back in Sarajevo, in conjunction with the Dobrinja War School Center, given conditions in the besieged settlement.

Gimnazija Dobrinja

To reiterate a passage from the July 1992 "Basic Work Program" concerning objectives and tasks, future developments in education, "especially secondary education and socialization," indicated the need "to generate worthy proposals to appropriate institutions for the establishment of a secondary school in Dobrinja" (Nastavni centar, 1992: 6). At approximately the same time, in the "Annals" of Gimnazija Dobrinja, dated 19 July 1992, on the very same day that the Teacher's Council for the War School Center was appointed, the entry notes that the "Basic Work Program" was adopted. The entry continues, "In the program the need was emphasized for the establishment of the gimnazija in Dobrinja within the Section for Secondary Education." In other words, "the establishment of a secondary school in Dobrinja" is now interpreted as "the establishment of the gimnazija in Dobrinja." In this regard, it is clear that the creation of a gimnazija, an academic secondary school designed to prepare students for the university, was viewed by Smail Vesnić, and by many secondary school educators, as a critical element in the establishment of a secondary school system to serve the entrapped students in besieged Dobrinja.

There were three prominent gimnazija in Sarajevo at the beginning of the siege. Prva (First) gimnazija was located on Zmaj Jove Jovanović (today Gimnazijska) Street directly on the boundary line between Centar and Stari Grad municipalities on the east end of the city. Prva gimnazija had the longest tradition to include, at the very least, two prominent alumnae: Ivo Andrić, the noted writer, who won the Nobel prize for literature, and Vladimir Prelog, who won the Nobel prize for chemistry. Druga (Second) gimnazija, located in an open parklet of Sutjeska Street in Centar Municipality, was recognized for its mathematics and computer science academic tracks. Treća (Third) gimnazija was located on Vilosonovo šetaliste (Wilson Promenade) in Novo Sarajevo Municipality, then the frontline along the Miljacka River. Treća gimnazija, the newest of the three, dated back to 1948 and was noted for natural sciences and mathematics, and marked among its alumnae, Sven Alcalaj, the Bosnian ambassador to the United States during the recent war.

Četverta (Fourth) gimnazija was a relatively recent creation serving students in Ilidža Municipality on the outskirts of the city to the west which was occupied by enemy forces during the early months of the siege. Mješovita srednja škola Peta (Fifth) gimnazija i birotehnicka škola (Comprehensive Secondary School Fifth Gimnazija and Office Technical

School) was a unique mixture of an academic gimnazija and vocational-technical school. Located in the large apartment complex of Alipašino polje in Novi Grad Municipality on the western end of the city, the school became the Školski centar "Pero Kosorić" (Pero Kosorić School Center) during the war, named after Pero Kosorić Square in the Hrasno area, a temporary administrative adaptation designed to serve secondary students living in the large apartment complexes on the western side of the city.

With 23 vocational-technical secondary schools in Sarajevo, and but four gimnazija with the outset of the siege, the three primary gimnazija stood out as prestigious secondary schools that carried a high profile in Sarajevo educational circles. In this regard, the creation of a gimnazija in besieged Dobrinja was intended to provide a similar high profile for a secondary educational system where no secondary schools had previously existed. The intent was, for all practical purposes, to create something from nothing. The idea of Smail Vesnić, to develop the focus upon the creation of a gimnazija would, in turn, create a similar focus upon the creation of an entire secondary school operation. The gimnazija as the center of attention would provide both a physical location and an administrative locus for all secondary schooling in Dobrinja, academic and vocational-technical alike. In the words of Behija Jakić, a teacher at Treća gimnazija who became one of the secondary school coordinators, "Gimnazija Dobrinja became the center of everything. All of the work that we did to coordinate the work of secondary schools was coordinated through the gimnazija" (2004).

On 9 August 1992, the entry in the "Almanac" of the Dobrinja War School Center noted that Ismet Hadžić, commanding officer of the 1st Dobrinja Brigade, and Fuad Babić, the commanding officer of Civil Defense Headquarters, visited the Center that day along with a group of other guests. The entry reads:

> After their departure, three shells fell in front of the press center [nearby]. That caused panic. Four people were injured from the Teaching Center, two slightly and two heavily. Paintings were damaged, the entrance door destroyed, mirrors broken ... In the press center four people were also injured, two slightly and two heavily. (Nastavni centar, 1992-1993)

On 20 August 1992, an entry in the "Annals" of Gimnazija Dobrinja, well before it was even operational, noted that "a report on the economic justification for a gimnazija in Dobrinja was completed" (Gimnazija Dobrinja, 1992-1995). A similar entry in the "Almanac" of the War School Center, dated 23 August, noted the "creation of materials for the initiative for opening of the gimnazija in Dobrinja" (Nastavni centar, 1992-1993).

On 26 August 1992, Smail Vesnić sent a working document to the Ministry of Education, the Sarajevo City Assembly, and the Novi Grad Municipal Assembly, outlining the case for creating the new gimnazija. Under the heading of both the Sarajevo Pedagogical Institute and the Dobrinja War School Center, the subject of the document read: "Delivery of a Development Plan Concerning the Opening of a Gimnazija in Dobrinja." The document noted that at the 6 August 1992 meeting of the Teacher's Council of the War School Center that adopted the July 1992 "Basic Work Program," the Council "set in motion the initiative for opening the gimnazija in Dobrinja" on the basis of the developmental plan. According to the document, the initial design was to create four class sections for 128 first-year secondary students, or 32 students per section, and the developmental plan offered four items to clarify the initiative:

> 1. Opening of a gimnazija in Dobrinja is consistent with ... a secondary school type of gimnazija in the context of the development and reformation of secondary education in the Republic of Bosnia and Herzegovina.
>
> 2. With over 120,000 residents, Sarajevo's Novi Grad Municipality has only one secondary school in its entire territory (the Electroengineering School).
>
> 3. Among a poll of future secondary school students, 173 students committed themselves for registration for the first class of the gimnazija which would be opened in Dobrinja.
>
> 4. The geographic situation of Dobrinja, the social and age composition of the residents and the residential housing plan on this territory with now over 45,000 residents are sufficient explanatory factors for setting this initiative in motion. (Vesnić, 1992)

The development plan also reviewed the difficult conditions that confronted the Teacher's Council in its efforts to create the new gimnazija to include available space, teaching equipment, and instructional resources. Particular concerns were expressed for subjects such as chemistry, biology, and physics classes, as well as music and the arts, but the plan also noted that over 10,000 books had been collected for the gimnazija library located in the War School Center.

To repeat a portion of the article, "Gimnazija opens in Dobrinja?" cited in a previous chapter, that appeared in *Oslobođenje*, 28 August 1992, just two days after delivery of the developmental plan outlining the case for the new gimnazija, the subheading noted that a "Gimnazija in Dobrinja [is created] with four sections." While the article updates the reader on the educational situation in Novi Grad Municipality, which includes Dobrinja and the Airport Settlement, and notes the new developments for elementary education and the three Dobrinja elementary schools, the reference here concerns the status of the proposed gimnazija:

> The War Presidency of Novi Grad Municipal Assembly supported the initiative of the Teaching Center in Dobrinja concerning the formation of four sections of the gimnazija with 160 students, in view of the fact that currently in Dobrinja the teaching staff has permission for the work of one secondary school institution ... Although only a small portion of the secondary school students of Dobrinja will attend this gimnazija, this initiative that came about in wartime deserves the attention and support of all authorized authorities. (*Oslobođenje*, 1992: 6)

Although perhaps a backhanded acknowledgement of the place of the new gimnazija which "only a small portion of the secondary school students will attend," the focus of the article upon support for the gimnazija in Dobrinja suggests the importance of the initiative. If only a relatively small number of students would attend the gimnazija, why place this emphasis upon it at the expense of other secondary schools? In this regard, the prominence given to the opening of the gimnazija highlights the importance of creating it in the first place and, in a backhanded way, also gives attention to the larger number of students who attend those other secondary schools, most notably those students who attend vocational-technical schools. In this regard, the creation of the gimnazija would prove to be the basis upon which to reconstruct secondary school operations in a settlement where no secondary school had existed in the years preceding the siege.

During summer and fall 1992, there was steady movement towards the creation of Gimnazija Dobrinja and the subsequent creation of a secondary school system. On 3-4 September 1992, for example, the entries in the "Almanac" of the War School Center refer to the "Delivery of a Developmental Plan" for opening the gimnazija in the following manner:

> 3 September 1992, *Thursday*: A development plan was completed on the opening of the gimnazija in Dobrinja and delivered to certain institutions in the city (City Assembly; Ministry of Education, Science, Culture, and Sport; Novi Grad Municipal Assembly).
>
> 4 September 1992, *Friday*: Smail Vesnić, the director of the Center, com-

pleted the development plan for the opening of a gimnazija in Dobrinja and, with materials, took it into the city to Novi Grad Municipal Assembly, Assembly of the City of Sarajevo, and to the Ministry of Education, Science, Culture, and Sport. Promises were given that the gimnazija in Dobrinja will be opened. (Nastavni centar, 1992-1993)

On 2 October 1992, the "Annals" of Gimnazija Dobrinja noted: "The Presidency of the Sarajevo City Assembly adopted the report on establishing a gimnazija in Dobrinja" (1992-1995). A five-member commission, with Smail Vesnić as commission chair, was formed to hire the new teaching staff. Yet a series of October entries in the "Almanac" of the War School Center remind the reader of just how difficult the situation was at the time in besieged Dobrinja and provide a background for the work of education which was taking place:

> 7 October 1992, *Wednesday*: It is again a cold morning without water, electricity, and gas. Walking to work, everywhere you look you can see a fire in front of the buildings or balconies. It seems the city is on fire ... During the day there was a lot of shelling in Dobrinja. (Nastavni centar, 1992-1993)

While the entries in the "Annals" of Gimnazija Dobrinja are quite matter-of-fact, the "Almanac" entries often relate conditions of the siege, weather conditions, and the state of morale at the time. These October entries continue to note another "cold rainy morning," or "a cold, wet, and sad morning," that "there is still no electricity, war, and gas," and attest to the severity of conditions under siege:

> 22 October 1992, *Thursday*: The morning is cold and wet. Finally the electricity started coming on. Oh God, how we look forward to things that naturally belong to us, which are returned to us for the moment. (Nastavni centar, 1992-1993)

In the introduction to the section on basic objectives and tasks of the "Work Program" for the Secondary Education Section of the November 1992 "Basic Work Program," the importance of creating a gimnazija in Dobrinja is emphasized once again:

> To be able to achieve the educational objectives and tasks in the future more fully, a need for the establishment of a gimnazija in Dobrinja was presented. The reasons for this are not only the distance to Sarajevo and the war activities, but the great number of students and teachers in Dobrinja ... The conditions for verification of this school are being created. The starting school premises have been secured for first-year [of high school, i.e., ninth grade] students. (Nastavni centar, 1992: 41)

The introduction provides additional information on the status of the gimnazija, the organization of classes, and the preparations for new students and teachers:

> Activities on securing other teaching equipment that is needed for verification of this school are underway. This means that with the start of the classes we are organizing, the new gimnazija in Dobrinja starts with work as well. The gimnazija will start with the four first-year classes [four ninth grade sections]. An advertisement is already being prepared for accepting students and teachers. Instruction will take place under the professional supervision of the Pedagogical Institute of Sarajevo. (Nastavni centar, 1992: 41)

The "Work Program" also notes the interest of those Dobrinja students who had attended one of the other city gimnazija prior to the war in attending the new gimnazija. "In accordance with the wishes expressed by first-year students, a great number of them are interested in enrolling in the gimnazija, and that is, of course, the reason for opening the gimnazija in Dobrinja" (Nastavni centar, 1992: 43).

With the anticipation that came with the new gimnazija, amidst cold and rainy fall months, with the days getting shorter and cold frosts, and amidst intermittent shelling of the settlement, these days were critical in the preparation for the gimnazija opening. However, these days were also critical in constructing the administrative framework for organizing the work of all Sarajevo secondary schools in Dobrinja as an outgrowth of Gimnazija Dobrinja since, in the words of Behija Jakić, "all of the work that we did to coordinate the work of secondary schools was coordinated through the gimnazija" (2004).

An "Almanac" entry, dated 18 November 1992, noted that "the students are asking about the start of the new school year, and parents and students about the beginning of the work of the gimnazija." As late as November 1992, however, as noted in regard to elementary schooling, the 1992-1993 school year had yet to begin which meant a delay in the opening of secondary schooling as well. We might remember the reference to elementary schools and that "the concept of the 'little schools' has been accepted at the city level and when the security situation is assessed, the 1992-1993 school year may begin" (Bulja, 1992). Analogous to the situation initiating the new school year for elementary schools, the "Work Program" of the Secondary Education Section reads:

> With the approval of the Pedagogical Institute of Sarajevo and the City

Secretariat for Education, Science, Culture, and Sport, at the end of November 1992, we began preparations and programming, in similar fashion, for regular instruction in the 1992-1993 school year. (Nastavni centar, 1992: 40)

It appears that the Dobrinja War School Center had by now compiled all relevant information on schooling at both elementary and secondary levels as seen in the November "Work Programs" of both the Elementary Education and Secondary Education Sections. As noted, the secondary "Work Program" proposed a "reduced teaching plan and program" of 18 weeks to be offered "in the planned time, from mid-December 1992 to mid-June 1993," an indication of the intentions to begin the new school year. However, December entries in the "Almanac" indicate that preparations were still underway.

> 3 December 1992, *Thursday*: Preparations are in progress for holding the meeting of the Teacher's Council for elementary and secondary schools related to the start of the new school year in the elementary and secondary schools. Regular consultations of professors and students are held. Regular training was held for members of the Armed Forces of RBiH. A meeting of the members of the 2nd Battalion of the 5th Hill Brigade [the new name of the 1st Dobrinja Brigade].
> Around 2:15 P.M., two shells fell behind the building of the Teaching Center. The director's office suffered damage (broken windows). Luckily no one was hurt. Today shells are falling all over Dobrinja. In the neighboring "Preporod" [a business], Professor Muminović is giving a lecture by the title of "War and Morality." (Nastavni centar, 1992-1993)

A 7 December entry in the "Almanac" reads that "preparations are in progress for the start of the new school year in elementary and secondary schools." Another December entry reads:

> 22 December 1992, *Tuesday*: The whole day was spent on completing the "Basic Work Program" of the Dobrinja Teaching Center for 1993, as well as the report on work in 1992. One big and important job for the Dobrinja Teaching Center was completed. The programs were reviewed, put together, and packed. The director of the Dobrinja Teaching Center, Smail Vesnić, will take them into the city tomorrow [to the City Secretariat for Education]. We hope that everything is alright ... Applications have begun to come in concerning the announcement of openings for teachers in the future gimnazija in Dobrinja. That is proof that in war, it is important that one thinks mainly of peace. (Nastavni centar, 1992-1993)

Another winter month went by, with references to the lack of water, electricity, and heat, and the references to the shelling and the snipers continue, as well as to the harsh conditions that served as the backdrop to schooling. In mid and late January, the "Almanac" entries suggest that classes would soon get underway at the new gimnazija:

> 22 January 1993, *Friday*: A relatively peaceful day, without shelling and shooting. At the Dobrinja Teaching Center, regular activities with students are being carried out. The last preparations are being carried out for the start of the new school year. The new school year should start on Monday 25 January 1993 ... It can be said for the first time that the gimnazija in Dobrinja is beginning with work in wartime conditions. This undertaking would have been hard to realize in peace, but how much will, love, and effort is needed in these difficult times? (Nastavni centar, 1992-1993)

On Monday, 25 January 1993, Gimnazija Dobrinja formally began classes. The entry in the "Annals" of Gimnazija Dobrinja was simple and

"Gimnazija Dobrinja: Rođena je u toku ratu." "Gimnazija Dobrinja: Born during the war." On Monday, 25 January 1993, Gimnazija Dobrinja formally began classes with a history lecture by Smajo Halilović entitled, "The Social and Political Situation in the Republic of Bosnia and Herzegovina." Smail Vesnić, director of the Dobrinja War School Center, here referred to as the Dobrinja Teaching Center, was the new director of Gimnazija Dobrinja as well. Photo courtesy of Gimnazija Dobrinja.

matter-of-fact referring only to "the first day of classes at the gimnazija in Dobrinja." It also included a reference to the first class taught, a history lecture by Smajo Halilović on the topic, "The Social and Political Situation in the Republic of Bosnia and Herzegovina." It should be remembered that Professor Halilović was responsible for the initial history curriculum for secondary education in the July "Basic Work Program." On the other hand, the entry in the "Almanac" of the War School Center expressed the struggle to create the gimnazija in as well as the hope that Gimnazija Dobrinja would serve not only as an educational center for the organization of secondary schooling but as a cultural focus of the Dobrinja community as well:

> 25 January 1993, *Monday*: A big ceremony at the Dobrinja Teaching Center. Today the newly-opened gimnazija in Dobrinja began with its work. For now, first and second-year students from all Sarajevo secondary schools will be in the territory of Dobrinja. The gimnazija was formally opened by the director of the Dobrinja Teaching Center, Smail Vesnić, in the presence of a large number of students, parents, teachers, and guests. (Nastavni centar, 1992-1993)

The entry, after noting the class of Professor Halilović, continues with a sense of hope for the future for students, teachers, and their families:

> It is expected that this gimnazija, besides educational activities, will be a center of cultural and other manifestations in Dobrinja and wider. The opening was very humble. Time will prove the importance of this school for all the inhabitants of Dobrinja. After the ceremony, the first working and teaching day in the 1992-1993 school year continued. We wish to all students and teachers and their parents much luck and success, but the most we can wish them is peace and a free Republic of Bosnia and Herzegovina. (Nastavni centar, 1992-1993)

On the last page of the "Work Journal" of Dobrinja 2A for first and second-year secondary students, someone wrote the words below in bold, capital letters to commemorate the opening of Gimnazija Dobrinja and, in turn, the resistance of teachers and students to the enemy. The words offer a legacy of their efforts, as seen in the "Work Journals" of all the war schools of Dobrinja, to whomever would someday read such a mundane school document and, in this regard, I am proud to say that I can pass on this legacy to whomever reads this book:

> *Gimnazija Dobrinja*
> *Rođena je u toku rata*
> *Ratni dnevnici i ostaci granata, kojima su odoljeli učenici sa svojim profesorima*

Gimnazija Dobrinja
Born during the war
War journals and the remnants of shells, all of which the students and
their teachers managed to survive. (Gimnazija Dobrinja, 1992-1995)

Secondary School Organization
in Dobrinja and in Sarajevo

As a complement to the November 1992 "Work Program" compiled by the Secondary Education Section, Ilija Šobot and his colleagues also compiled a three-volume set entitled, "Data on Teachers and Students: Secondary School, 1992-1993 School Year." This document reveals in painstaking detail the nature of the relationship between the organization of secondary schooling in Dobrinja and the secondary schools of Sarajevo. In this regard, it provides a wealth of data on schools, students, and teachers to indicate the incredible amount of work accomplished. The document includes a listing of each of the 27 secondary schools/secondary school centers in Sarajevo at the time of the war whose students were trapped in Dobrinja, and would attend classes there under the administration of the Secondary Education Section and Gimnazija Dobrinja, but would nevertheless maintain their enrollment in their respective schools.

The document includes information on the number of students and classes for the 27 secondary schools/centers, as seen in Table 4.2, along with rosters of all students enrolled in each school. The data include the list of names for the secondary school coordinators, although no names are listed for selected schools, as well as the names of each of the secondary instructors for each of the secondary subject area classes. It should be pointed out here for selected schools that the terminology used for the schools/centers in Table 4.2 is the same terminology used in the document where the names of the vocational-technical schools are often the common, abbreviated names.

The numbers cited in Table 4.1 indicate a total of 790 secondary students based on data from the November 1992 "Work Program" compiled by the Secondary Education Section from their surveys of the local Dobrinja communities. The numbers in Table 4.2, however, indicate a total of 595 secondary students based on data from student registration that was compiled from the respective secondary schools. While there appears to be a discrepancy of approximately 200 students, the explanation for the discrepancy appears to lie in the registration of first-year students in the gimnazija. In this regard, the student rosters for the gimnazija indicate that only second, third, and fourth-year students were enrolled. In other words,

Table 4.2
Data on Secondary School Students in Dobrinja and the Airport Settlement, Their Secondary Schools of Register, and School Coordinators, in the 1992-1993 School Year

Secondary School	Coordinator	Class I	II	III	IV	Students
1. Prva gimnazia	Mirsada Balić	0	7	8	9	24
2. Druga gimnazija	Momčilo Simić	0	4	12	6	22
3. Školski centar "Igmanski Mars" (Ilidža)	Momčilo Simić	0	0	0	2	2
4. Treća gimnazija	Senada Kulenović	0	14	11	2	27
5. Peta gimnazija/ Birotehnička škola	Branka Pavlović	3	8	15	6	32
6. (Školski centar "Pero Kosorić")	Branka Pavlović	0	0	0	0	0
7. Grafička škola	Branka Pavlović	2	8	3	2	15
8. Trgovačka škola	Azra Baluković	14	7	14	8	43
9. Ekonomska škola	Gordana Kordić	6	14	12	10	42
10. Ugostiteljsko-turistički školski centar	Muhamed Duranović	11	8	7	0	26
11. Zubozdravstvena škola	Gorana Lukić	14	10	2	2	28
12. Medicinska škola	Gorana Lukić	13	13	6	8	40
13. Škola za medicinske sestre	Gorana Lukić	17	14	3	0	34
14. Elektrotehnička škola	Amir Ajanović	13	11	11	4	39
15. Elektroenergetska škola	Drago Lončar	9	19	9	2	39
16. Mašinska tehnička škola	Rade Soko	4	12	6	5	27
17. Škola metalskih zanimanja	Rade Soko	1	17	12	1	31
18. Školski centar "Buro Pucar Stari" (Vogošča)	Rade Soko	0	0	0	0	0
19. Željeznički školski centar	Darinka Šobot	9	18	13	8	48
20. Saobraćajna škola	Edina Knežević	2	7	5	3	17
21. Tekstilni školski centar	Nisveta Jamak	2	4	3	1	10
22. Poljoprivredno-veterinarska i prehrambeni školski centar	Tatjana Tešanović	3	15	5	1	24
23. Građevinsko-geodetski školski centar	Medžida Mulić	3	10	6	3	22
24. Drvno-tehnička škola	Mirsad Kurtović	0	0	1	2	3
25. Šumarski školski centar	Mirsad Kurtović	0	0	0	0	0
26. Muzička škola		0	0	0	0	0
27. Škola primijenjenih umjetnosti		0	0	0	0	0
Totals		126	220	164	85	595

Source: Nastavni centar (1992-1993).

there are no class rosters for first-year students in the gimnazija listed in Table 4.2. If we remember the discussion concerning the proposal for opening the gimnazija in Dobrinja, the plan was to create "the formation of four sections of the gimnazija with 160 students" who would, of course, be first-year students. Over a four-year period, Gimnazija Dobrinja would realize its full complement of students in years one through four with the admission of 160 students each year.

It would appear, therefore, that the numbers in Table 4.1, as revealed in the gimnazija rosters of first-year students, indicate that those first-year students living in Dobrinja, who would enroll in a gimnazija for the purposes of pursuing an academic track to the university, are choosing to enroll in Gimnazija Dobrinja—and Gimnazija Dobrinja is not listed here. If these figures are taken into account, leaving only a discrepancy of about 40 or so students, which might be explained by the lack of data from five or six of the schools/centers listed, then the secondary student numbers are approximately the same.

The difficulty of gathering such data on students of high school age living in Dobrinja who once attended all 27 Sarajevo secondary schools/centers is noteworthy to say the least. The complexity of organizing these students, across four secondary grade levels, to attend classes in their individual subject areas, according to a regular class schedule, dependent upon an academic or vocational track, with but one central school location, dispersed at perhaps 14 available premises, is even more noteworthy. In this regard, the organization of secondary schooling in Dobrinja is a microcosm of the organization of secondary schooling in Sarajevo and must be discussed at the marcolevel as well.

Dated April 1993, a Pedagogical Institute document entitled, "Information on the Beginning of Instruction in Secondary Schools, 1992–1993," provides data from across Sarajevo city to clarify the relationship between the organization of schooling in Dobrinja and the organization of Sarajevo schools. First, the data indicate the extent and the complexity of the relationship between Gimnazija Dobrinja and the 27 secondary schools/centers viewed within the framework of the 72 local communities across what remained of the four Sarajevo municipalities. The document states that, "in general, every secondary school received the obligation to organize instruction in a region ranging from three to five local communities" (Pedagoški zavod, 1993: 5). It is clear that Gimnazija Dobrinja, as the only secondary school in the settlement, received the obligation to organize instruction in the seven school regions of Dobrinja.

In fact, secondary schools all across Sarajevo received similar obligations to organize instruction in the local communities around the schools, or around their relocated administrative offices, given their location near the frontlines or the status of their school buildings. Thus a school like Treća gimnazija, for example, originally located in Novo Sarajevo Municipality in the center of the city, was relocated to Stari Grad Municipality on the eastern end of the city, upon the destruction of its school buildings. There in its relocated administrative offices, Treća gimnazija "received the obligation to organize instruction" in four local communities in Stari Grad Municipality: Bistrik, Kovači, and Sumbuluša I and II.

In this regard, based upon the Pedagogical Institute document, at the outset of the 1992-1993 school year, Table 4.3 indicates the assignments of secondary schools by local communities across Sarajevo, and I will list these assignments in full here to indicate the extent of secondary school organization across the city. The terminology used in Table 4.3 is the same terminology used in the document which cites the complete names of the schools/centers, in contrast to Table 4.2 where the common, abbreviated name for the schools are often cited. There are 27 secondary schools/centers cited in both documents and, for the most part, the terminology is clear enough to indicate that the schools cited are the same schools and the names can be easily matched. There are exceptions, however, and these will be clarified in the discussion, but there are several inconsistencies, however, between documents, and hence, the two tables.

For example, the two school centers cited in Table 4.2, "Igmanski Mars" Ilidža and "Buro Pucar Stari" Vogošča, are not cited in Table 4.3, perhaps because both Ilidža and Vogošča municipalities were under the control of the enemy and these school centers could no longer function. Školski centar "Pero Kosorić" and Peta gimnazija are listed separately in Table 4.2, but Peta gimnazija and Birotehnička škola together form the Pero Kosorić Center in Table 4.3. Četvrta gimnazija and Škola za mentalno retardirane učenike (the School for Mentally Retarded Students), listed in Table 4.2, are not listed in Table 4.3, perhaps because none of their students lived in Dobrinja. Given these differences, 25 of the 27 schools/centers cited in Table 4.2 are also cited in Table 4.3. One of 28 secondary schools or school centers in Sarajevo, Gimnazija Dobrinja is simply referred to here in the document as responsible for organizing instruction under the Dobrinja War School Center which has responsibility for all seven Dobrinja school regions. In this regard, Table 4.3 provides an overview of secondary school organization and responsibilities and the place of

THE WAR SCHOOLS OF DOBRINJA

TABLE 4.3
SECONDARY SCHOOL OBLIGATION FOR THE ORGANIZATION
OF INSTRUCTION BY SARAJEVO LOCAL COMMUNITY IN THE 1992-1993
SCHOOL YEAR

Schools	Sarajevo Local Communities
1. Mješovita srednja poloprivredno–veterinarska i prehrambena škola	Podtekija Skenderija Mahmutovac Mjednica Širokača
2. Srednja muzička škola	Logavina I and II
3. Mješovita srednja ugostiteljsko–turistička skola	Breka
4. Srednja stručna trgovinska škola	———
5. Školski centar "Pero Kosorić" (Mješovita srednja škola peta gimnazija i birotehnička škola)	Olimpijsko Selo Mojmilo Otoka Petar Đokić Kumrovec Avdo Hodžić 25 Novembar
6. Zubozdravstvena škola (Srednja zubotehnička škola)	Trg Oslobođenje II Koševo Džidžikovac
7. Srednja škola za medicinske sestre–techničare	Višnjik Park Podhrastovi
8. Srednja medicinska škola	Mejtaš I and II Bjelave
9. Srednja škola primjenjenih umjetnosti	———
10. Prva gimnazija	Trg Oslobođenje I Centar Hrid Jarčedoli
11. Druga gimnazija	Ciglane
12. Mješovita srednja građevinsko–geodetska škola	Soukbunar Babića Bašta
13. Srednja mašinska tehnička škola	Koševo I
14. Mješovita srednja elektrotehnička škola	Adem Buć Marijin Dvor M. Obradović
15. Četvrta gimnazija	Koševsko Brdo Crni Vrh Gorica

(Table continued on next page)

TABLE 4.3
SECONDARY SCHOOL OBLIGATION FOR THE ORGANIZATION OF INSTRUCTION BY SARAJEVO LOCAL COMMUNITY IN THE 1992-1993 SCHOOL YEAR (CONTINUED)

Schools	Sarajevo Local Communities
16. Šumarski školski centar (Mješovita srednja drvna–šumarska škola)	Omer Maslić Blagoje Parović
17. Grafički školski centar (Srednja grafička technička škola)	Medeseta
18. Željeznički školski centar	Hrasno Brdo Trg Heroja Ivan Krndelja
19. Gimnazija Dobrinja	Nastavni Centar
20. Srednja economska škola	Baščaršija I and II
21. Saobračajni školski centar (Mješovita srednja saobraćajna škola)	Velešići Donji Velešići Gornji Pofalići Donji Pofalići Gornji
22. Treća gimnazija	Kovači Sumbuluša I and II Bistrik
23. Tekstilni školski centar (Mješovita srednja tekstilna škola)	Vratnik I and II Gazin Han Sedrenik I and II
24. Drvna tehnička škola (Mješovita srednja drvno–šumarska škola)	Mladost Ivo Andrić Jedinstvo 6 April
25. Srednjoškolski centar Velešići	Podhrastovi II
26. Mješovita srednja škola za elektroenergetiku	Bratstvo Jedinstvo
27. Srednja škola metalskih zanimanja	Ivo Lola Ribar Aneks Petar Dokić
28. Škola za mentalno retardirane učenike	Pavle Goranin Staro Hrasno

Source: Pedagoški zavod (1993: 6-9).

Gimnazija Dobrinja within the organizational framework for secondary schooling across the four Sarajevo city municipalities.

Several points need to be made here as qualifications to the Table 4.3 data regarding the comparison of schools or local communities between prewar, wartime, and postwar eras. First, the names of the schools are recorded in the Institute document as they existed at the time given war conditions, the consolidation and restructuring of schools as the result of the war, and the creation of school centers from individual schools. Second, the postwar era has seen the creation of new schools and the restructuring and renaming of old ones, so the names may not necessarily be the same over time. Third, the number and the names of the local communities are based upon the situation at the time as they existed in the four remaining municipalities of the city. Many local communities have since been renamed, just as many locations in the city were renamed, and new local communities have since been recast out of the older ones adding to the number and the confusion. Fourth, school obligations changed over time so that schools assigned local communities at one point in time would be assigned responsibility for different local communities the following year given the school's own particular situation and changing wartime conditions.

The example of Treća gimnazija again illustrates the organizational complexity of the secondary school system during wartime. Originally located in Novo Sarajevo, relocated to Stari Grad, and then back to a different location in Novo Sarajevo, the situation and conditions of Treća gimnazija, and therefore its school responsibilities, changed greatly over the years of the siege. In April 1993, at the beginning of the 1992-1993 school year, Treća gimnazija had no school buildings, yet was given administrative responsibility for schooling for the four local communities in Stari Grad, cited previously, yet retained responsibility for its own students who were enrolled in the school at the time. As of 1 April 1992, at the outbreak of the war, there were 1,297 students enrolled at Treća gimnazija as, what is termed, their school of register or home school (*matična škola*). As of 1 March 1993, almost one year into the war, the number of registered students had dropped to 318 (Pedagoški zavod, 1993), although by the beginning of the next school year, the number had increased to 362 (Treća gimnazija, 1992-1995).

With no school buildings, Treća gimnazija, in administrative terms, was responsible for the instruction of all secondary students living in the four local communities it was assigned for the 1992-1993 school year and, although some of its own students lived in those four local communities, the majority of its 362 students lived in local communities all across the city. Viewed from another perspective, these 362 Treća gimnazija students attended not only the war schools that were established by Treća gimnazija in the four assigned local communities, but they attended another 51 local community war schools all across Sarajevo. In other words, Treća gimnazija students attended a total of 55 secondary schools across the length and breadth of Sarajevo city, including Gimnazija Dobrinja, but

139

still maintained their enrollment in Treća gimnazija as their school of register (Treća gimnazija, 1992-1995).

The example of Treća gimnazija serves to clarify the organization of secondary schooling in Dobrinja and the role of Gimnazija Dobrinja within the organizational structure and, of course, the role of the Secondary Education Section under the administration of the Dobrinja War School Center. To the best of my calculations, there were at least 27 students who were enrolled at Treća gimnazija, based on 1992-1993 school year data compiled by the Secondary Education Section, but living, and now trapped, in Dobrinja unable to travel into the city proper to attend the war schools under Treća gimnazija administration. These 27 students would attend 31 different classes organized for gimnazija students at the 14 classroom locations organized by Gimnazija Dobrinja which "received the obligation to organize instruction" in the school regions of Dobrinja and the Airport Settlement. Of note is that, as gimnazija students, they would attend classes along with students from the other Sarajevo gimnazija at Gimnazija Dobrinja which was responsible for the instructional process. At the same time, these Treća gimnazija students, while attending classes in Dobrinja, still maintained their enrollment at Treća gimnazija as their school of register.

In the documents of the Secondary Education Section, Senada Kulenović, a chemical engineer who worked at the Occupational/Industrial Safety Institute, is cited as the Treća gimnazija coordinator in Dobrinja. These school documents indicate that at least 22 different subjects and 31 different class offerings were available to Treća gimnazija students, including four foreign languages (English, German, French, and Latin) befitting the academic focus of a gimnazija. In addition, a variety of specialized vocational classes were offered, and Civil Defense became a standard course offering as a curricular subject. The documents further indicate that at least 40 different instructors taught Treća gimnazija students in three of the four secondary grades (there was no enrollment of first-year or ninth grade students at that time) that included four separate academic tracks or streams for third-year and fourth-year gimnazija students (Nastavni centar, 1992-1993).

The "Work Program" of the Secondary Education Section noted that "there are students from all types of schools. The fewest number of students are tenth, eleventh, and twelfth grade students from the gimnazija" (Nastavni centar, 1992: 43). Although there were five gimnazija located in the city municipalities, the numbers cited here are based upon data from the three primary Sarajevo gimnazija. No figures are cited for Četverta gimnazija or the Fourth Gymnasium. As for Peta gimnazija, the Fifth Gymnasium, located in the occupied suburb of Ilidža, there is some confusion about which students are enrolled in gimnazija programs. So, the data from the three primary Sarajevo gimnazija indicate that 24 second class or tenth grade gimnazija students, 22 third class or eleventh grade students, and 27 fourth class or twelfth grade students were listed on their respective gimnazija class rosters. To the best of my calculations, a total of 73 gimnazija students in three grade levels registered to attend classes in Dobrinja for the 1992-1993 school year. As noted, there was no listing of first-year or ninth-grade students who would enroll at Gimnazija Dobrinja instead of enrolling in the other city gimnazija.

These figures suggest that there were approximately 522 students who would attend vocational-technical schools all across the city but who were trapped in Dobrinja and registered for classes under the administration of Gimnazija Dobrinja and the Secondary Education Section. There are coordinators listed for 22 vocational-technical schools, to the best of my calculations, including the Pero Kosorić School Center which includes Peta gimnazija, but this number is problematic since many vocational-technical schools were consolidated as a result of the wartime conditions. The lack of basic equipment and specialized technical resources required to operate these schools and the lack of opportunities for students to exercise their specialized skills was a major problem for vocational-technical education.

A group of students of the Economics Secondary School, under the heading on the chalkboard, Dobrinja Teaching Center, pose for a photograph during the 1993-1994 school year. Photo courtesy of Miroslav Kordić.

These schools ranged from the Economics Secondary School to the Comprehensive Electroenergy Secondary School to the Comprehensive Wood-Forestry School to the Railway School Center. In addition to a regular offering of core subjects, almost every one of these schools offered a variety of specialized vocational tracks and hence specialized subjects to meet the needs of their students, not to mention the expertise required of their instructors. The incredible variety of programs and courses that were somehow offered these students enrolled in selected occupational or vocational tracks is a testimony to those "experts" with diverse profiles living in Dobrinja. Along with the Music School, there were a total of 23 vocational or technical schools/centers which, in addition to the four gimnazija already cited, indicate a total of 27 Sarajevo secondary schools and their secondary school students who were represented in besieged Dobrinja, although there is a lack of student data for five or six of these schools. Nevertheless, the data compiled by the Secondary Education Section of the Dobrinja War School Center to initiate the 1992-1993 school year indicate that approximately 790 secondary school students who were originally registered at 27 different secondary schools throughout Sarajevo city would attend classes in the Dobrinja school regions. These students attended classes under the administration of Gimnazija Dobrinja and the Secondary Education Section while still maintaining enrollment, via their school coordinators, in their home schools back in Sarajevo, with the hope that one day they would return to their home schools upon the end of the war.

NOTE

[1] In the former Yugoslavia, the *gimnazija* was a prestigious academic secondary school designed to prepare students for the university. I will use the term *gimnazija* throughout as a reference to both Gimnazija Dobrinja as well as the other Sarajevo *gimnazija* rather than the English translation, gymnasium, which may perhaps suggest another meaning.

Mirani Ratni Dani

Peaceful War Days
The 1992-1993 War School Year

CHAPTER FIVE

Surviving in an Honest Manner

Night was falling. She was standing by the window and watching tracks in the snow. The tracks led from her doorway to the market and backwards.

It was during the war and winter had already come. Her children did not have a father. He was killed very young. She was also a very young widow with two three-year-old children. She herself did not know how to provide food for her children. There was no electricity, water, gas, wood and the food was getting less. She stood like this, by the window, asking herself what to do next. She thought how everything would be easier if her husband was here.

Suddenly, someone appeared from the shadow of the nearby market. Why was he exiting the shop window in a strange way? She realized that something was mischievous. As the strange figure got closer to her doorway, a strange chill started to grow within her. Yes, she recognized him.

It was her neighbor who lived in the apartment above. He wore a black raincoat and a black hat. He carried a bag on his back which was clearly very heavy. He lived alone without a wife or kids. His balcony was filled with piles of wood. He often arrived with some kind of bag or sack.

He brought some kind of sack from the market, went into his apartment and then with an empty sack back to the market. And he did this several times. His footprints were embossed in the snow.

Why was he doing this so cautiously and during nightfall?

It was obvious that this was not an honest deal. She carried on watching him like this with tears in her eyes. She was pondering over the possibilities of her survival together with her family, but one must survive in an honest manner.

—Ivona Muratović, 6th Grade
Skender Kulenović Elementary School

The Slippery Beginning to the 1992-1993 War School Year

In one sense, Dobrinja was further along in the efforts to reorganize schooling than the rest of Sarajevo city. The "stairway schools" that sprang up as early as spring and summer of 1992 at the onset of the siege were the very first schools in Sarajevo city to adapt instruction to wartime conditions well in advance of the directives of the City Secretariat for Education. The Work Programs of both the Elementary and Secondary Education sections reveal that Dobrinja school administrators, under the direction of the Dobrinja War School Center, were addressing the organizational problems of schooling in a systematic fashion as early as June and July 1992. Furthermore, these administrators had developed systematic plans of operations to initiate schooling and, in the process, to address the particular problems of elementary and secondary schooling seen in the refined Work Programs of November 1992.

Under the direction of the Elementary Education Section, the elementary "Work Program" was designed to integrate teachers, students, and classrooms of the "stairway schools" into the administration of the three elementary schools that functioned before the war, but now had no school buildings and no permanent physical locations. Under the direction of the Secondary Education Section, the secondary "Work Program" was designed to integrate teachers and students from 27 Sarajevo gimnazija and vocational-technical secondary schools into the framework of a new proposed gimnazija that had no previous history. Forced by the isolation of a siege within a siege to confront the educational realities of schooling months earlier than the schools in Sarajevo proper, Dobrinja educators were in the process of forging "a model of educational work" not just for Dobrinja but what would eventually become a model of educational work for the elementary and secondary schools of Sarajevo as well.

It would be noteworthy to conclude the previous chapter, or to begin this chapter, with the 25 January "Almanac" entry on the opening of Gimnazija Dobrinja, to mark the end of one difficult period and the beginning of another. In this regard, the opening of Gimnazija Dobrinja was a major event that provided hope for the future in the besieged settlement, a focal point for schooling in an actual building with the three elementary school buildings in ruin. Unfortunately, two days after the opening ceremony, a single, difficult-to-read, 27 January entry in the "Annals" of Gimnazija Dobrinja indicates only that "Instruction was not held because of the shelling." An entry on the same day in the "Almanac" of the War School Center clarifies the Gimnazija entry:

> 27 January 1993, *Wednesday*: At 7:45 A.M., a merciless cannonade shelling of Dobrinja began. The first shell fell close to the Teaching Center near the Red Cross, and others were falling all over Dobrinja. Great material damage was done, but let that be the greatest evil. Luckily, there were no victims until noon. Hopefully there will not be any after, because people have gone to the shelters. There was no school in the newly-opened Gimnazija. Classes have been postponed for some better times. A small number of people came to work. (Nastavni centar, 1992-1993)

One day later, the "Almanac" entry reads, that "compared to yesterday, today was almost completely peaceful, and that "regular instruction was held for students in [first-year] class I and [second-year] class II of the Gimnazija and other secondary schools." Over the next two weeks, entries in both the "Almanac" and the "Annals" alternate between regular class sessions at the Gimnazija and the cancellation of these sessions because of the war. A late January entry in the "Almanac" reads:

> 30 January 1993, *Saturday*: The usual activities at the Teaching Center. Regular instruction was organized at the Gimnazija ... The day was relatively peaceful until the afternoon when five shells fell in Dobrinja and killed five people. Day by day, innocent people are being killed in this difficult fight for freedom, which will come in spite of everything. (Nastavni centar, 1992-1993)

Although regular classes were being held over the next week at the Gimnazija, and in the dispersed elementary school classrooms located in the local school regions, the shelling of Dobrinja had become so severe by the second week of February that it was seriously disrupting any semblance of a regular school routine. Two early February entries in the "Almanac" indicate something of the situation:

> 9 February, *Tuesday*: The constant shelling of Dobrinja in recent days is not permitting regular instruction to be held at the Gimnazija in Dobrinja. Instruction lasted until 11:00 A.M. on the morning shift and then it was stopped ... Luckily, in the Teaching Center, until now, there were no injured.

> 10 February, *Wednesday*: The days in Dobrinja are going by on some sort of war schedule. The snipers are doing their dirty work, and the shelling is constant. All that interferes with the regular activities of the Teaching Center. Besides that, instruction is held regularly, but it stops during

the time of the shelling. But that must pass. Other activities have been completed in the Teaching Center—work with students, preparations for the opening and the beginning of work in the elementary schools. (Nastavni centar, 1992-1993)

Although the administrative framework was now in place, the reference to beginning work in the elementary schools is another indication that the new school year had, officially, yet to get underway. Even though both elementary and secondary schooling was taking place on an intermittent basis at various locations, the regular 1992-1993 school year, as determined by the Ministry of Education and the City Secretariat of Education, had yet to begin for both Sarajevo and Dobrinja schools as late as February 1993.

On 27 February, the entry in the "Annals" of Gimnazija Dobrinja records the formation of a commission by the Minister of Education of the Republic, Nikola Kovač, to determine the working conditions of the Gimnazija. At the same time, the entry also refers to the continual shelling of the settlement referred to in the Center entries for early February:

> At 2:00 P.M., four shells hit the area between the Press Center and the Military Hospital. At that moment, two of our students were killed. They didn't have instruction that day. Mirjana Malešević was a first-year [grade nine] student and Samir Poljo was a second-year [grade ten] student.

By the next day, the 28 February entry reads:

> Due to the danger of shelling, instruction will not be held until further notice. (Gimnazija Dobrinja, 1992-1995)

One week later, the 6 March entry noted a meeting of the Teacher's Council, followed by an "Announcement to Parents" from the Dobrinja War School Center that appeared in the Gimnazija "Annals," to be cited here in full:

> You probably know that with the approval of the parents, the Teaching Center has organized certain activities for a more successful start of this school year. In that regard, all necessary organizational preparations for students of elementary and secondary schools on the territory of Dobrinja were carried out. That is how, at the end of January in the local communities of Dobrinja 2A and 2B [the location of the Teaching Center and Gimnazija Dobrinja], regular instruction for secondary students began. Since hostile activities have increased in the last couple of days, regular instruction is suspended until further notice. With the approval of the Minister for Education, Science, Culture, and Sport, of the Republic of Bosnia and Herzegovina, we are committed to assist elementary and secondary students in the following way:

In the coming period, students will receive instructional sheets for all subjects separately. The instructional sheets contain information on the learning material which the students need to cover, the dates on the textbook, and other necessary literature, the location and type of assistance which teachers will be offering as well as information on the steps to authenticate the adoption of the learning material. Practically, the students will, with the possible help of parents, and instruction and consultations with teachers, learn at home and, at a scheduled time, take partial examinations. Grades will be entered in the work journal separately for every student. The number of instructional sheets will vary between six and twelve depending on the type and scope of the subject. Examinations are taken in order. After passing one exam, another instruction sheet is given, and so on. We are aware of the fact that this is one of the more difficult ways because the lack of textbooks and school literature is clearly noticeable. Nevertheless, we consider that with the maximum engagement of the teachers, we will be able to reduce this problem and succeed in achieving satisfactory results. When necessary security conditions have been met, we will begin with regular instruction. Until then, the instruction sheet will be an intermediate and firm connection between teachers and their students.

Best regards to students and parents. (Gimnazija Dobrinja, 1992-1995)

To reiterate the words of Abdulah Jabučar, deputy minister of education of the Bosnian Republic at the time, the "Guidelines on Educational Activities" for the operation of schools "committed every school to work, regardless of conditions—to adapt to the actual situation" (1997: 295). In a paper delivered at the 18 April 1994 education conference in wartime Sarajevo, entitled, "Modification and Application of Linear Programmed Instruction in Gimnazija Dobrinja in Sarajevo," Smail Vesnić speaks to the guidelines proposed by Minister Jabučar as it applies to the schooling situation in Dobrinja.

It is January 1992. War activities are very intense so the factor of security has significantly influenced the way and *the level of adaptation of the programmed materials to the entire situation* [my emphasis]. Realization of the written assignments as well as other forms of written examinations of the instructional materials were conducted in groups or in another way which is appropriate to the situation in the local community as a basis of organization of educational activities. All other issues and needs for educational activities were resolved in accordance with the given situation considering the principles that the entire organization of these activities need to be filled with a high level of security for the students and teachers. (1994: 2-6)

The implementation of "linear programmed instruction" (*linearno programiranje nastave*) in the words of Professor Vesnić, was an instructional adaptation to wartime conditions in Dobrinja. This form of instruction "in which the students independently work on the written program assignments" and "in which the content and the way of learning have been well-determined" by the teacher allows individualized instruction consistent with the curricular objectives "considering the lack of textbooks and other literature" available to students (1994: 2). Such instructional programs place a heavy responsibility upon the teacher since s/he must prepare "instructional sheets" (*nastavni listići*) for the students in the absence of textbooks and curriculum materials. Professor Vesnić explains:

> The essence of the organization for educational activities through instructional sheets is that, in principle, a student of any school receives on average, for every subject, every two weeks, an instructional sheet in which, in accordance with the expressed principles, the [instructional] material [to be assigned] in that period belongs in accordance with the plan. Besides that, on the sheets there is information on textbooks, collection of assignments, and other necessary literature. The information on the time and place where assistance is given to students is given as well. (1994: 3)

The adaptation of both curriculum and instruction for students attending not only the new gimnazija, but for all elementary and secondary students as well, was designed to continue the process of schooling under the most difficult of wartime conditions. Gimnazija Dobrinja was an attempt to reconstruct schooling in a central school location but, given the intense shelling of the settlement during late January, February, and early March 1993, such a traditional school model was problematic. In this regard, although instruction was performed at Gimnazija Dobrinja when possible, secondary schooling in Dobrinja returned to the "stairway school" model of elementary education during these difficult times, with at least fourteen secondary classroom locations in the local communities of the settlement. The difficult wartime conditions forced Dobrinja educators not only to localize the schools in terms of classrooms, but forced teachers to adapt the school curriculum for individualized instruction in order to meet the needs of the students. Thus, in an article entitled "Education and War" from *Dobrinjski spektar* (Dobrinja Spectrum) that appeared in the "Annals" of Gimnazija Dobrinja along with the 13 March 1993 entry, the following passage is noted: "Teachers are adapting to the conditions of war, endeavoring to implement the teaching plan normally, balancing between teaching and danger."

With the opening of Gimnazija Dobrinja on 25 January 1993, schooling for secondary students was initiated in Dobrinja over a month before the official beginning of the school year in the rest of Sarajevo city on 1 March 1993. It should be noted, however, that the majority of secondary students in Dobrinja had not attended school since the beginning of the siege and the official end of the 1991-1992 school year on 15 May 1992. These secondary students, many of whom wanted to apply to one of the University faculties, were well behind many of the elementary students who attended classes in the stairway schools during the summer and fall months in order not to lose the school year. If we remember the question of Fata Trle, one of the elementary coordinators for Dobrinja 2A, expressing the fundamental concern in the 28 November 1992 meeting of the Teacher's Council, "I would like to ask whether this school year will be recognized because this needs to be said to the parents?" (Bulja, 1992).

In this regard, the beginning of classes at Gimnazija Dobrinja well before the official start of the Sarajevo school year was intended to make up for over one-half year of lost classes to ensure that the secondary school year would be recognized as well. The operation of the stairway schools from the beginning of the siege ensured, given Smail Vesnić's response to Fata Trle, that "if all this is well-organized, this school year will probably be recognized," at least for elementary school students (Bulja, 1992). The 10 February notation in the Center "Almanac" noted the "preparations for the opening and the beginning of work in the elementary schools" which appears as a reference to the beginning of the new school year as the three Dobrinja elementary schools assumed administrative responsibility for instruction in the stairway school classrooms of the local Dobrinja communities. The 13 March 1993 entry in the "Annals" of Gimnazija Dobrinja summarized the situation at the time noting that "secondary education is in progress, while preparations for elementary education are underway." The "Annals" of Dušan Pajić-Dašić Elementary School reiterate that "in March 1993, preparations for the beginning of the school year were in full swing" (1992-1995).

The official 1992-1993 school year for all Sarajevo schools that operated under the administration of the City Secretariat for Education was designed to run for 18 instructional weeks, from 1 March to 9 July, "plus one more week in reserve," until 16 July 1993, while "the instructional plan and program have been reduced by 50 percent" (*Oslobođenje*, 1993: 4). From the beginning of the siege in spring 1992, it had taken approximately eleven months to reorganize schooling across Sarajevo city. In a June 1993 article in *Prosvjetni list* entitled, "The School Year is not Lost," Mehmed

Hromadžić, citing Fahrudin Isaković, the secretary of the City Secretariat for Education at the time, responds to critical comments concerning the delayed opening of the 1992-1993 school year:

> To organize and perform instruction for secondary school students in occupied, destroyed, constantly shelled and sniper-exposed Sarajevo—is equal, without exaggeration, to real heroism. In conditions when bombs were falling for days, hours, months, and weeks—a full 15 months, one shift after another, when snipers, anti-aircraft guns, and other deadly iron from hill-billies from the surrounding Sarajevo hills did not allow us "to open an eye"—we had to gather students and teachers together and not allow the school year to be lost. Besides all war conditions, in spite of those people from the hills and 101 reasons "against it," it was decided to start with "war schools"—in one real, safe, and applicable way of organizing instruction ...
>
> In this way, some schools started in December, two schools in November, and the schools in Dobrinja started in September. (1993: 3)

Hromadžić is partially right here citing the Dobrinja schools although he no doubt equates their earlier start to the stairway schools and the beginning of the regular school year. The critical point here is that in spite of legitimate reasons not to even begin the belated 1992-1993 school year, this statement in an official government newsletter makes it quite clear that a belated and truncated school year served a larger purpose than simply classroom instruction. In this regard, the Hromadžić article concludes with the following statement:

> We are already taking into consideration the new school year. That organization as well as progress will depend on war conditions and for now we foresee that the school year should be divided into three sessions. As soon as this savageness of cannons and other artillery from the hills comes to an end, everything will be much easier ... We are planning to start with the 1993–1994 school year in the beginning of September ... Experience from this school year will be useful for us in the new school year, so all of us who have been involved in the implementation of those tasks are expecting that this school year will be more successful. (Hromadžić, 1993:3)

To refer back to the 8 September 1992 article in *Oslobođenje*, "War Determines the Term," the reference to a "slippery beginning" of the 1992-1993 school year for the schools of the RBiH is a most appropriate reference for the schools of Dobrinja. To reiterate a small portion of the article here:

> The preparation of plans for registration in the secondary schools in the

Republic is in progress. The authorized ministry states that the date of the beginning of the school year will be given later because it highly depends on war operations and the situation at the front.
Therefore, it can be spoken about some kind of "slippery" beginning of the school year. Municipalities will individually decide about the beginning of the school year depending on the circumstances. (1992: 4)

The heart of the matter was to not "lose" the school year to an uncivilized enemy who besieged the citizens of Sarajevo from the hills above the city. Even in spite of wartime conditions, the message was that schooling, as an essential fabric of the normal life pattern, would continue for Sarajevo students albeit in altered form.

It should be noted, however, that parents, students, and teachers alike across Sarajevo, and especially in Dobrinja, had very serious concerns about beginning the school year amidst the snipers and the shelling of the settlement. Perhaps the stairway schools in the same apartment building where one lived were one thing, but the thought of children walking to classes through trench lines to separate buildings was something else. Many parents simply didn't want their children to risk their lives for school. I have cited Edina Dmitrović in my Treća gimnazija book who, as an elementary teacher during the early years of the war, and a parent, expressed these concerns in the following manner:

> We were frightened. We were frightened because it was too much responsibility. We were frightened for ourselves, for our families. But to be involved in such a risk, to invite other people's children and get them killed, that was too high a risk for most of us ... two-three weeks thinking, meetings, talking. Most women teachers were against it. We said, "To hell with school, let them be alive." I don't want to be responsible. I don't want somebody's mother to look at me and say, "You killed him." (1996)

Edina's concern as a parent and teacher living in the city were echoed by Narcis Polimac, the new director of Dušan Pajić-Dašić Elementary School, who lived in Dobrinja 2:

> They were shelling Dobrinja, and people were getting killed. People asked if we were crazy trying to organize school. What were we doing trying to organize school when people were getting killed on the streets? I asked myself what I was doing. These were questions of our responsibility for the children.
>
> Schooling was a part of the organization of civilian life under siege. It was important for the children to go to school, not to lose school years. The alternative was to stay in a dark basement. The idea was to

create a normal life for children. School was an illusion of a normal life. (Polimac, 2006)

Ilija Šobot, likewise a parent and teacher, and manager of the Secondary Education Section of the War School Center, who lived in Dobrinja 5, expressed similar concerns about the situation in Dobrinja, about his efforts to organize the secondary schools, and about the severity of his responsibilities towards the students:

> There was the problem of whether or not to organize education in Dobrinja. The first months were very difficult because of the danger. There was especially great danger from the shelling. The parents didn't want their kids to come to school. I couldn't sleep at night because I thought about the dangers to children going to school. Every day I hoped for the students for an end to the war.
> We went door to door to determine the numbers of students. There were snipers and there was shelling. In this atmosphere, there were arguments between teachers and parents about all this. The first time it was very difficult, but after they saw the organization and the work effort, they felt better about sending their kids to school. (2001)

Given his role as manager of the Secondary Education Section responsible for the organization of secondary schooling throughout the settlement, and coordination with the 27 secondary schools in the city, Professor Šobot was directly responsible for all the students and the teachers, who had their own concerns as well. To recruit teachers was also quite difficult under wartime conditions, he noted, and there was no money to pay them, but he made the same efforts to recruit the teachers as he did to recruit the students:

> I went door to door to recruit the teachers as well. It was very difficult to get teachers at first. I went around to their homes, their apartments, and recruited them. It was especially difficult with the women. They were teachers—and they were mothers
> We recruited about 80 teachers for the secondary schools. Once they began to work in the schools, they were to sign in every day. The signature was important. Their signature was evidence that they were alive. (2001)

Nevertheless, with the efforts of dedicated educators like Ilija Šobot, Seniha Bulja, and Smail Vesnić, not to mention the three school principals at the time, Aida Musić, Simon Bolivar Elementary School, Narcis Polimac, Dušan Pajić-Dašić Elementary School, and Faruk Jabučar, Nikola Tesla Elementary School, the 1992-1993 school year would soon get underway with 29 March as the target day for the first day of classes throughout all of the Dobrinja school regions, in contrast to the 1 March date in Sarajevo, given the intense shelling during the early weeks of March. In fact, the new school year began in selected sites in the local school regions and, within three weeks afterwards, in virtually all school sites. Classes would run for 18 instructional weeks based on a curriculum reduced 50 percent in order to adapt the instructional process to the abridged school year. While a truncated version of the regular academic year, the 18-week session was designed to establish the organizational framework for the instructional process in the schools of Sarajevo city under the administration of the City Secretariat for Education. In other words, the intention was that the belated and truncated and very difficult 1992-1993 school year would serve as a trial run for the 1993-1994 school year to follow. Over those next 18 weeks in the war schools across the settlement, until the target day for the last class on Saturday, 31 July 1993, at least if instruction began on 29 March, the routine of school days became established once again for the students and teachers trapped in the besieged settlement.

Peaceful War School Days
The 1992-1993 War School Year

In regard to the new school year in Dobrinja, the "Minutes" for the meeting of the Teacher's Council of the Gimnazija provide insight into the organization and operation of schooling in the besieged settlement. The "Minutes" begin with the 20 January 1993 meeting and note that "the Work Program for the 1992-1993 school year" is based upon "18 working weeks" in which "to program and realize 50 percent of the instructional year," in other words, to adapt the curriculum to a condensed school year. At the secondary level, "the organization of instruction in the 1992-1993 school year in Dobrinja" is no small matter, "because in Dobrinja, about 800 students are left and about 80 teachers and teaching assistants," with about 250 of these students enrolled in the first and second-year classes (Gimnazija Dobrinja, 1992-1995).

These numbers refer to the data compiled by the Secondary Education Section, as noted in the November 1992 "Work Program," cited in the previous chapter, that indicate a total of 790 secondary students registered for their schools (Nastavni centar, 1992:60). While classes in Gimnazija Dobrinja were up and running on 25 January 1993, the "Minutes" for the Teacher's Council meeting, dated 30 March 1993, referring to "the organization of instruction in war conditions," indicated that "secondary and elementary school is continued on 29 March 1993," setting in motion the 1992-1993 school year, although the local war schools had to adapt to the war situation in their respective regions. By 30 April 1993, according to Ilija Šobot, as related in the "Minutes" of the Teacher's Council, there were a total of 729 students attending 29 class sections (Gimnazija Dobrinja, 1992-1995).

The "Work Journals" (Dnevnik rada) of the secondary class sections organized by local school regions are consistent with the Gimnazija Teacher's Council "Minutes" and also indicate the beginning of the 1992-1993 school year on 29 March 1993. For example, the entries in the "Work Journal" for the "Ratna škola Gimnazija Dobrinja" (Gimnazija Dobrinja War School) for one of the first-year class sections, I/5, located in the region of Dobrinja 3A and 3B, begin on 29 March with English language and Bosnian language classes. The English language exercises include "School is Fun: Questions and Answers," "Verb 'to be' tenses," and "the Present Tense." Geography and German language classes were held the next day, with Mathematics, Biology, Chemistry, Physics, History, Latin, and Art classes held during the six-day week in the first week of school. A total of 18 students were registered as gimnazija students in class I/5 of Dobrinja 3A/3B, located on the northeast side of the settlement just below Mojmilo Hill. However, their schools of register (*matična škola*), the schools where they were enrolled before the war, included "all secondary schools of the city of Sarajevo," but specifically, the other city gimnazija. Eight students originally registered for Prva gimnazija while two students registered for Druga gimnazija. Fifteen different faculty taught fifteen different courses under the direction of the section coordinator, Nisveta Jamak.

The "Work Journal" for the second-year class section II/7 in Dobrinja 5, on the northwest corner of the settlement just below Mojmilo Hill, adjacent to enemy-occupied Nedžarići, also indicates the school year began on 29 March 1993. At least 26 students registered for the Gimnazija Dobrinja War School although the home schools of the great majority of these students were vocational-technical or professional schools. Whereas the gimnazija sections usually contained students from the city gimnazija almost exclusively, the professional school sections usually included students from a variety of these schools from throughout the city. Thus the home schools of the 26 students were at least nine different professional schools to include the Medical Secondary School, the Metalworker Professional

Secondary School, and the Railway School Center, among others. Two students were originally registered at gimnazija as well. Fifteen different instructors taught 15 different classes to include all the core subject areas as well as Civil Defense and Basic Information Science and Accounting under the direction of Sonja Sučić, the section coordinator (Gimnazija Dobrinja, 1992-1995).

The "Work Journal" for the first-year class section I/4 for students in Dobrinja 1 and Dobrinja 2B indicates that classes were held on Jawaharlal Nehru Street #1 in the immediate area of the Salvador Allende and the Emile Zola stairway schools once located nearby. At least 15 different instructors taught at least 16 different subjects to include the core subject areas, English, German, and Russian language, and Civil Defense and Protection. A total of 31 first-year students, all but two of whom were enrolled in vocational-technical schools in the city, attended classes there.

Included among the ten professional schools were students enrolled at the Economics Secondary School, the Medicine Secondary School, and the Electroengineering Secondary School. One of these students was Ibrahim Sejfović who, as an 8th grade during the previous year, had attended the Salvador Allende Stairway School organized by Seniha Bulja on the edge of Dobrinja 2B. The "Work Journal" for class section I/4 records that instruction began on 25 January 1993, with the opening of Gimnazija Dobrinja, and continued through 31 December 1993, indicating the class section that was organized to complete instruction for the 1991-1992 school year continued to function through the 1992-1993 school year, and on into the 1993-1994 school year as well. On 17 August 1993, just four days before the end of the 1992-1993 school year, at the end of his first year of secondary school, Ibrahim Sejfović was severely wounded chasing a soccer ball from his apartment into the street when a shell exploded sending shrapnel through his body.

Whereas the coordination of secondary education evolved out of the opening of Gimnazija Dobrinja, with class sections also operating in the local communities, the organization of elementary education reverted back to the educational administration of the three Dobrinja elementary schools that existed before the war. With the three elementary schools assuming administrative responsibility for the stairway schools in their respective regions, these elementary schools were responsible for the beginning of the new school year for the students who had attended the stairway schools. Since conditions varied within the settlement depending upon a variety of factors to include physical location, war activities, not to mention classroom space available, the assumption of administrative responsibility varied as well dependent upon these factors.

In this regard, the entries in the "Almanac" of Simon Bolivar Elementary School, for example, which was responsible for the local school regions of Quadrant C5 and Dobrinja 2A in the center of the settlement, indicate the increasing activity of teachers as the new school year approached. The February entries highlight these preparations and, by 12 March 1993, an entry makes reference to the beginning of the 1992-1993 school year:

> There was a meeting in the Teaching Center regarding the beginning of school. We received new assignments and a new curriculum in compliance with the Ministry of Education. School will last from April to August 1993. It is important to engage parents in this new form of work. (Osnovna škola Simon Bolivar, 1992-1995)

The next few weeks note that listings of students were compiled by address and grade and that teaching assignments were distributed. The 7 April entry notes that "it is necessary to fit an 18-week syllabus into nine teaching units and present them in written form for the children." At the 11 April faculty meeting, Aida Musić, "a music teacher who, in this wartime chaos ... worked with a large group of students in her apartment," in other words, a stairway school teacher, was nominated to be the new school director. It should be noted that Aida's husband, Omer Musić, as cited in Chapter One, was still on the frontline along Prištinska Street of Quadrant C4 defending the settlement.

During this time, there were ongoing efforts to acquire classroom spaces, or *punkts*, suggesting the ongoing concerns over physical conditions and, once these spaces were acquired, to construct secure passageways to these locations. In November 1992, for example, Azra Kujundžić notes that there were 11 punkts for the stairway schools in Quadrant C5 and Dobrinja 2A, although two of these locations were in adjacent premises (1992-1993). The *Monografia* of Skender Kulenović (Simon Bolivar) notes the state of the situation in preparation for the new school year:

> In the period of January-April 1993, all special preparations for organization of the instructional process are performed.
>
> In collaboration with the Army of BiH [and] the Dobrinja local communities, 16 punkts are secured for performing the instructional process. The punkts are situated in basements, garages, shops, and private apartments, and needed furniture is secured in different ways, ... from burned schools and abandoned apartments ... The number of punkts by

streets in Dobrinja 2 settlement was nine, and in Quadrant C5 seven. (Osnovna škola Skender Kulenović, 1992: 13)

With these classroom punkts now under the administration of Simon Bolivar Elementary School to begin the 1992-1993 school year, major efforts were made to ensure these punkts were connected in secure and systematic fashion. Across Dobrinja 2A and Quadrant C5, routes were designed to lead from punkt to punkt to ensure the safety of teachers and students. Sniper screens were constructed out of wooden platforms and garbage dumps, sandbags lined the walkways and protected the entrances to the punkts, and trenches were dug in more open locations. In fact, a tunnel was actually dug under the ruins of the Simon Bolivar school building which led to trenches in the exposed areas on either side of the school, as well as under the main roadway to connect Dobrinja 2A to the punkts in Quadrant C5.

In addition to securing an adequate number of punkts for classrooms, another significant problem was securing physically adequate punkt locations where children would be spending their days. The problem is indi-

Sniper screens were constructed in systematic fashion across Dobrinja to prevent open fields of fire for enemy snipers at either end of the settlement. Here, the outer screen along the roadway was constructed from busses overturned on their sides topped by a row of cars. The inner screen was constructed from overturned cars topped by rows of sandbags. Photo courtesy of Mevsud Kapetanović.

cated by entries in the Simon Bolivar "Almanac" which, in the narrative at the outset of the 1992-1993 school year, notes the following concerns:

> In the area of Dobrinja 2A, the largest school spaces are in the A-bomb shelter and in the Teacher's Center in Dobrinja. The conditions in the A-bomb shelter are obviously very difficult—there is no natural light or air conditioning, so the students work under candlelight (made of tallow) in a very cold place with no fresh air.

Approximately four months into the school year, another entry concerning the punkt at the A-bomb shelter in Dobrinja 2A appears in the "Almanac," dated 17 July 1993:

> School was interrupted at the punkt in the A-bomb shelter. The children's health is seriously affected as a result of conditions in this space. The school administration addressed the military and civilian authorities with the request that some other space should be provided for those children, because the conditions without natural light and minimum air conditioning are damaging for the children. This decision about the continuation of classes was supported by the parents as well. (Osnovna škola Simon Bolivar, 1992-1995).

Nevertheless, in spite of concerns over conditions at the classroom punkts at the outset, the 13 April entry in the "Almanac" indicates that "the first classroom premises have been prepared on Sarajevskih Ilegalaca (Sarajevo Underground Fighter) Street #3" and, in capital letters, that "CLASSES ARE BEGINNING!" In her personal journal, Azra Kujundžić documents the state of events over the next week with particular concern for the continual struggle to find classroom locations in Quadrant C5 and Dobrinja 2A:

> 13 April 1993: prepared the first premises for performing instruction of elementary education at Sarajevo Underground Fighter Street #3.
>
> 14 April 1993: obtained "Lemes" premises on Mak Dizdar Street for the needs of the school.
>
> 14 April 1993: obtained an apartment at our disposal at Ivica M. Ratka Street #9.
>
> 15 April 1993: meeting of the Teacher's Council of Quadrant C5 took place scheduled by the newly-selected director Aida Musić. Then made a schedule of class periods for the premises on Mak Dizdar and Sarajevo Underground Streets.
>
> 16 April: meeting of the Teacher's Council of Dobrinja 2A took place

which was scheduled by Aida Musić. Obtained new premises for work at Vase Butozana #21.

17 April: obtained an apartment at Koste Abraševića Street #11 for the needs of instruction of this divided settlement.

21 April: finally it is possible to say that Quadrant C5 included all the children of this settlement in the process of performing instruction of elementary education. (Kujundžić, 1992-1993)

In similar fashion, the "Annals" of Dušan Pajić-Dašić note the following in narrative form:

> Preparations for the beginning of the school year were overseen by the director, Narcis Polimac. In order for the school year to begin, several tasks needed to be completed. In all neighborhoods, a list of all students was made according to the streets in which they live and their respective classes ... Along with compiling lists of students, teachers were also sought.
>
> The first meeting of the Teacher's Council of the school was held on the 26th of March. Up to the 10th of April, five more meetings were held. In these meetings, all necessary preparations for the beginning of the school year were completed.
>
> Regular classes started on the 12th of April 1993. (Osnovna škola Dušan Pajić-Dašić, 1992-1995)

Thus the entries in the various school journals chart the routine of schooling during the spring months as both students and teachers became accustomed to the work of the new school year. These entries gradually begin to attest to the routinization of schooling seen most notably in the "Almanac" of the War School Center, but also in the "Annals" of Gimnazija Dobrinja which notes the progress of secondary education, in the "Almanac" of Simon Bolivar Elementary School which notes the progress of elementary education in Quadrant C5 and Dobrinja 2A, and the "Annals" of Dušan Pajić-Dašić Elementary School which notes the progress of elementary education in Dobrinja 1, Dobrinja 2B, and Dobrinja 3B. These entries note the many Teacher's Council meetings, the continuing enrollment of students, and the consultations and examinations for students, along with personnel matters that concerned the teachers. The entries of the War School Center note performances put on by students, cultural and religious events to include the Catholic mass, and the appearance of a variety of visitors to include, for example, General Ismet Hadžić, the commanding officer of what was now the 5th Motorized Brigade responsible for the defense of Dobrinja.

Thus three "Almanac" entries of late March read simply:

> 27 March, *Saturday*: There were no big events at the Teaching Center, except for the daily activities in the work with students of the Gimnazija and other secondary schools.
>
> 29 March, *Monday*: At the Teaching Center, regular activities are being carried out with the students of the secondary schools and the Gimnazija. Shooting and shelling in Dobrinja, as usual.
>
> 30 March, *Tuesday*: A day without significant activities, except for the regular work with students, which is a lot, but has become a normal thing at the Teaching Center. Sporadic shooting continues in Dobrinja as well as some shelling. (Nastavni centar, 1992-1993)

The 28 April entry reads in similar fashion, "Daily activities at the Teaching Center: exams, consultations, instruction sheets. Everything is done like in a beehive, as if it is not war." On 4 May, the entry reads simply, "Regular activities are taking place at the Teaching Center." Such entries appear with more regularity and attest to the routine of daily activities at the War School Center in particular. Such entries indicate that as the schools assumed responsibility for the administration of the instructional process, the responsibilities of the Center for educational administration slowly began to move into the background. Entries in the Gimnazija "Annals" are similar noting, for example, on regular occasion, that "classes are regularly being held." The daily routine of the school day, and the weekly routine of the six-day school week, serve to chart the course of the 18-week school year. Perhaps the most notable such entry appeared in the "Almanac" of the Center on 9 July 1993—"A peaceful war day."

By late spring 1993, with the 1992-1993 school year well underway, the normality of "shooting and shelling in Dobrinja, as usual," was well accepted as a facet of everyday normal life under abnormal siege conditions, as noted in the following "Almanac" entry:

> 17 May 1993, *Monday*: Days, weeks, months, years, everything from the beginning. It is always some new Monday and the war is still on ... At the Teaching Center, it is like peace. The youth are attending classes, learning, singing, laughing, and life must go on. (Nastavni centar, 1992-1993)

Of course, the war would disrupt the routine at times to remind teachers and students that teaching and learning still took place in the midst of the siege. Although the shelling and the snipers were a continual problem through spring, intruding into the entries from time to time, the reality of wartime conditions would again dominate the entries and break the routine of schooling, once again taking lives of students and teachers in the process.

"Massacre in Dobrinja" screamed the headline in *Oslobođenje*, dated 2 June 1993, in bold, capital letters. On 1 June, at 10:30 in the morning, two mortar rounds fired by "chetnik criminals from Lukavica landed in the midst of an improvised soccer game in Dobrinja 3, in a parking area between two buildings, killing 13 people and wounding at least 104. Among the 13 dead were Damir Trebo, age 13, and Adnan Mirvić, age 15. "Explosions, the smell of powder, blood, shrieks of pain ... In only ten seconds Dobrinja returned to reality" (Džemidžić, 1992: 3). The "Almanac" entries read:

> 1 June 1993, *Tuesday*: A nice May day ... This was a terrible day for Dobrinja and its residents. Fifteen dead and over 80 wounded. Horrible! Horrible! All of them were youth of Dobrinja, who for a moment had wanted to stop the war and were killed and injured competing in who's better in a game. All educational activities were cancelled.

> 2 June 1993, *Wednesday*: Because of yesterday's gory day in Dobrinja, awareness of the safety of children at the Teaching Center has increased. Even though the fear exists that unexpected shelling will begin, classes are being held according to schedule. (Nastavni centar, 1992-1993)

The director of Civil Defense operations in Dobrinja, Ismet Kumalić, contacted Azra Kujundžić directly by phone and give an order to cancel all classes for security reasons. The response in the Gimnazija "Annals" noted that "classes are cancelled with no need or reason. Director Vesnić warned the directors of the elementary schools and us to make the teachers pay more attention." Regular school activities resumed on 3 June, and the "Almanac" entry the next day read:

> 4 June 1993, *Friday*: Morning classes at the Teaching Center are being held. A large number of students attended. Students and teachers are trying to do their best, just like in the time of peace, to do their assignments in order to, for a short time at least, to forget the horrors of the war. The youth shall succeed. (Nastavni centar, 1992-1993)

The schools continued their instruction through June, interrupted at times by the shelling and the snipers, but students continued to attend classes in shifts, take examinations, and conduct a variety of school activities. Relatively normal conditions prevailed for several weeks when heavy shelling resumed trying the sanity of all Dobrinjans trapped within the siege. To provide a better sense of wartime conditions, and the attempts to both live life and conduct schooling in spite of these conditions, a series of "Almanac" entries are presented here that chronicle the situation in Dobrinja with some continuity through the month of July 1993:

> 5 July 1993, *Monday*: A peaceful sunny morning, but only until 9:00 and after it became hell. Shells searching for new victims. Children are by the river from early morning. They do not know that an alert bloodthirsty eye is watching them. The dull impact of a shell, a scream, and then silence ... A motionless body of a girl, the scream went silent ... She was only 11 years old and she only wanted water. Elma Muhić is dead. A student of the fifth grade of elementary school. A general danger is in force. In spite of that, there are students at the Teaching Center and there is work being done, but with reduced intensity.

> 9 July 1993, *Friday*: A peaceful war day. The July sun is drying up the last drop of sweat while waiting in the queue for water. A long line of white canisters, while the owners are watching over them from somewhere nearby. There will be water and this drought created unnaturally will not last long. And this man here, used to all the problems of war, is determined in one thing, he shall endure! Many students are visitors of

Waterlines: In the shadow of Mojmilo Hill, the residents of Dobrinja come out of their basements and shelters to stand in line for water during a lull in the fighting where they were easy targets for gunners in the hills above the settlement. Photo courtesy of Mevsud Kapetanović.

these queues; when they are not in class they are learning their lessons in those white lines.

12 July 1993, *Monday*: An ordinary working day. Classes of all subjects are being held as planned. In the late afternoon, hell in Dobrinja again. While waiting in line for water eleven people were killed and 16 injured. Quadrant C5 is in deep mourning for God knows what time. Ilhan Jelovac and Ajdin Krilić were killed.

13 July 1993, *Tuesday*: An unusually peaceful day. The students are extremely silent, completing their tasks and sharing great sorrow, commenting on the death of their two school friends while waiting in line for water. Everyone is aware that they can be next, but there is no panic because everyone thinks that they will survive. (Nastavni centar, 1992-1993)

The headline of the 13 July issue of *Oslobodenje* replicated the headline of the 2 June issue in bold capital letters: "New Massacre in Dobrinja."

The interior of Skender Kulenović Elementary School, formerly Simon Bolivar, after the intense shelling on 18 July 1995. While standing in line for water at a pump inside the ruins of the school building, nine people were killed and at least twelve people were wounded when the school, which was originally destroyed by shelling on 15 May 1992, was shelled once again. Today a memorial inside the school commemorates those who were killed during the shelling. Photo courtesy of Mevsud Kapetanović.

163

According to the article, 13 people were killed and 15 badly wounded while waiting in line at a water pump in Quadrant C5. Such a daily routine suggests that the only explanation for such attacks on innocent civilians in line for water is that they were easy and deliberate targets of the enemy (Džemidžić, 1993: 1). The photographs of Mevsud Kapetanović show these long lines of ordinary people who waited in desperation to fill canisters and carry them back to their apartments, carrying them up flights of stairs in buildings with no running water and no electricity to run pumps or elevators (n.d.). In regard to the two students who were killed, Ilhan Jelovac was a second-year student registered at Prva gimnazija while Ajdin Krilić was a second-year student registered at Druga gimnazija. Both were students in the II/8 class section of 40 gimnazija and professional students who attended the war school in Quadrant C5 (Gimnazija Dobrinja, 1992-1995).

In his book written during the time, *Seasons in Hell: Understanding Bosnia's War*, Ed Vuilliamy provides a sense of the atmosphere in besieged Sarajevo, of the desperation that was setting in, and of the psychological pressures of living under siege (1994):

> By the summer of 1993, the Bosnian capital had become almost deaf to good news. Something had snapped; whatever it was that had enabled the city to endure, that had steeled its will to survive, had fractured … Gordana Knežević, deputy editor of *Oslobođenje*, called it "a clear strategy: to strangle the city until it becomes so desperate, it commits suicide. They don't need to take Sarajevo, they just need us to kill ourselves with fear and prison psychosis." … At the grim mercy of the ultimatum, Sarajevo's End Game was under way … But now the whole city was imploding. (Vuilliamy, 1994: 304-309)

Dobrinja was Sarajevo at its most extreme, however, a Sarajevo community almost totally cut off from the heart of the city. The "specific circumstances in Dobrinja during the war (Blockade and isolation, the long period and intensity of diverse exposure to constant threats and dangers, a high percentage of separated families)," are noted by Renko Đapić, et al., in a study, "War Traumas of the Children of Dobrinja" (1997: 27). Here the authors note "the relation between exposure to war torture and traumatic reactions," and thus they write of "the torture of Dobrinja" and, in particular, of the effect of this torture on Dobrinja's children. "Primarily, in Dobrinja, the fight for survival was in order for there to be any possibilities to think out other life activities … The number of objective exposures to war horrors of the children of Dobrinja exceed that of children in other parts of Sarajevo" (1997: 25). In other words, the situation was even more desperate in Dobrinja than in the rest of Sarajevo and, therefore, perhaps even more desperate for Dobrinja's children.

The "Almanac" entries continue to record the relentless shelling, as well as the snipers, through July and into August and the efforts to maintain the routine of the school year:

> 19 July 1993, *Monday*: A peaceful July day. A peaceful day on the political scene of Bosnian reality but not on the military plan. The shells that go from Lukavica towards Igman are psychological pressure for the people of Dobrinja. Besides the all day and all night shelling, the youth of Dobrinja are in the Teaching Center and work as if there is no war. Afternoon classes last until late, although the sign for general danger is in force.

> 21 July 1993, *Wednesday*: What appeared to be a peaceful day for Dobrinja turned into hell around 1:30. There were new victims. The bloodthirsty beast can never get enough of human blood. It is swimming in it today too. How far does that human mind reach?

> 22 July 1993, *Thursday*: General danger! Sarajevo is being shelled from all sides. Just a few pedestrians can be seen on the streets. However, students in a smaller number are at the Teaching Center. They don't care about the shells that have been fired in the thousands today. They are here to learn and nothing more. However, for the students of the afternoon shift, the danger is higher and only the bravest come to the Teaching Center.

> 24 July 1993, *Saturday*: Although there is general danger, classes are on at the Teaching Center. No sign of shooting being stopped. Shells are daily life. They were falling like rain today as well. At 12:00 the regular meeting of the secondary school coordinators was held. Classes in the afternoon shift went on as planned.

> 31 July 1993, *Saturday*: A working July day. The shells have gone silent a bit, but the sniper is searching for his new victim. Not even the signatures from Geneva are preventing the wild beast in its fascistic intent. To kill and only to kill.
> The students are very regularly visiting the Teaching Center. In spite of danger from snipers they appeared ... A regular meeting of the secondary school coordinators was held.

> 6 August 1993, *Friday*: A relatively peaceful day without shells. Sniper fire is at every corner. The students are given instructions on how to cross the streets. This is a daily responsibility of all the teachers. Despite that danger, students are present at the Center in large numbers. (Nastavni centar, 1992-1993)

The videos made by Mevsud Kapetanović during the siege from his studio in Dobrinja 1 just off the frontline attest to the desperation. Here we see elementary students walking to classes through trench lines and into sandbagged classrooms to protect them from shelling. Here we see secondary students running across the sandbagged bridge over Dobrinja rijecka, the creek that runs east-west through the settlement, ducking for cover, yet flashing victory signs at the snipers on either end (n.d.).

The Student-Soldiers of Dobrinja
Extending the 1992-1993 School Year for Justified Reasons

In the schools of Dobrinja, the 1992-1993 school year was intended to conclude on 21 August 1993, and the "Almanac" entry notes that "today the students used their last day in this school year to affirm their knowledge with a grade." A following notation cites the meetings of the secondary Teacher's Councils which decided "that the school year be prolonged until 29 August 1993." Just four days later, on 25 August, the "Almanac" notes that the enrollment process is continuing for the 1993-1994 school year, but that "there are many who will extend this school year until 15 September 1993 for justified reasons." Given that the "Almanac" notes the continuing preparations of teachers and the enrollment of students for the 1993-1994 school year, the entries offer no clarification of an extended 1992-1993 school year.

In the "Annals" of Gimnazija Dobrinja, the entries record events not only for the gimnazija but for all 27 other secondary schools to include vocational-technical schools as well. Here the references to an extended school year become clearer since the extensions are a very particular concern to many secondary school students. A series of entries from late August into September and October 1993 clarify those references with particular concern for the student-soldiers in the Army of Bosnia and Herzegovina (ARBiH):

> 27 August: It's very lively on the premises of the Gimnazija. School is ending in a hurry. Enrollment documents are delivered ... Classes are extended until 15 September, mainly for the fighters of the ARBiH, children with no parents, wounded children, and all those who took credits for the calluses and the work.
>
> 28 August: It's the last day of the first-year class extension. There were some requests for extension of class. Over 100 requests were taken. At 12:00, coordinators for the professional classes held a meeting. At 2:00 the Board

for all four classes of secondary school held a meeting. It has been decided that classes will be extended for two more weeks, which means until 15 September. The beginning of the next school year is uncertain.

18 September: Classes started on time. A great number of exams were held this morning for students without one or both parents, students who were injured or who had another kind of family tragedy. We extended classes until 15 November this year because of them. We hope that will help them.

30 September: All planned classes were held. Consultations and exams go on intensively. Special services to members of the ARBiH every day. It's a real pleasure to help these courageous and strong young men. We have enough time and will to help them through the lessons as best we can.

24 October: Morning mass for Catholics. After mass, exams and consultations for the fighters of the ARBiH and others who are allowed to take the exams. The situation is very dangerous in Dobrinja. No one mentions the regular classes. Until next time! (Gimnazija Dobrinja, 1992-1995)

These entries in the Gimnazija Dobrinja "Annals" are reflected in other school documents to include, most notably, the permission request forms, applications, or petitions (*molba*), submitted by students to extend the school year given their own personal circumstances. One such request for an extension reads as follows:

> I am submitting a request for an extension of the 1992–1993 school year because I am unable to regularly attend school (because of the activities of snipers by my apartment and entrance, and the activities of snipers and shelling on the way to school). I kindly ask you to acknowledge my request. (Gimnazija Dobrinja, 1992-1995)

The student, Darije Tufekčić, was a student at the Electroengineering Secondary School. He lived at Jawaharlal Nehru Street #9, a small side street that ran directly towards the front entrance of Dušan Pajić-Dašić Elementary School, occupied by the army, and perpendicular to the frontline on the eastern end of Dobrinja. For enemy snipers on the other side of the frontline, who sometimes used the steeple of the Orthodox church as a snipers' nest, such streets provided a clear line of sight directly into the heart of the settlement. Darije's request was characteristic of many of those students who attempted to attend classes under the shelling and the snipers.

Another such request, for an extension to take an examination, was submitted by Ermin Alamerovič who lived at Nikola Demonja Street

#5, a small side street just down from Seniha Bulja's Salvador Allende Stairway School in Dobrinja 2B, and just across from Jawaharlal Nehru Street. Although Ermin was a student at Treća gimnazija, the request is submitted to Gimnazija Dobrinja and the Secondary Education Section, dated 28 August 1983, "the last day of the first-year class extension," and one of "over 100 requests" that were submitted to the secondary schools for extensions. Ermin's request reads:

> I would like the above-mentioned authority to give me approval for an extension to take the examination for the second-year class in Dobrinja. The reason why I did not take all the examinations from the second year of the gimnazija on time is that I was wounded on 1 January 1993. The wounds from the shelling prevented me from attending consultations for three months, and as a result, I could not take the examination. I sincerely hope that you will understand me and that my request will result in a positive solution. (Gimnazija Dobrinja, 1992-1995)

Attached to the request is a "certificate from the hospital and a recommendation of the hospital." The certificate from Dobrinja Hospital-Sarajevo notes that Ermin was wounded "from a shell explosion" on the right side of the thoracic cage, on the right side of his lower leg, and on both sides of his hip regions. It was signed by Dr. Xoussef Hajir, the most prominent doctor who worked under the most difficult conditions in the makeshift Dobrinja branch hospital that was created in response to siege conditions.

Another request, dated 13 September 1993, was submitted to the Teacher's Council of Gimnazija Dobrinja by Kenan Bahar who lived at Grada Kalgarija (Calgary City) Street #8/IV, named after Calgary as the preceding Winter Olympic city, in Dobrinja 3A, just below Mojmilo Hill. Kenan's request for taking the examination for the third-year class of the Trade Technical Secondary School (Srednja stručna trgovinska škola) reads as follows:

> Because of my commitments in the armed forces of the Army of BiH, I was not able to regularly attend the third-year classes of the Trade School. Therefore, I would like to ask you about the possibility to take the examination until the 15 November 1993 deadline. (Gimnazija Dobrinja, 1992-1995)

Attached to Kenan's request was a certificate from the Command of Military Unit 5453, Military Unit 5021–Sarajevo, which indicates that Kenan was a member of the unit from 15 March 1993, and signed by General Ismet Hadžić himself.

As noted in the entries, "special services" were extended to those students who served in the military, in what was referred to as the Armed Forces (*Oružane snage* or OS) of Bosnia and Herzegovina (OSBiH) at the outset, in the Territorial Defense forces, for example, and then as the Army (*Armija*) of the Republic of Bosnia and Herzegovina (ARBiH). We might remember here the July 1992 "Basic Work Program" and the survey instruments for both elementary and secondary students that included the question—"Are you a member of the Armed Forces of BiH?" (Nastavni centar, 1992: 11-12). The knowledge of those students who served in the armed forces provides a better sense of how the school in which they were enrolled, and the teachers who served as their instructors, might better accommodate their particular situation when, for example, requesting "special services" such as an extension of the school year.

In fact, many of the male students, especially in the higher classes, were soldiers who served in the defense of the settlement alternating between attendance in the classroom and duty on the frontline. Some of these students would find themselves in classrooms during the day and in trenchlines during the night, finding little time for sleep if they chose to attend classes. Some would miss days or weeks or a semester of classes, or perhaps even a year or two. To reiterate the words of the November "Basic Work Program" concerning class attendance for these student-soldiers during the war:

> This number changes very often, because students leave, and more often return. A great number of students in the higher years are active in units of the ARBiH, so these students need to receive special attention. This especially relates to the outlying regions of Dobrinja. When looking at the divisions of Dobrinja, the majority of students are from the center of the settlement: Dobrinja 2A, Dobrinja 2B, and Dobrinja 3A. (Nastavni centar, 1992: 43)

Outer Dobrinja included Dobrinja 1, or what remained of Dobrinja 1, on the southeast edge of the settlement, Dobrinja 5 on the northwest edge facing Nedžarići, and Quadrant C5 facing the airport, what remained of the Airport Settlement. The students who lived in the region of outer Dobrinja were directly on the frontlines and found themselves defending their homes from the beginning of the first assaults on the settlement.

To reiterate the words of Halil Burić here, the manager of the Higher Education Section, "My students were on the frontlines. They were defending Sarajevo—and Bosnia, our country." Professor Burić emphasized the importance of professors and teachers making every effort to accommodate these student-soldiers regardless of the circumstances. Of particular note here is that the documents indicate that these students were enrolled in the class sections of their local school regions and yet registered for their home schools as the situation stood at the beginning of the war. The reality that many of these students found themselves on the frontlines defending Dobrinja did not detract from an understanding of their situation by dedicated faculty such as Halil Burić. "It was very important for them to think about normal things," he said, about classes and examinations, for example, "as a means to forget the war, at least temporarily" (2001). The reality of the war, however, was that many of these students were killed on the frontlines while defending Dobrinja.

The issues of *Dobrinja—Ratne novine,* published first by the 1st Dobrinja Brigade, which became the 5th Hill Brigade, then the 5th Motorized Brigade, and then the 155th Hill Brigade, document not only the transformation of the Bosnian Army but, at times, the casualties suffered by the Brigade's soldiers. The January 1993 edition of the 5th Hill Brigade was a special issue, for example, devoted in its entirety to the "martyrs and killed fighters" *(šehid i poginuli borci)*, the former a reference to Muslim soldiers and the latter to soldiers of other faiths, most notably Bosnian Croats who were Catholic, who were killed in action. "They gave their lives for the freedom of the Republic of Bosnia and Herzegovina," read the headline that salutes them followed by an introduction by Ismet Hadžić, the commanding officer of the Brigade. There is a photograph and personal data for each of the soldiers, although photos and data were not available for several of them.

Nevertheless, of the 135 soldiers commemorated in the special issue who died in the defense of Dobrinja since the onset of the siege, at least 14 of them were 20 years of age or younger. One of the soldiers, Denis Bosankić, a recent graduate of Simon Bolivar Elementary School, was 15 years of age when he was killed on 17 June 1992 defending the Quadrant C5 frontline during the mid-June 1992 assaults on the settlement (Porča, 1993). The story of Denis' young life appears as follows in *Dobrinja—Ratne novine*:

Denis Bosankić: MORE THAN A BOY

All those who gave their lives and served in the Army, and did not live to become adults and celebrate their legal age with dear "buddies," will have the freedom fight of their graduating class justified because Bosnia and Herzegovina will be free, sooner or later. A fifteen-year-old-boy, Denis Bosankić, the son of Hamed and Ljubinka, gave his youth and his life to the permanent foundations of his own state.

As soon as the war broke out, and the defense was organized on the streets of Dobrinja, Denis joined his colleagues and offered to be there for them, to give his contribution in the defense of their settlement C-5, Dobrinja, and Bosnia and Herzegovina. Because he was under age at that time, the commander explained to him that he was not obligated to fight since that was a responsibility of adults. Denis and other boys, who voluntarily joined the Army, performed courier's tasks in the beginning of their engagement. When the TO was established and the military units were originated, it was very difficult to bring the boys back to their homes.

Patriotism, friendship and love for his settlement, his city and his friends, drove Denis to re-register at headquarters, because all under-age youth were earlier deleted from the lists and returned to their homes as the organizers wanted to protect the lives of the young people. Denis, Seval, Damir, and others forced their parents, sometimes even using blackmail, to give their permission with their signature so that their sons could join the Army and defend their neighborhoods. That was the time when Denis was the happiest boy in the whole world, because he was given a semiautomatic rifle, and he believed that nothing could do him any harm, not even a bullet or a shell. Twenty-four hours a day, he served as a courier to the commander, Mirsad Belko, and even slept in the headquarters—he was that eager and willing to help out and fulfill all of the tasks that were assigned to him.

When the chetnik monster began to operate in settlement C-4, and eventually captured it on 17 June 1992, Denis and his other friends on the first front line gave their contribution to prevent further advancement of the enemy troops towards settlement C-5. He didn't know how to say "I will not," or "I cannot." After all, he was always trying to be the first one to finish the assignment and be the role model for everyone else. He always claimed that they could not do us any harm, because we had a clear goal and we wanted to fight for justice and common coexistence.

With such a vision of common coexistence, and the struggle of all the people in this region, after a whole-day shelling, with blisters on his feet from running to headquarters and back to the front line, bearing munitions for his friends, he was hit by a chetnik shell on the way back from the completed assignment. Because of Denis, and the others who were killed, we do not have a moral right nor are we allowed to pause and stop fighting when faced with the aggressors, no matter what direction they come from. Because of them, we have to keep up the fight until the final liberation of our beloved, and one and only Homeland of Bosnia and Herzegovina.

One year after the youngest fighter of our Brigade, Denis Bosankić, was killed, his family, friends and comrades gathered to evoke memories of this courageous young man. This is a huge and irretrievable loss for all of us; this was a boy who outgrew himself by giving his life and his youth to the freedom of his Homeland. He has become a legend, unforgotten, and remains in our hearts. (Topalović, 1993: 15)

Almost one year later, the twelve pages of another the November-December 1993 special issue of *Dobrinja–Ratne novine* published by the 5th Motorized Brigade commemorated another 147 soldiers who died over the year. Some 15 of these soldiers were 20 years of age or younger to include Ismar Kadrić, another 15-year old soldier, and Saudin Bolić, age 16 at the onset of the war (Porča, 1993). It is interesting to note that the photographs of many of these 147 soldiers were photos from their early years, perhaps to show their youth, or perhaps since many families were refugees in their own community, these photos were all that they had. Yet these two issues commemorate 282 soldiers who died in defense of Dobrinja alone, of whom 29 of these soldiers, or one-tenth of the casualties, were 20 years old or younger. And these figures represent only the casualties through the first years of the siege of Dobrinja.

Given the efforts made to provide such "special services" for the student-soldiers who were risking their lives on Dobrinja's frontlines, the school documents provide an indication of the adaptations made by the Dobrinja War School Center to accommodate the needs of these students. Such requests for extensions of the school year, or extensions to take school examinations, especially during the early war years, became a particular form of instructional adaptation by teachers to ensure that those students did not lose another school year if possible. As Smail Vesnić notes in his Foreword to this book, "Thus, up until June 1993, in a grace period, student-fighters stood for 352 examinations before their professors." It is also clear that the grace period for admission to the secondary schools, as well as admission to the next class or grade level, extended well beyond into the fall months of the 1993-1994 school year (2005).

In this regard, another such request to extend the deadline for attending school, dated 21 September 1993, was submitted to the Teacher's Council of Gimnazija Dobrinja by Almir Trle, citing that he was a second-year student of the Railway School Center (Željeznički školski centar), and a member of the ARBiH from 27 August 1992. The request reads as follows:

> I am asking the Teacher's Council to give me approval to attend the second-year classes until 5 November, which is the extended deadline.
> I was unable to register earlier because of my obligations to the Army of RBiH. I have had little free time, because I was on the frontline in Dobrinja 1 and the Airport Settlement, and my obligations included

digging trenches and cleaning weapons, as well as spending time on assignment on [Mount] Igman.

I sincerely hope you will help me and fulfill my request, and I am grateful to you in advance. (Gimnazija Dobrinja, 1992-1995)

Almir Trle was registered as a second-year student at the Railway School Center in class section II/2, along with 30 other professional students and one gimnazija student, a total of 32 second-year students who attended what was termed the vocationally-oriented schools (*usmjerene škole*) class section from Dobrinja 2A (Gimnazija Dobrinja, 1992-1995).

Another of these student-soldiers was Damir Hadžić, a 16-year old, second-year student at the time and, like Almir Trle, also registered at the Railway School Center. When the 1991-1992 school year came to an end, Damir found himself defending his home and family "but," in his own words, "I was not the youngest." Damir lived in the area known as Quadrant C5, directly across from the airport and, at the beginning of the war, directly on the frontline, "300 meters from my apartment. That's how I found myself in a unit of the Territorial Defense" in another one of those groups of ragtag defenders that held the line in Dobrinja, who were eventually transformed into the 1st Dobrinja Brigade. "I didn't feel patriotism at that time," he said, "We only felt the need to defend our families. Patriotism only came later. It was only later that I realized what we were fighting against" (2001).

Once the frontlines had stabilized, Damir found himself in a special brigade running weapons and supplies through "no man's land" across the airport runway between Bosnian government-held territory in Butmir and encircled Dobrinja. "You're talking with a man who ran across the airport more than 450 times," he told me, "perhaps seven times a night," an extremely dangerous assignment. In fact, French UNPROFOR troops who patrolled the airport would shine their spotlight on anyone observed crossing the runway to escape or enter Sarajevo, thus providing fair game for Bosnian Serb snipers at either end of the airport and resulting in numerous civilian casualties. All this took place before the Dobrinja-Butmir tunnel (D-B Tunnel) under the airport runway had been constructed between January-July 1993 when it was opened as a military facility under control of the 1st Corps of the Bosnian Army. It was young men like Damir Hadžić, whose mission was to carry supplies across the airport runway into besieged Dobrinja, who served as the lifeline into besieged Sarajevo. "During that time, I wasn't thinking about my schooling," he said to me in all honesty. "I was thinking about war, and about weapons" (2001).

Although enrolled as an electrical technician student in the Railway School Center, and registered for classes in Quadrant C5, he remembered the loss of the 1992-1993 school year, in which "I spent only three nights in my own home during the whole year," while serving on the Dobrinja frontlines. Although Damir lost his entire third class year, he somehow managed to return to his schooling one year later in time for the 1993-1994 school year, "as a soldier-student," he said, in order to finish his last two years of secondary school (2001). Indeed, in the "Work Journal" of Quadrant C5, Damir was registered as a third-year student in the III/7 class section, one of 32 students, to include 25 professional students and 7 gimnazija students, who attended classes at Gimnazija Dobrinja in order to continue his education (Gimnazija Dobrinja, 1992-1995). In his words, "the Dobrinja Teaching Center and Gimnazija Dobrinja gave him a chance to finish his education" (2001).

Searching through the school records, I came upon Damir's "Request for Registration" (*Zahtjev za upis*), dated 15 July 1993, submitted to the Teacher's Council of Gimnazija Dobrinja, which read as follows:

> I am asking the Teacher's Council of the General Gimnazija Dobrinja to enable me to register and complete the third-year classes of secondary school. From the first days, more precisely, from 15 April 1992, I was engaged in the armed forces of the Army of RBiH, which I am proving with the attached certificate number dated on 16 February 1993.
>
> Since I am continuously engaged, I am not able to regularly attend classes, so I am asking you to provide me with instructions and literature in order to prepare myself and take the class examination. My home school is the Sarajevo Railway School Center, and I am training for the educational profile of electrical technician. (Gimnazija Dobrinja, 1992-1995)

Attached to Damir's request is the certificate signed by Mirsad Belko, the company commander, and Alihodža Safet, the battalion commander, dated 16 February 1993. The certificate is a standard official form, with Damir's name filled in, that indicates he was a member of the 1st Company, 3rd Battalion, 5th Hill Brigade (formed out of the 1st Dobrinja Brigade), since 15 April 1992, as he stated, from the very beginning of the war. At the top of the request, dated 17 July 1993, and signed by Smail Vesnić, is the notation that Damir's request for assistance with his schooling had been approved (Gimnazija Dobrinja, 1992-1995).

Damir remembers that "my teachers were understanding of my duty with the army." Somehow he somehow managed to graduate from secondary school, alternating duty on the frontline and on the airport runway with classes that he was able to schedule, with "the non-stop efforts of my teachers." He offered that the times were "unbelievable experiences for everyone, but especially for guys my age" remembering "the high level of solidarity of his generation." For a 16-year old student who rushed to defend the C4 frontline during the mid-June 1992 assaults on the Airport Settlement, Damir remembered what he and his friends shared during those difficult times. "What we had in common," he said, "is that we all defended our homes." At the time of this writing, Damir is the youthful mayor of Novi Grad Municipality, which includes Dobrinja and the Airport Settlement, along with the 2001 annexation of a portion of Dobrinja 4 that had been part of Srpska Sarajevo (Serbian Sarajevo) and the Republika Srpska. "The war caught me at that age," he reflects, "and I came to the realization that we had to live in a different community" (2001).

Naselje Nastavnika i Učenika Heroja

A Settlement of Teacher and Student Heroes
War School Years and War School Legacies

CHAPTER SIX

One day in May, a line of people in succession was crossing from Dobrinja over Mojmilo Hill. There was no shooting. I had thought that the war was winding down. That night, I calmly fell asleep but loud firing awoke me. Startled, we all descended into the basement. Here, I fell asleep again. Another loud bang above our heads woke me up. The war was not over.

In the morning, when it quieted down, I went to the apartment. I entered my bedroom. I could not recognize it, damaged walls, broken windows, pierced pillows and blankets. All the clothes from the big wardrobe were scattered on the floor. All my dear books and toys which I had so carefully kept over the years were destroyed. This badly shocked me. But I settled down a bit, when in this mess I noticed my favourite patchwork doll. I hugged her firmly and I did not want to be separated from her.

Later during the war, I received presents several times from unknown children from all around the world. There were lots of different toys, including two dolls. However, my damaged patchwork doll was my dearest toy because together we had survived all the horrors of war. She became my most faithful friend. I often play with her. And when I put her away in order to study, she does not get angry.

—Asja Makarević, 6th grade
Skender Kulenović Elementary School

Fall 1993
The Beginning of the 1993-1994 War School Year

On 19 August 1993, as the 1992-1993 school year was concluding in Dobrinja, the "Almanac" of the Dobrinja War School Center notes that "official preparations for enrollment of secondary school students in the new 1993-1994 school year have begun." These preparations continued through the next week and concluded on 26 August, "the last day of enrollment into the secondary schools." The significance of these preparations is expressed as follows:

> 30 August 1993, *Monday*: Extremely crowded. The Teaching Center is a meeting place for youth. It is wonderful to work with the youth; they are our future. That is why the work and effort collecting and submitting their enrollment papers to all the secondary schools in Sarajevo is an easy and dear task. Many will know in a day or two which road in life they will take. Good luck, good luck!!! (Nastavni centar, 1992-1993)

The 1993-1994 war school year was scheduled to begin in Dobrinja on 6 September 1993 in accordance with the beginning of the school year in Sarajevo. However, the 6 September entry in the "Almanac" indicates that "the beginning of the new school year has been postponed. It will begin on 13 September 1993 in the Gimnazija and 20 September 1993 in all other secondary schools." Indeed, the 13 September entry reads: "First working day in the new 1993-1994 school year in the Gimnazija. The students of the first year of the Gimnazija began their class at 8:00 A.M. and the second and third-year students are in class from 9:00 A.M." The next day's entry reads that "the morning work at the Gimnazija went in perfect order. Classes were held as planned. Afternoon classes were held as well and the number of students that managed to finish this school year increases" (Nastavni centar, 1992-1995).

For the elementary schools of Dobrinja, the entries in the "Annals" of Dušan Pajić-Dašić Elementary School and the "Almanac" of Simon Bolivar Elementary School indicate that the new school year did begin as scheduled on 6 September 1993. The Simon Bolivar "Almanac," however, records an ominous beginning:

> Unfortunately, we are still under the same conditions, in the same premises, and with the same fear for the lives of our students. There is still constant shelling in the entire city and also in Dobrinja. The snipers are shooting all over the city, which will not affect the beginning of the

school semester. Teaching methods will be adjusted in order to meet the needs of the kids; the kids will not spend time on the streets where their lives are jeopardized by the shelling, and they will not only gain some knowledge but also will be able to express their attitude towards the war, the cruelty of everyday living. (1992-1995)

The "Annals" of Dušan Pajić-Dašić Elementary School provide an overview of events in narrative form rather than a chronicle of the school year as recorded in the "Almanac" of Simon Bolivar, or the "Annals" of Gimnazija Dobrinja, for example. The narrative notes that the school year was organized into two semesters: in the first semester, four shifts of classes met in 30-minute sessions six times a week, and 40-minute sessions in the second semester. The first two shifts met 7:30 A.M.-1:30 P.M., while the second shifts met from 2:00 P.M.-6:00 P.M., extended to 6:55 P.M. second semester. "Classes are taught according to the curriculum ... In comparison to last year [and the reduced curriculum of 18 weeks], this year we have prepared thoroughly to ensure that the curriculum will be fulfilled."

Given the original location of the school on the eastern end of the settlement, Dušan Pajić-Dašić had responsibility for elementary education in the regions of Dobrinja 1, Dobrinja 2B, and Dobrinja 3B, which were "outer regions" exposed to the frontlines. At least 15 classroom locations were scattered across these regions to include basements, apartments, and a former daycare center, while several other locations were acquired during the year. The "Annals" note that "classes are organized in several locations for security reasons. Therefore, the number of teachers is somewhat higher than there would be under optimal conditions." Approximately 45 teachers were responsible for the organization and instruction of classes which included history, geography, mathematics, physics, biology, chemistry, music and art, Bosnian language, along with three foreign language classes: English, German, and French.

From a figure of 625 students at the end of the 1992-1993 school year, the "Annals" note that the number of enrolled students gradually increased from 687 at the beginning of the 1993-1994 school year to a total of 757 students at the end of the first semester with 70 new students enrolling for school (See Table 6.1). In contrast, during the 1991-1992 school year, some 2,860 students were attending the school, "making it the largest school in the city and the republic" prior to the war. Nevertheless, it is clear that student enrollment during the war school years was showing a gradual increase.

The 1993-1994 school year was designed to operate for 30 weeks

Table 6.1
Number of Students and Classes in Dušan Pajić-Dašić (Osman Nuri Hadžić) Elementary School at the beginning of the 1993-1994 School Year

Grades	Students	Classes
Grade 1	43	3
Grade 2	93	3
Grade 3	96	3
Grade 3-4 combined	16	1
Grade 4	79	3
Grade 5	94	3
Grade 6	81	4
Grade 7	77	3
Grade 8	108	4
Totals	687	27

Source: Osnovna škola Dušan Pajić-Dašić (1992-1995).

over two semesters, but because of interruptions for security reasons, most notably, the shelling of the settlement during the fall months, and the lack of heating for classrooms during the winter months, the 15 weeks of the first semester extended until 2 April 1994. The second semester began on 4 April and lasted 15 weeks with interruptions extending the school year until 25 August 1994. In Dobrinja 3, on the northeast corner of the settlement, just below the ridgeline of Mojmilo Hill, still occupied by the enemy, special conditions applied. Here the beginning of classes was delayed by two weeks in both semesters and there was but one class for all students grades 1-8, and one combined class for all students grades 3-4.

By the end of the 1993-1994 school year, the figures recorded in the "Annals" of Dušan Pajić-Dašić Elementary School indicate that a total of 734 students who attended classes received grade reports, an increase of 47 students from the beginning of the year, 23 less than reported to classes during the first semester. Only "three students [in grades 1-3] had one or two Ds and Fs, but were allowed to advance to the next grade."

In regard to the secondary schools, the "Minutes" of the Teacher's Council of Gimnazija Dobrinja, dated 20 September 1993, provide a breakdown of the numbers of students registered in the Dobrinja regions at the beginning of the 1993-1994 school year as seen in Table 6.2. These numbers are consistent with the breakdown of numbers seen in Table 4.1 for the 1992-1993 school year, although there are gaps in the numbers, especially for Quadrant C5, as well as for Dobrinja 5. Given similar number of enrollments, it would appear that these gaps may be due to the consolida-

TABLE 6.2
NUMBER OF SECONDARY SCHOOL STUDENTS BY REGIONS OF DOBRINJA
AND THE AIRPORT SETTLEMENT AT THE BEGINNING OF THE 1993-1994
SCHOOL YEAR

Region	Class				Totals
	I	II	III	IV	
Quadrant C5	27	0	0	0	27
Dobrinja 1	38	13	44	0	95
Dobrinja 2	130	108	103	86	427
Dobrinja 3	48	51	62	30	191
Dobrinja 5	47	24	0	0	71
Totals	290	196	209	116	811

Source: Gimnazija Dobrinja (1992-1995).

tion of class sections with C5 students attending classes in Dobrinja 2, for example, although there is no explanation of the numbers provided.

The totals indicate an increase of 21 secondary students for the 1993-1994 school year, with a significant increase of 88 students from the previous year enrolled in the first year of secondary school. Of the 811 total, 207 of these students were enrolled in the Gimnazija. Consistent with the reorganization of school regions, Dobrinja 2A and 2B are now consolidated into Dobrinja 2 and Dobrinja 3A and 3B are now consolidated into Dobrinja 3 (Gimnazija Dobrinja, 1992-1995). Much of Dobrinja 2, 2A and part of 2B, was an inner school region and somewhat more protected from the frontlines which may be the reason for the higher number of students.

The "Minutes" of the Teacher's Council, dated 12 January 1994 provide a breakdown of student numbers that might be compared to student numbers for the 1992-1993 school year as seen in Table 4.2. These numbers indicate a decrease of 92 students from the beginning of the 1993-1994 school year, as seen in Table 6.2, but a comparable number of students to the 1992-1993 school year. The major discrepancy from the previous school year is the figure of 237 students who are registered for the first year of secondary school, a figure that is based upon the 77 students who are registered for Gimnazija Dobrinja. Since the Gimnazija did not come into existence until 25 January 1993, it was, therefore, not listed in the documents cited.

As I noted in Chapter 4, it is important to consider the prospective number of Gimnazija students when considering the total number of secondary students enrolled in both the gimnazija and the vocational-technical secondary schools. With 86 students registered for Gimnazija Dobrinja, the 719 figure is consistent with the approximate number of students from the previous year when considering prospective Gimnazija students. The difference between the beginning of the year and the mid-year figures suggest the fluidity of the situation amidst the intensity of the shelling during the fall and winter months. However, when viewing the numbers over time, they attest to a certain stability of the situation in Dobrinja, or at least the efforts on the part of the teachers to create a sense of stability, since the numbers of students enrolling at the secondary level were not declining. Thus the "Minutes" of the Teacher's Council record a total of 782 students by the end of the 1993-1994 school year.

There are 25 secondary schools/centers cited in the "Minutes" (See Table 6.3), to include Gimnazija Dobrinja, in contrast to the 27 schools cited in the document, "Data on Teachers and Students: Secondary School, 1992-1993 School Year" (Table 4.2), excluding Gimnazija Dobrinja. As noted in the discussion of discrepancies between Tables 4.2 and 4.3, schooling responded to changing war conditions, and thus the two school centers in the occupied suburbs of Ilidža and Vogošća, and the Applied Arts School, are no longer included in the secondary school lists since secondary students no longer continued to register for these three schools.

Entries on 19-20 September in the "Almanac" of the War School Center indicate that, although preparations were continuing, the 1993-1994 school year for secondary vocational-technical students did not begin as scheduled on 20 September. The 19 September entry in the "Annals" of Gimnazija Dobrinja reads: "The beginning of the next school year for students of the other secondary schools, which was planned for Monday, 20 September, was cancelled because of the unsolved problems with premises in the Teaching Center." In fact, the beginning of school for these students was delayed several weeks, until 4 October, when the "Almanac" entry reads: "Today the premises of the Teaching Center are in the hands of the General Gimnazija. The problem that lasted for several months was finally resolved. The students of all secondary schools are in classes. Good luck!"

"The problem" that delayed the opening of the school year for secondary students was a turf war, or perhaps a culture war, between advocates for education and the schools and what the "Almanac" refers to as "cultural workers" or the "culturals." These were local politicians who infused nationalist politics into Dobrinja's schools, and into the Dobrinja War School Center and Gimnazija Dobrinja in particular, through the mechanism of

TABLE 6.3
DATA ON SECONDARY STUDENTS IN DOBRINJA AND THE AIRPORT SETTLEMENT AND THEIR SECONDARY SCHOOLS OF REGISTER DURING THE 1993-1994 SCHOOL YEAR

	Secondary School	Class				Students
		I	II	III	IV	
1.	Prva gimnazia	0	7	8	9	24
2.	Druga gimnazija	0	5	12	8	25
3.	Treća gimnazija	0	14	11	2	27
4.	Četverta gimnazija	0	0	2	0	2
5.	Peta gimnazija/ Birotehnička	3	8	7	6	24
6.	Grafička škola	2	8	3	2	15
7.	Trgovačka škola	14	7	14	8	43
8.	Ekonomska škola	6	14	12	10	4
9.	Ugostiteljsko-turistički školski centar	11	8	7	0	26
10.	Zubozdravstvena škola	14	10	2	2	28
11.	Medicinska škola	13	13	6	8	40
12.	Škola za medicinske sestre	17	14	4	0	35
13.	Elektrotehnička škola	12	12	11	3	38
14.	Elektroenergetska škola	7	19	9	2	37
15.	Mašinska tehnička škola	4	12	5	5	26
16.	Škola metalskih zanimanja	1	18	12	1	32
17.	Željeznički školski centar	46	15	20	12	93
18.	Saobraćajna škola	2	7	5	3	17
19.	Tekstilni školski centar	2	4	3	0	9
20.	Poljoprivredno-veterinarska i prehrambeni školski centar	3	17	4	1	25
21.	Građevinsko-geodetski školski centar	3	9	6	3	21
22.	Drvno-tehnička škola	0	0	2	2	4
23.	Šumarski školski centar	0	0	0	0	0
24.	Muzička škola	0	0	0	0	0
25.	Gimnazija Dobrinja	77	9	0	0	86
	Totals	237	230	165	87	719

Source: Gimnazija Dobrinja (1992-1995).

the civil defense authority and local community office, at the expense of the teachers and students. Here in Dobrinja, these individuals were local politicians from the Party of Democratic Action (SDA), the party of the Bosnian Muslims, which came to be seen as the third nationalist party, vis-à-vis the Serbian Democratic Party (SDS) representing Serbian nationalist aims, and the Croatian Democratic Union (HDZ) representing Croatian nationalist aims. In educational terms, the battle for a heterogeneous Bosnia living "a common life" together was being waged within the schools of besieged Dobrinja with nationalist political figures of the SDA while, at the same time, the battle was waged on the frontline against military forces attempting to implement Serbian nationalist aims of the SDS.

In this regard, Sabiha Miskin, the director of Gimnazija Dobrinja at the time of this writing, views Smail Vesnić as "a great fighter," as "a fighter for the school," and "a fighter for the students and teachers." She perceived Professor Vesnić as someone who had the interests of the students and teachers at heart and as someone representing "the common life" of a heterogeneous Bosnia, with a vision of "common schools," in a confrontation with local nationalist politicians. Director Miskin offered the following words to me on the struggles of the time:

> Smail Vesnić was trying to bring in the best teachers, including Serbs and Croats. The SDA didn't like this. Note the documents. Note the references to the Civil Defense command and the Local Community. They were trying to throw him out, take his office space, replace the Gimnazija with a Cultural Center. They even came onto the school premises while classes were being held. Who? Ismet Kumalić. Why? They were stupid people.
>
> We were qualified educators who were in these positions trying to do our jobs. They were stupid people who were trying to shut us down. (Miskin, 2001)

I asked Director Miskin if I might quote her directly, given the implications of such statements, especially for a school director. She laughed it off saying that she didn't care what these people thought. Here I offer her my admiration for her courage.

In reference to the Civil Defense command and the Local Community, Director Miskin was suggesting that I examine the "Annals" of Gimnazija Dobrinja to see for myself what she was talking about. Indeed, the entry of 12 March 1994 in the "Annals," almost six months after the start of the 1993-1994 school year, indicates the nature of this struggle:

Mister Fahro Isaković, secretary of the City Secretariat for Education, declared by the phone that the people from the local community [*mjesna zajednica* or MZ] are blaming the school for not putting in use the rooms at C5 Block. They didn't put it in use and now the Gimnazija is responsible. Actually, a group of people is behind this ... all led by Ismet Kumalić, ex-commanding officer of Civil Defense [*civilna zatišta* or CZ]. They are so determined to disturb our work. But, our work wins. There are still exams! We're working and everything will be OK. (Gimnazija Dobrinja, 1992-1995)

In this case, the politicization of Dobrinja entered Gimnazija Dobrinja through the space afforded the Cultural Information Center of the Dobrinja Local Community, promoted by the Civil Defense commander, Ismet Kumalić,[1] who, at the same time, had become the Dobrinja Local Community commissioner (*povjerenik*).

"A local community is a main autonomous community based on a territorial principal," wrote Miodrag Višnjić, whom I cited in my Treća gimnazija book, in his analysis of the role of local communities within the political system of the former Yugoslavia:

> In a large number of local communities there are very intensive social and humanitarian, educational, cultural, artistic, recreational, sport, firefighting and other activities, depending on the needs and interests of the working people and citizens ... By joining activities and resources of working people and citizens, organizations of joint activities and communities of self-governing interests in many local communities, many communal buildings have been constructed ... buildings for cultural and educational, health and other needs. A broad range of activities are developed by almost all local communities especially in the field of national defense and social self-protection ... The role and influence of a local community, in large extent, needs to develop within a municipality, because that is ... the only way for affirmation of a local community in the entire social and political system. At the same time there is no self-governing municipality without self-governing relations developed in local communities. (1979: 5, 18-19, 42)

Prior to the war, however, these local community offices were minimally staffed and responsible for such matters as local grievances, social functions, and civil defense activities in a peacetime setting. In 1992 at the beginning of the war, Novi Grad Municipality was organized into 28 local communities while, as noted in Chapter One, Dobrinja and the Airport Settlement, located within the municipality, were organized into five local communities. During the siege, however, with the political reorganization of greater Sarajevo, local communities were reorganized across the city as well and, on 28 November 1992, the five local communities of what remained of Dobrinja and the Airport Settlement were reorganized into a single Dobrinja Local Community (Općina Novi Grad, 1998). In the process, the local communities took on a prominent role in civil defense activities assuming far greater political power than they possessed prior to the war.

The Dobrinja War School Center, since it "received its premises in the 'Games Club'" on the 9 July 1992 order of Ismet Hadžić, moving into the building on 12 July 1992, shared the space with any number of community and cultural organizations to include, for example, a women's chorus organized by Azra Kujundžić. With the Dobrinja Local Community organization in place on 28 November 1992, the problem of space in the War School Center became part of the larger discussion over the administration of education in Dobrinja which came to the fore after the opening of Gimnazija Dobrinja on 25 January 1993. Although the record is incomplete, there are a series of documents to include memos, letters, and resolutions that record the events of spring 1993, but I will cite only a selected few here that indicate the efforts of the Dobrinja Local Community to close the Dobrinja War School Center.

On 1 April 1993, a "Decision Concerning the Opening of the Dobrinja Cultural-Information Center" (CIC) was issued by the Dobrinja Local Community and the Local Community Council under the signature of the commissioner, Ismet Kumalić, that noted, with the opening of the new CIC, "the Dobrinja Press Center, the Dobrinja Teaching Center, the Dobrinja Arts School and Music School, as other independently-established forms of cultural activities in Dobrinja, are to stop work." In individual letters directed to the War School Center, as well as to the Press Center, the Arts School, and the Music School, dated 9 April 1993, Ismet Kumalić explained that the aims of the CIC were the "consolidation and coordination of all cultural and informational activities going on in the region of the local community." Furthermore, the letter reiterated that, "On the basis of this Decision, all former forms of the organization of cultural and information activities, except the cultural educational association [newly created by the CIC], are to stop work" and will henceforth be organized "as part of the Cultural-Information Center in accordance with special plans and programs ...In this manner, we hope to considerably improve the quality of cultural and informational activities" for all residents of the settlement (Kumalić, 1993).

In a 15 April 1993 response, Smail Vesnić first wrote to Ismail Haverić, Municipal Secretariat for Business, Public Services, and General Administration and Budget, Novi Grad Municipality, reviewing the work of the Center for preschool, elementary, secondary, and higher education, and citing the need for the space provided with the founding of the Center. A second letter followed, "Request for Reconsideration of the Provisions of the Decision of the Council of the Dobrinja Local Community," that was sent to the Presidency of Novi Grad Municipality, the Executive Committee of Novi Grad Municipality, and to the Municipal Council of Dobrinja Local Community, and reads as follows:

> We are asking you to please examine the Decision of the Council of the newly-formed Dobrinja Local Community concerning the abolishment of the mentioned institution [Teaching Center]. We are convinced that the Teaching Center needs to exist especially in this situation when secondary schools and students do not have other institutions for realizing their rights. We are asking that as part of the examination of this Decree, you appreciate the results achieved which are known by all organs of government in the Republic, the City, and the Municipality, as well as by the citizens of our settlement. Also, we ask that you please support the posture of the Ministry of Education, Science, Culture, and Sport of the RBiH concerning the work of the Dobrinja Teaching Center which is familiar with the organs of government of Novi Grad Municipality Sarajevo, which itself recommends that you support the Teaching Center in the subsequent period. (Vesnić, 1994)

Such correspondence continues through spring and summer 1993 which, in the "Annals" of Gimnazija Dobrinja, appear as a struggle over the limited space available to the Gimnazija in the administrative offices of the Teaching Center. With students from all the secondary schools attending classes there, taking examinations, or meeting with teachers, the space of the former "Games Club" was extremely restricted, while the CIC occupied classroom space in the Teaching Center as well. On 6 August, for example, the entry in the "Annals" reads:

> This morning's classes started at 7:30. Everything is full already at 9:00. We asked the Local Community to give back to the Gimnazija the space that was given to them since the day the Gimnazija was established. If we had opened a newspaper shop, they would help us more. They are strangling us. Why? No phones; they have been taken away from us. We have no place to leave our documents. The Railway School gave one evidence notebook to the Gimnazija (thanks to Ilija Šobot). In the afternoon, professional classes lasted until 8:00 P.M. (Gimnazija Dobrinja, 1992-1995)

187

A series of entries from both the Gimnazija "Annals" and the Center "Almanac" illustrate the progression of the struggle during August and September 1993, at the close of the 1992-1993 school year, and at the beginning of the 1993-1994 school year:

11 August 1993, *Wednesday*: It is unusually crowded. The school year is slowly brought to an end. Neither the students nor the teachers can understand the behavior of the "culturals," that they are keeping the doors of their premises locked while students are taking exams standing up. Those responsible in the Center are awaiting a reasonable solution. That is why the director of the Center went to consult with the Local Community. ("Almanac")

13 August 1993, *Friday*: Classes held as scheduled. Students are passing the exams. Certain safety measures are taken. Still, it's crowded. We get little or no help. We are interrupted in this work by the Cultural Information Center, containing one man and one classroom taken away from the Gimnazija. Lazy and worthless people gather there just to interrupt us. Until when? In the afternoon, the professional classes. Work is getting done, despite the interruptions. Classes ended at 7:00 P.M. ("Annals")

23 August 1993, *Monday*: Intensive activities. Lots of examinations and consultations are done. It's the third day of the enrollment procedure. A great number of new students are enrolling. The commander of the 5th Motorized Brigade, Ismet Hadžić, visited the Gimnazija concerned for the problems with space. We're expecting better results. There's no electricity for two days. Next year will be better. ("Annals")

8 September 1993, *Wednesday*: Lots of examinations and consultations done today. We are getting ready for the next school year. The unresolved space problems are still making it hard for us to begin. Anti-aircraft machine guns from Nedžarići are shooting at the entrance of the Center and Gimnazija, all day long. Luckily, no one is hurt. ("Annals")

8 September 1993, *Wednesday*: Consultations and examinations are still on. The number of students that are completing the school year successfully is increasing.

The famous "culturals" still do not understand why they need to leave the premises that are not even theirs. They are disrespecting the laws and the decisions of the municipality. They are just simply ignoring all the written decisions. Simply unbelievable that such behavior is still tolerated by the authorities. ("Almanac")

10 September 1993, *Friday*: School activities are very intensive. Lots of examinations and consultations are done. Representatives of Novi Grad Municipality visited the Gimnazija. They couldn't understand what the native population could do. They are also surprised that it's them who are disturbing the work. It's decided that the occupied space should be freed right now. It's because of them that classes start on Monday only for the Gimnazija. ("Annals")

10 September 1993, *Friday*: The Teaching Center was visited by the Municipal Commission in order to see the premises of the Gimnazija. The other party, the "culturals," and the Local Community authorities are using these last inhuman insinuations in order to nullify everything achieved in the Gimnazija, even with an unbelievable lie claiming that the Gimnazija was established by the Cultural Information Center, which is a lie. How can something that is not established, establish something else? ("Almanac")

This series of entries provide an indication of the struggle for education between teachers and administrators of the War School Center and the politicians of the Local Community who came into power through political reorganization of the Sarajevo local communities during the siege and, in the process, were promoting their own narrow, exclusionary political interests. The contempt for these "lazy and worthless people," as noted, the "famous 'culturals,'" suggests that they ignored the decisions of the civil government of Novi Grad Municipality under which the premises were given to the War School Center at the outset of the war for educational purposes. On 22 September 1993, a letter from the Municipal Secretariat for Business, Public Services, and General Administration and Budget, Novi Grad Municipality, signed by Ismail Haverić, "temporary utilization of workspace for Gimnazija Dobrinja," was sent to Dobrinja Civil Defense Headquarters and the Dobrinja Local Community Council which, referring to previous correspondence, noted simply. "It is important that you execute the relocation of the Cultural-Information Center to other premises, so that schooling in the Gimnazija could proceed without being disturbed" (Haverić, 1993). The "Annals" entry of 4 October notes that the "culturals" finally left the premises which meant that secondary students could now begin the 1993-1994 school year:

> Today, all students of the professional schools started with classes. Finally, the CIC (Cultural Information Center) left the premises of the Gimnazija. Classes were formed and schedules have been made. It was crowded. Ilija Šobot, Smail Vesnić, together with Izet Kodić, a teacher at

the Trade School, work late. We rearranged the classroom and invented new working space. Successful! (Gimnazija Dobrinja, 1992-1995)

The entries also give an indication that in the midst of the political struggle, teachers and students were nevertheless engaged in classes, examinations, and consultations, and that the War School Center was a very busy and hectic place. It should further be noted that these educational activities all took place in the midst of the siege as well suggesting another reason to cite the series of entries. Thus, as noted on 8 September 1993, anti-aircraft guns from Nedžarići to the west, located adjacent to Dobrinja 5, were shooting at the entrance to the Center. There was no electricity at times, or no gas, no telephones, no water, no services, creating extremely difficult conditions in which to conduct educational activities for students in the first place.

Yet the entries indicate that classes for both gimnazija and professional students were finally underway and suggest the organization and scope of operations for Gimnazija Dobrinja as the locus for secondary education:

> 5 October: Classes started on time, as usual. Certain corrections have been made concerning the classes. The Gimnazija finally got the rooms that belonged to it. Classes go on in three shifts. Exams are getting done in a hurry. Good luck!

> 6 October: Work at the Gimnazija is going well. We've got the bell. Drago Mandić, professor of Civil Defense and Protection, gave this bell to the school. We have formed 35 class sections. Twenty-eight [secondary] schools and over 800 students. Another 200 students are not quite done with last year. A diligent professor, Ada Purić, is successfully solving current problems. It's better that no one steps in her way. (Gimnazija Dobrinja, 1992-1995)

Dobrinja Is Covered in Fog

At approximately the very same time, however, the severity of the siege intensified throughout Sarajevo city in general and across Dobrinja in particular. For example, the initial entry for the 1993-1994 school year in the "School Annals" of Treća gimnazija in Novo Sarajevo Municipality in the center of the city reads as follows:

> Life and work in the city are still extremely difficult. The war is not stopping even beside a number of signed ceasefires. Most frequently, there is no electricity, gas, fuel, water, telephone lines, communication,

organized transport, and what is especially difficult is no food. Being out on the street is extremely dangerous because of the shelling of the city and underhanded snipers. Everyday civilians are being killed and wounded.

The war continues and the work continues, and in such conditions a new, and that is second war school year. The entire work is being done with great effort and support of the employees and of the students, with great risk and exposure to danger. (Treća gimnazija, 1992-1995)

In Dobrinja, the siege first appears as a backdrop in the midst of the political struggles and the beginning of classes at the start of the new school year. However, in October, with the professional school classes beginning, the siege comes directly to the forefront in the entries of both the War School Center and Gimnazija Dobrinja. It is clear from the nature of these entries, and the progression of school days through the month of October, that the siege has intensified and that the shelling and the snipers are overwhelming the process of schooling. In response, the teachers, concerned for the safety of their students, have to make very

A load of crutches arrives at the entrance to the Dobrinja hospital located in the Dobrinja 2 complex. There was no hospital in the settlement at the beginning of the war; however, with Dobrinja totally surrounded at the onset of the siege and cut off from Sarajevo proper, a group of doctors trapped inside the settlement created the hospital in response to the casualties of the siege. Photo courtesy of Mevsud Kapetanović.

difficult decisions concerning the operation of the schools. A series of entries through the month of October 1993, from the "Almanac" of the War School Center, illustrate the difficulty of the situation:

7 October 1993, *Thursday*: The premises of the Teaching Center by day are more and more like a real school. Class sections have been formed and the work is done in three shifts. There are many problems and they are all solved along the way. The major problem is the problem of fear for the safety of the students.

At 3:00 the shell that fell very close by to the Gimnazija could have had unforeseeable consequences, but fortunately it didn't.

8 October 1993, *Friday*: Yet another difficult war day. Once more shells are planting fear and death. Three students of the gimnazija have been injured today. They have been lightly injured. The students were outside the Teaching Center. Immediately after, all students were warned not to stand in front of the building. Classes are held according to schedule. (Nastavni centar, 1992-1993)

The 8 October Gimnazija entry noted that a shell exploded 50 meters from the entrance to the Center at 2:30 in the afternoon wounding the three students who were standing outside. These shellings intensified through October interrupting classes and forcing teachers and administrators to decide whether classes were worth the risk either at central locations like Gimnazija Dobrinja or the war school classrooms in the school regions. In the "Annals" of Dušan Pajić-Dašić Elementary School, the narrative notes the regular interruption of classes during the year for security reasons with one of "the longer interruptions" beginning 10 October and running through 13 November 1993.

In fact, every teacher with whom I talked would share the experience of shellings outside their schools, their classrooms, their *punkts*, of shells just missing their students coming or going to classes, of life and death decisions whether or not to cancel classes. As I noted in the Treća gimnazija book, most talked about how lucky they were, but others lamented the responsibilities of the situation. In besieged Dobrinja, students were killed and wounded more frequently than in Sarajevo proper coming and going to school, but also in water lines and bread lines. In general, the bitterness on the part of Dobrinjans to this day lies in the belief that civilians in the most vulnerable of situations were deliberately targeted by enemy gunners. The very same feeling on the part of Dobrinja's teachers lies in the belief that innocent students were deliberately targeted at these classroom locations which everyone agrees were known by the enemy. Since the enemy held much of the high ground encircling Dobrinja, it is hard not to reach a similar conclusion.

One week later, the 17 October Gimnazija entry notes the severity of the shelling in Dobrinja but the shelling of Sarajevo as well:

> All planned professional classes were realized. Sarajevo has been attacked from all sides. Shells are falling on Dobrinja too. Classes were partially cancelled. The coordinators of secondary schools held a meeting and discussed the organization of classes. During the afternoon, lots of shells exploded, over 15 people were wounded ... Classes cancelled in the whole block. (Gimnazija Dobrinja, 1992-1995)

The same day, newspaper accounts in *Oslobođenje* testify to the intensity of the October shelling. One headline reads, "152 MM Shells on Sarajevo," citing the 152 millimeter howitzers that pounded the city. According to the article, UNPROFOR counted 517 shells that fell on Sarajevo the previous day killing six and wounding 55. On 18 October, there was a "New Attack on Sarajevo" with the shelling of the entire city (*Oslobođenje*, 1993). With no end to the heavy shelling, the "Almanac" of Simon Bolivar Elementary School states that "from 16 October to 1 November, instruction was suspended by the decision of the Presidency." The "Almanac" of the War School Center records the situation at the time:

> 18 October 1993, *Monday*: General danger! [*Opšta opasnost!*] Classes have been postponed until further notice.
>
> 21 October 1993, *Thursday*: Classes are still not being held. However, the Teaching Center is full of students. Exams are taken. Everything is flowing through the Center except for water which is so needed. What is it with water, electricity, and gas except for searching for new victims by the enemy? The world continues to silently watch the victims with a canister of water.
>
> 22 October 1993, *Friday*: A peaceful war day in Dobrinja, but not for the city. It is hell in the city. Shells are falling like at the beginning of the war. Weird, the beasts are never lacking in that damn food.
> But life goes on. Students of the secondary schools in Dobrinja, just like brave fighters, are making that life complete at the Teaching Center and that is how they are standing up to the human beasts from the hills.
>
> 24 October 1993, *Sunday*: Regular Catholic mass was held. They are praying to God for peace. That is not the case in Stupni Do, a village near Vareš where Catholics have completed the most bloody job today

in front of everyone. They destroyed everything that was living in that village. Is it possible that there are such beasts living among us? (Nastavni centar, 1992-1993)

On the same day, 24 October, the headline in *Oslobođenje* read, "Over a Thousand Shells on Sarajevo," citing five dead and 37 wounded, but "the defense line remains firm" (1993). The "Almanac" entry here refers to the massacre of Muslim villagers by Croat paramilitaries of the HVO, the Croatian Defense Council, hence the Catholic reference, in the village of Stupni Do, located just to the north of Sarajevo in central Bosnia where warfare erupted between Bosnian Croats and Bosnian Muslims. The "Almanac" entries for the latter part of October read:

> 28 October 1993, *Thursday*: A somewhat peaceful war day. But that is not the case in the center of the city. Shells are destroying everything from early morning. How long will this last and how long will the world tolerate this?
>
> Because of all this there are still no classes but students are frequent visitors of the Teaching Center. We are hoping that reason will take over and that the end of the war will come soon and that students like in all free countries will be able to go to school freely.
>
> 30 October 1993, *Saturday*: The Center is being organized. With every day school space is more organized and better despite the humble possibilities. Last night's attack on Dobrinja warns that there will be no classes soon.
>
> A meeting of the group of coordinators was held and the realization of the Work Program for the 1993-1994 school year was discussed. (Nastavni centar, 1992-1993)

The shelling continued into the winter months. Shells continued to find their victims, and it was only a matter of time that schools were hit once again and schoolchildren became casualties while attending classes. The shelling of fall 1993 left Dobrinja in a state of shellshock and traumatized the population trapped inside the siege. With a lack of food and water, along with the onset of winter, with minimal or no electricity and gas, Dobrinjans were struggling to survive much less to teach and learn. The 24 December entry in the Gimnazija "Annals" reads:

> Yesterday's hell has its effect today too, to the psyche of Dobrinja's residents. The shells that exploded near the Gimnazija didn't take any victims, but they upset the parents and the students, and most employees at the Gimnazija. Anyway, we're working regularly today. (Gimnazija Dobrinja, 1992-1995)

In the shadows of Mount Igman, fog enshrouded the settlement "pressing down on everything that breathed and thought," to reiterate Ivo Andrić here. "Fear spread over [Dobrinja] like a bank of fog ... the kind of great fear, unseen, imponderable, but all-pervading, that comes over human communities from time to time, coiling itself around some heads and breaking others" (1993: 381). The "Almanac" of the Dobrinja War School Center recorded the heavy fog that hid the ridgeline of Mount Igman on those cold and wet November days, partially cited in the first chapter of the book, recording the events of the day in the following manner:

> November 1993, *Wednesday*: It is a cold November day. Dobrinja is covered in fog and it's making that atmosphere even colder. Through the heavy fog, the heads of the students can be seen running down to the Teaching Center. They are rushing through the fog because they do not believe that it can protect them from the snipers ... It is cold at the Teaching Center, but warm as well. The students are safe there, and it is easier for them. There is no electricity, there is no water, there is no gas, there is no freedom, but there is the strength to overcome all this and there is so much will to win. The road to freedom is difficult and

The devastated ruins of the townhouses on the old frontline along Prištinska Street that runs through the east end of the C4 Quadrant of the Airport Settlement—six years after the end of the war. Photo courtesy of Mevsud Kapetanović.

bloody, and so dear ... That is best known by the fighters of our Army, but also every citizens of our suffering country because the aggressor equally attacks the lines of fighters and ordinary citizens.

It is 3 November 1993 today. The day when the War School Center practically stops its work. However, everything that was achieved in this Center during the difficult 1992 war year will be remembered by generations of youth of this time, but also all others because the Center, with its few denizens defied a brutal enemy and gathered the youth of Dobrinja together to give them points of freedom and light between two impacts of shells ... That is how life went on as well as defiance. That is how there was joy and sorrow in the Center. That is how the Center was left with pride and with the richness of new knowledge. Many will be happy in the end that the difficult 1992-1993 war year found them here in Dobrinja, that they were the students of the first generation of the Gymnasium. (Nastavni centar, 1992-1993)

There was no previous hint in the "Almanac," or in any other school documents that I have reviewed, to indicate that 3 November 1993 would be the last day of operation for the Dobrinja War School Center. It was clear by now, however, with the resumption of the 1993-1994 school year at its regular time in September, that the new school year was the beginning of a new school era. Based on trials and errors of the belated and truncated 1992-1993 school year of 18 weeks, teachers and administrators had reorganized the work of schooling under siege conditions and, in the process, adapted both curriculum and instruction for the war schools across Sarajevo city. With the resumption of the regular school year in Sarajevo, the teachers and administrators who worked under the administration of the Dobrinja War School Center had, under the most difficult of siege conditions, reconstructed the administrative framework for both elementary and secondary schools in the besieged settlement as well.

In a settlement where all three elementary schools were in ruin, these educators had reorganized the work of schooling in the stairway schools of the local school regions during the summer and fall months of 1992. During the fall and winter months of 1992-1993, elementary educators resurrected the administrative framework of the three elementary schools to begin the 1992-1993 school year. At the same time, secondary educators constructed the administrative framework for secondary schooling from nothing, to include 27 gimnazija and professional schools, in a settlement where no secondary school had even existed and then created a gimnazija to serve, in the words of Behija Jakić, as "the center of everything."

In the process, they wrote "Basic Work Programs" to reorganize the school curriculum for elementary and secondary education and developed "linear programmed instruction" to carry the instructional process to the students. With the beginning of the 1993-1994 school year virtually on time, with the stairway schools functioning under the administration of the three elementary schools, and with both gimnazija and professional school classes underway at Gimnazija Dobrinja, the administration of elementary and secondary education was now in the hands of the respective schools themselves. In this regard, the organization and operation of the schools of Dobrinja was now directly under the administration of the Sarajevo City Secretariat for Education.

In other words, the Dobrinja War School Center had served its purpose, turning over its responsibilities directly to the school administrators and, in the process, working its way out of existence although seven months previously, the Dobrinja Local Community had attempted to close it down. And here, at this point, the nature of the story changes. With the 1993-1994 school year well underway, the story of the war schools of Dobrinja under the administration of the Dobrinja War School Center becomes another story, a story based on the routine of schooling for the individual Dobrinja schools as they sought to adapt the routine of teaching and learning during the regular school year in the local school regions for which they now had administrative responsibility.

A particularly poignant entry in the "Annals" of Gimnazija Dobrinja, two days after the closure of the War School Center, partially cited in the Preface, reflects the mood of the times:

> November 1993, *Wednesday*: A rainy morning, just like human souls. Blood on the sidewalk and one life less as a result of last night's shelling. How long is human blood going to flow down the streets, and the world still watch and say nothing?
>
> It's dangerous so the kids can't go to school, again. Classes are cancelled. Just the same, in the schools, life will go on. Students are passing their exams in great numbers. Lots of them are completed successfully.

Four days later, the "Annals" record another shelling:

> November 1993, *Tuesday*: It's a cold November day. It's been washed with the blood of innocent victims, innocent children from the 1 May War School and their teacher Fatima Gunić, the wife of the well-known journalist, Vehid Gunić.
>
> What are these youth guilty of? Who took their right to live? One becomes speechless searching for an answer.

The students of the Gimnazija and the other schools are still not coming to classes. (Gimnazija Dobrinja, 1992-1995)

With the headline, "Massacre in Front of a School," the 10 November issue of *Oslobođenje* recorded the slaughter at the school in explicit terms. The subheading read, "Chetnik shells have once more massacred our fellow citizens, this time on Alipašino polje, when deadly projectiles fell just in front of a school and wiped out the youngest." These shellings occurred in the Alipašino polje and Otoka areas in Novi Grad Municipality on the western end of the city. A selected portion of the article reads as follows:

> Another massacre in Sarajevo yesterday. The Alipašino polje settlement was shaken around 11:00 by explosions. Screams, panic, escape, dead and wounded, puddles of blood, sirens. . . . Several dead, dozens wounded, at only one place. Automobiles were trying to transport the wounded and those who can were helped to hospitals ... Most of the wounded are children, 22 of them. The injuries are various, on practically all body parts. Six of them have very serious injuries. Eight are kept for further treatment." (*Oslobođenje*, 1993: 1)

There was another shelling the following day, 11 November, and another headline, "Massacre Again in Sarajevo," with a photograph of four dead children, "innocent victims of yesterday's shelling." At least "eight civilians were killed, 42 were wounded, unfortunately, mostly children," in one shelling, while at least five were killed and 35 wounded in another. The casualties from the previous day's massacre were revised upward to at least nine killed and another 70 wounded (1993: 1). In the "Almanac" of Simon Bolivar Elementary School, the 10 October 1993 entry records events through 12 November, to include the 9 November school shelling, in the following manner:

> On 9 November 1993, in Alipašino polje, a tragedy happened—a school was hit by a shell and three students were killed while a lot of them were seriously injured. As it is very dangerous to live in this city, the monsters should at least be prohibited from slaughtering children. (Osnovna škola Simon Bolivar, 1992-1995)

The same entry in the "Almanac" cites the Institute for Researching Crimes against Humanity (Institut za istraživanje zločina protiv čovječnosti) which was testing elementary students who lost one or both parents, and those who were forced to leave their homes, to determine the manner in which they were affected by the war. According to the entry, there were multiple-choice questions as well as short essays "on how they imagine their lives to be after the war is finished, how they imagine their lives in peace," which were then submitted to the Pedagogical Institute in Sarajevo. I was unable to track down these tests through the Institute, although Aida Musić, the director of Simon Bolivar Elementary School, today Skender Kulenović, provided me with poetry and essays that she indicated were written by her students for this purpose. At this point, I will leave it with the "Almanac" entry where she recorded her thoughts at the time:

> After we reviewed a couple of the completed tests, the effect they had on us, the readers, was quite depressing—the scars that this war is leaving behind on the lives of those young human beings are horrifying. Their childhood, which was interrupted, has been transformed into a sudden and harsh coming of age. Their sense of joy and optimism are all being destroyed because they lost their parents, and they had to face the disappointment which is the result of their loss. The greatest pain is the hopelessness which is so very present among a certain number of the students—it is the hopelessness of those young people who are just taking a stride into life. (Osnovna škola Simon Bolivar, 1992-1995).

War School Legacies

The "Almanac" of Simon Bolivar Elementary School contains a copy of the "Invitation" sent to selected guests to attend the ceremony celebrating the change of names of the school to be held at the Dobrinja War School Center on Friday, 6 April 1994, and from that day onward, the school would be known as the Skender Kulenović Elementary School. The 6 April entry reads:

> The school changed its name from Simon Bolivar to Skender Kulenović, and this change was the reason for teachers and students to present their work in public for the first time since the beginning of the aggression. The school director, Aida Musić, presented to all the guests the story of how the war schools were founded and what obstacles and successes they have been facing in such a difficult time. The students presented everything they have achieved in the course of free-time activities. The project entitled, "School in Flames," received three literary and three arts awards. (Osnovna škola Simon Bolivar, 1992-1995)

The project refers to the shelling of Simon Bolivar Elementary School on the very last day of the truncated 1991-1992 school year as cited in Chapter Two. In the words of Mustafa Smajlović, writing on 10 April 1994 in *Dobrinja danas* (Dobrinja Today), "'The school does not exist, but its students and teachers do,' it was said, on changing the name of the school 'which went up in flames' on 15 May 1992. From the cultural-entertainment program, which was arranged by the students and teachers, and which was enthusiastically received by all those present, we picked out the best literary and artworks on the theme, 'SCHOOL IN FLAMES.'" The Smajlović article, entitled "The Schools Will Carry the Names of Our Writers," continues as follows:

> The sixth of April will be remembered among Dobrinjans by marking a day of state security [and] in an exhibition of student pictures of the Arts School and in celebrations on the occasion of changing the names of two of Dobrinja's elementary schools.
>
> The celebrations on the occasion of changing the names of two schools were held in the shelter in Dobrinja 3A and in the Teaching Center in the presence of a great number of Dobrinjans, students, parent, and teachers, and the representatives of CZ [Civil Defense], MZ [Local Communities], the 5th Motorized Brigade, and UNPROFOR. As we know, Simon Bolivar School henceforth will carry the name of writer and poet SKENDER KULENOVIĆ, [and] Nikola Tesla the name of writer and storyteller ĆAMIL SIJARIĆ. (1994: 1)

Thus Simon Bolivar was renamed Skender Kulenović Elementary School, after the writer and poet from the Bosnian Krajina, and Nikola Tesla was renamed Ćamil Sijarić Elementary School, after the writer and storyteller from the Sandžak (1994: 1).

For some reason, Smajlović does not mention the third elementary school, Dušan Pajić-Dašić, renamed Osman Nuri Hadžić, after the educator and writer from Mostar. However, the school "Annals" note that "at the beginning of 1994, with the decision #1080 of Novi Grad Municipality, the school was given a new name, and called Osman Nuri Hadžić (Osnovna škola Dušan Pajić-Dašić, 1992-1995). These names, of course, reflect a particular Bosnian-Herzegovinian literary tradition befitting the creation of a new identity for the children of a new state. It should be mentioned, however, that Nikola Tesla, the noted electrical engineer who invented the Tesla coil, was a graduate of Sarajevo's Prva gimnazija, and although the emphasis was on Bosnian writers, the fact that Tesla was Serbian might have had something to do with it.

The narrative of the "Annals" of what was now Osman Nuri Hadžić Elementary School continues through the remaining months of the 1993-1994 school year. The latter paragraphs record the number and percentage of students receiving excellent and good grades; only three students in the

TABLE 6.4
NUMBER OF STUDENTS AND CLASSES IN OSMAN NURI HADŽIĆ
(DUŠAN PAJIĆ-DAŠIĆ) ELEMENTARY SCHOOL AT THE BEGINNING
OF THE 1994-1995 SCHOOL YEAR

Grades	Students	Classes
Grade 1	61	3
Grade 2	56	3
Grade 3	116	5
Grade 4	106	4
Grade 5	93	4
Grade 6	111	5
Grade 7	100	4
Grade 8	83	4
Totals	726	32

Source: Osnovna škola Dušan Pajić-Dašić (1992-1995).

1st-3rd grade had one or two D or F grades but "were allowed to advance to the next grade."The eight-page overview concludes the year as follows:

> Altogether, at the end of the year, for 1st-8th grade, there were 734 students divided into 28 class sections. 300 students, or 40.87 percent received excellent grades and 266 students, or 36.23 percent received good grades. The average grade is 4.14. 725 students, or 98.74 percent received excellent behavior marks and 9 students received good behavior marks.
>
> Considering the incredibly difficult conditions under which this school year was conducted, and the difficult safety issues in the first semester, the faculty decided that learning and behavior in the 1993–1994 school year was excellent ...
>
> Summer vacation will be shorter than usual, and the 1994–1995 school year starts on 5 September. (Osnovna škola Dušan Pajić-Dašić, 1992-1995)

The narrative for the 1994-1995 school year is 10 ½ pages in length that replicates the same basic information of the previous school year and provides an overview of the administrative efforts of the school. "Regular instruction began on Monday, 5 September 1994" and continued through 3 July 1995 for students in grades 1-4, and grade 8, and until 15 July 1995 for students in grades 5-7. There are listings of teachers by class sections and subject areas, status of personnel changes, and comments on conditions in war school classrooms. Information is provided about the organization of classes that operated on three shifts from 7:30 A.M. until 7:25 P.M. With schooling organized on the quarter system, the number and percentage of students who received grades is cited for all four quarters taking up a major portion of the narrative. Meetings of the Teacher's Council for the school are cited as well.

In spite of wartime conditions, the 1994-1995 school year appears in the overview as a replication of the 1993-1994 school year. In this regard, the routine of a regular school year for students and teachers suggests a return to some semblance of normality, "the illusion of normal life," amidst the abnormal conditions of the siege.

In contrast to the frenetic pace of the individual entries in the journal of Azra Kujundžić, as she hurried across Quadrant C5 in her efforts to record student data in preparation for the 1992-1993 school year, the overview of both the 1993-1994 and 1994-1995 school years in the "Annals" of Dušan Pajić-Dašić/ Osman Nuri Hadžić appears almost conventional, befitting the "normal" routine of a regular school year. In some ways, the war itself appears to become part of the routine, breaking the routine at times, forcing cancellation of classes for extended periods, whereupon classes would resume once again. Because of security concerns, for example, or the lack of heating in classrooms during the year, classes were cancelled for a short period from 2-4 November, and for a longer period from 9 November-10 December 1994, as well as from 23-28 March 1995.

Towards the end of the 1994-1995 school year, however, the security situation deteriorated dramatically. The "Annals" concludes the school year with the following entry:

> In the last school quarter, regular classes were very brief because the safety conditions in the city of Sarajevo, including our settlement, got worse. Regular instruction was held until 26 April 1995. Since that date, regular instruction was not held. Yet, the contacts with children have not stopped. We looked for ways of making contacts with the kids so that their safety is not jeopardized. From 15 May, we have had a kind of instructional classes [tutoring] for our kids. Namely, the students were coming to school twice a week, and they stayed at school for a very short time, during which their teachers would give them instructions and homework to be completed at home. However, as soon as the safety conditions became even worse, we decided to give up this form of instruction. In order to finish this school year, the classes were divided up into smaller groups of students who were gathering in places which were considered the safest and the teachers would come to those places to visit the kids.
>
> On 31 May, at the Teacher's Council meeting, we came up with

a curriculum for working with students in the current conditions, and each teacher was designing their own program according to the one we designed as a group. The essence of the program was designed around the goal to give the students some short instructions, in the safest possible way, on how to master the remaining curriculum units following the instructions, on their teacher's suggestions, and the recommended literature. (Osnovna škola Dušan Pajić-Dašić, 1992-1995)

Here I would reiterate the reference in Chapter Five to "linear programmed instruction" as an instructional adaptation to wartime conditions "in which students independently work on the written program assignments" that are designed for individualized instruction consistent with the curricular objectives. Such forms of instruction place a heavy responsibility upon the teacher since s/he must prepare "instructional sheets" for the students in the absence of textbooks and curriculum materials. Coordination of the time and place where the assistance of teachers is available, amidst concerns over the security situation, is critical to implement this form of instruction (Vesnić, 1994: 2-3). And to reiterate once again the words of Abdulah Jabućar, deputy minister of education of the RBiH at the time, the "Guidelines on Educational Activities" for the operation of schools "committed every school to work, regardless of conditions—to adapt to the actual situation" (1997: 295).

To continue with the entry in the "Annals" of what is now Osman Nuri Hadžić towards the end of the 1994-1995 school year:

> It is critical to emphasize that despite very difficult security conditions, none of the students or teachers were casualties during class time and the course of work with the students. However, because of the frequent shelling during the school year, some students were casualties [outside of school]. Three of our students were killed: Sahir Kapo, 7th year student, Adnan Kržalo, 6th year student, and Aida Bukva, 2nd year student. A great number of students were heavily or lightly wounded.
>
> Despite very difficult circumstances and obstacles in work during the school year, we need to be satisfied with the success and behavior of the students. (Osnovna škola Dušan Pajić-Dašić, 1992-1995)

The "Almanac" of what was now Skender Kulenović Elementary School records several entries towards the end of the 1994-1995 school year as well that attest to the difficult conditions. On 26 April, the day regular instruction was stopped at Osman Nuri Hadžić, the entry notes that regular instruction was also stopped at Skender Kulenović for safety reasons. By 9 May, regular instruction was concluded as well. On 15 May, the entry notes:

The Teacher's Council considered the possibility of introducing instructional classes and all other forms of teaching in order to [implement the curriculum] which has not been covered so far, to review all of the content, and to finish the school year. It is critical to take care of the safety of the students. (Osnovna škola Simon Bolivar, 1992-1995)

The regular entries in the "Almanac" of Skender Kulenovic reflect the particular situations affecting the school and its students within the background of the war. These entries chart the course of school events, cite the organization of classes, and record the interruptions of the instructional process. In this respect, these entries in the "Almanac" are simply organized a bit differently than the narrative in the "Annals" of Osman Nuri Hadžić, yet they read in similar fashion, attesting to the routine of schooling in chronological fashion over the course of the school years. Given their similarity, it is clear, however, that both these documents reflect the concerns of the particular school, in contrast to those earlier documents of the War School Center that addressed education for all three elementary schools within the framework of the Elementary Education Section. There may be a better understanding of the particular school in these pages, but perhaps less of an understanding of schooling across the settlement.

The "Annals" of Gimnazija Dobrinja also chart the course of the school years and, as noted previously, describe events for the Gimnazija in particular with commentary at times concerning the professional schools. What distinguishes the entries in the Gimnazija "Annals" are the regularity of these entries, on virtually a day-to-day basis, that attest to the routine of what have become regular school years. In this regard, the entries for the 1993-1994 school year, as well as for the 1994-1995 school year that follows, are a marked contrast to the entries for the belated and abbreviated 1992-1993 school year, in which the primary concern was to simply begin with regular classes so that "the school year [was] not lost."

Given their regularity, and the substance of the entries, the record of Gimnazija Dobrinja tends to offer a more in-depth perspective than the documents of the two elementary schools, providing greater information on the war situation in Dobrinja, in Sarajevo, and throughout Bosnia. For example, entries in April 1994 refer to the status of the siege of Goražde, the situation in Brčko, and note the "safe zones" of Žepa, Srebrenica, Bihać, and Maglaj. The siege of Sarajevo is a regular presence here in the pages of the Gimnazija "Annals," as seen in the October and November 1993 entries, cited above, which document wartime conditions that affect the school on a day-to-day basis. Hence, they also record the manner in which the war alters the regular school routine, and the regularity of such entries indicates something of the regularity of the school year. Shelling and snipers continually disrupted the school routine, forcing cancellation of classes, as with the elementary schools, yet, at the appropriate times, the resumption of school amidst these conditions and the assumption of a regular class schedule served to verify the regularity of the 1993-1994 school year in the pages of the "Annals."

An interesting feature of the entries during spring 1994 concerns conditions under siege with an emphasis on the status of prices for food and goods. The entry on 3 May 1994 notes that, "In Sarajevo, prices are getting lower. The price of sugar dropped from 20 Deutschmarks (DM) to 5 DM. The price of potatoes dropped from 8 DM to 3DM, etc. Things will be better." The 5 May entry also notes that "prices are decreasing—coffee is already 25 DM."

Several entries address economic conditions and what passes for teachers' salaries:

> 6 May 1994, *Friday*: We barely have any supplies for school maintenance. We work in three shifts, even during the night. We have not received any income since September 1993. Instead of getting money, we received 10 kilograms of flour to be used for the next three months. Of course, how could we have expected more! And despite all that, we are working very hard.

> 20 May 1994, *Friday*: We have more goods coming into Sarajevo. Prices are continuously dropping down—you can get a dozen eggs for 10 DM. In school, each teacher got 5 kilograms of flour as their salary for the months of October, November, and December 1993.

> 23 May 1994, *Monday*: It is a regular school day today—classes are run in three shifts. This school year is slowly coming to its end. One more convoy with food arrived in Sarajevo today, and they passed by our school. Prices are still dropping down—potatoes are 3 DM. Let's move on. (Gimnazija Dobrinja, 1992-1995)

With very minimal monies for teachers' salaries that were paid on an irregular basis, Gimnazija records indicate the economic desperation of the teachers as early as the fall of 1992 and continuing through the length of the siege. A "list of workers from the Teaching Center who have received vouchers for lunch for November 1992," for example, contains the names of ten educators who accepted the vouchers. Even with the 1992-1993 school year up and running, a "request for allocation of family packets for teachers of the Gimnazija in Dobrinja," contains a listing of 107 educators who were working there as of 26 May 1993. Another such request, dated 11 June 1993, addressed to the Center for Peace and the humanitarian organization, "Women for Women," in Sarajevo, contains a listing of 38 Gimnazija teachers to receive food packets. In short, teachers, when they were paid their salaries, were usually paid in some type of goods rather than in monies, often months later than when their salaries were actually due (Gimnazija Dobrinja, 1992-1995; Nastavni centar, 1992-1995).

With the return of a 1993-1994 regular school year that operated over 30 instructional weeks, and with a central physical location for school administration and classrooms, and with the 1994-1995 school year on the horizon, the "Annals" of Gimnazija Dobrinja reflect the return to normality, or at least, "the illusion of normality," seen in the routine of teaching and learning amidst the difficult conditions of the siege. Indeed, creating this "illusion of normality," in the words of educators such as Mujo Musagić, Halil Burić, and Narcis Polimac, as noted in Chapter One, was the very purpose behind the creation of the Dobrinja War School Center which, in turn, created the conditions for the establishment of the regular operation of the schools. With the routine of the regular school year, neither of the two "Annals" or the "Almanac" that I have cited that chronicle the events of the school, even mention the demise of the fighting in fall 1995, the ceasefires that came with the peace talks, or the Dayton Peace Agreement of December 1995 that ended the war. No doubt the teachers and students were caught up in the routine of the regular school year which, of course, was a good thing, considering those early efforts to reconstruct the schools when nothing was there amidst the "siege within a siege" of Dobrinja.

NOTE

[1] While a number of names of individuals opposed to the work of the Dobrinja War School Center and/or Gimnazija Dobrinja appear in the Gimnazija "Annals" or the Center "Almanac," or various names are mentioned in interviews, it serves no major purpose to mention most of them. Ismet Kumalić is cited because, as director of Civil Defense Headquarters as well as director of the Dobrinja Local Community, he was directly involved in the situation. I have cited Ismet Čengić and Salko Halilović from my interview with Narcis Polimac in the Epilogue that follows, because they are political figures as well who were cited in other situations by other individuals.

The Struggle for "Common Schools"

EPILOGUE

How To Know the Truth

If the mountains could speak,
to tell the truth about the battle of good against evil.

If the rivers could speak,
to tell the truth about the victims that floated through them,
about the liters of blood that mixed with them.

If the concentration camps could speak,
perhaps they would tell the truth about the fear and torture of their prisoners.

If the graves could speak,
to tell the truth which head or arm belongs to whom.

If the fire could speak,
to tell the truth about how many victims vanished in its flames.

If the house could speak,
it would tell how many shells and shrapnel it received.

The truth would be known if the consciousness started to speak,
the consciousness of the whole world.

—Azra Ajanović, 8th Grade
Skender Kulenović Elementary School

With the closing of the Dobrinja War School Center on 3 November 1993, and the City Secretariat for Education assuming responsibility for the administration of Dobrinja's schools, there was no longer an Elementary Education Section to coordinate the efforts of the three elementary schools. The story of elementary education in the settlement now becomes the story of the three individual schools and their efforts to individually organize the instructional process for their respective school regions. Dedicated elementary teachers such as Azra Kujundžić no longer walked the streets of the school regions to meet under the auspices of Seniha Bulja, as manager of the Elementary Education Section, in an effort to coordinate elementary education across the entire settlement.

There was no longer a Secondary Education Section either to coordinate the efforts of the 27 Sarajevo secondary schools, through the work of the individual school coordinators, with Gimnazija Dobrinja. Nevertheless, Ilija Šobot, as manager of the Secondary Education Section, along with his colleagues, had constructed the administrative framework for secondary school organization with secondary students still registered at their respective schools. Secondary school coordinators now reported directly to the respective school directors in the administrative offices of their schools back in Sarajevo itself.

With the beginning of the 1994-1995 school year, Smail Vesnić, the school director of Gimnazija Dobrinja, and the former director of the Dobrinja War School Center, as employee #21, "departed from the school" on 18 September 1994, and employee #22, Ismet Salihbegović, the school director, "came to the school" on 19 September 1994. In the 11 pages of the "Annals" of Gimnazija Dobrinja for the 1994-1995 school year, with over two pages of personnel listings, another page of student numbers, another page listing graduating students, and over two pages with newspaper inserts, there is simply no substantive discussion that provides any background on the change in school directors nor is there any explanation for the change (Gimnazija Dobrinja, 1992-1995). Such a lack of information is rather puzzling, to say the least, since the replacement of Director Vesnić, the individual who was solely responsible for creating the school in the midst of the war, might be seen as a significant personnel move, not to mention a change in school directors.

The "Minutes" of the Teacher's Council meeting, dated 4 October 1994, however, note that "the meeting was opened by the former school director of Gimnazija Dobrinja, Smail Vesnić." The agenda items for the

October meeting included the work report for the 1993-1994 school year, the proposed work program for the 1994-1995 school year, and "the transfer of responsibilities to the new school director." The agenda reads:

> The work report from the 1993-1994 school year was submitted by the former director of the Gimnazija, Smail Vesnić. Those present were introduced with all the problems that were present. The general conclusion was that all the teachers of Gimnazija Dobrinja made enormous efforts in the realization of the Work Program. Special gratitude was expressed to all subjects in Dobrinja who helped out in the completion of the 1993-1994 school year.
>
> On 19 September 1994, the executive board of the City made a unanimous decision to appoint Ismet Salihbegović as the new director of Gimnazija Dobrinja and with congratulations he assumed his new duty. (Gimnazija Dobrinja, 1992-1995)

With these words in the "Minutes" of the Gimnazija that he founded, Director Vesnić relinquished his duties, with no formal thanks in the "Minutes," much less thanks in the Gimnazija "Annals." In my personal conversations with him, he has never expressed any indication that "the transfer of responsibilities" was based on anything other than a professional decision, that he had a very good professional relationship with his successor, Ismet Salihbegović, that he had accomplished his mission to organize the schools of besieged Dobrinja, that students were now attending classes on a normal routine of a regular school year, and that it was, simply, time to move on. In this regard, Director Vesnić has always preferred to let his work speak for itself, referring instead to the efforts of his colleagues and, in turn, those colleagues with whom I have spoken express nothing but admiration for his efforts, continually citing him as the single individual who was directly responsible for the reconstruction of schooling in Dobrinja during the siege.

To reiterate the words of Sabiha Miskin, the school director of Gimnazija Dobrinja at the time of this writing, concerning the struggle with the "culturals" preceding the 1993-1994 school year, Smail Vesnić was "a great fighter, a fighter for the school," and "a fighter for the students and teachers." As the school director of Gimnazija Dobrinja from its conception until the beginning of the 1994-1995 school year, "Smail Vesnić was trying to bring in the best teachers, including Serbs and Croats," if they were good teachers, yet, "they were trying to throw him out, take his office space, replace the Gimnazija with a Cultural Center ... once they were in power, they replaced him, and they moved into his office before he even had the chance to move out" (Miskin, 2001). In the words of Director Miskin, if I wanted to understand schooling in Dobrinja, "Note the documents. Note the references to the Civil Defense command and the Local Community" (2001).

These school documents were packed in twelve, large, cardboard boxes in the closet hallways of Gimnazija Dobrinja. With the assistance of Director Miskin, I carried these boxes of documents out to her car, loaded them into the car, and then unloaded them from the car, and carried them up the stairways and into my apartment in the Airport Settlement. I will cite only two such school documents here, dated October 1994, within a month after the change in school directors of Gimnazija Dobrinja, that suggest that the "culturals," even with the departure of Smail Vesnić, were continuing their efforts and, not simply meddle in the schools, but continue their efforts to shape school policy and administration.

On 11 October 1994, a meeting was held of "representatives of the Dobrinja MZ [Local Community], Dobrinja CZ [Civil Defense], the 5th Motorized Brigade, SDA Dobrinja, Gimnazija Dobrinja and representatives of community and religious life," to include Ismet Hadžić (Mutevelija) as the military commander, to include his Islamic title here, the new civil defense director for the Dobrinja Local Community, the president of the Dobrinja Local Community Assembly, Munir Jašarević, the imam of the Islamic Religious Community, and Asim Račić of the Islamic Relief humanitarian agency, among others. The "Minutes" of the meeting, dated 17 October 1994, note the topic: "The theme was the creation of conditions for students of secondary schools who are registered in secondary schools in the city to be able to attend classes in Dobrinja" (Salihbegović, 1994). In this regard, the "Minutes" clearly suggest a much wider involvement in the educational administration of secondary schools, on matters that had been left to school administrators such as Ilija Šobot, by the Dobrinja Local Community controlled by the SDA, the Bosnian Muslim political party, with two members of the Islamic community attending the meeting, not to mention the military commander, but no Catholic representative, for example.

On 19 October 1994, Ismet Salihbegović, the new director of Gimnazija Dobrinja, sent a letter to "SDA-MO Dobrinja," the SDA Local Organization, concerning the membership of the Management and Supervisory Board of the school.

> We are turning to you with the request that you help us in the election of members of the Management and Supervisory Board of Gimnazija

Dobrinja. Currently, these organs do not function because of the absences and commitments of some members. The solution of this problem is urgent because of all the more important decisions the Management Board of the Gimnazija introduces, but in the course of appointments to work vacancies. (Salihbegović, 1994)

There are two lists of current members of the Management Board. The first list includes the names of seven members, with references to Severin Montina, the director of the Republican Fund for Secondary Education, and one of the original members of the Teacher's Council of the Dobrinja War School Center, with the notation, "in the city, does not come to meetings," and to Halil Burić, once the manager of the Higher Education Section of the Center, with the notation, "in the city, comes to meetings with difficulty." A second list of current members includes only three names: Enes Kujundzić, deputy minister of education of the Republic, and another original member of the Teacher's Council of the Center, Ilija Šobot, the manager of the Secondary Education Section of the Center, with the notation, "does not work in the Gimnazija," and Seniha Bulja, the manager of the Elementary Education Section of the Center, with the same notation, both of whom continued their work with the schools of Dobrinja (Salihbegović, 1994). There is no explanation for the two lists as each list refers to "current members of the Management Board," and there is no indication who is up for reelection or who is going to be replaced in such an election. Whatever the meaning of the listings, the former members of the Dobrinja War School Center are identified in one way or another in what appears to be a new administrative personnel initiative. But regardless of those identified in the listings, the reality was that the school director of Gimnazija Dobrinja sent a memo directly to the SDA in the Dobrinja Local Community requesting their assistance in replacing members of the Management and Supervisory Board of the school.

In a particular sense, the "culturals" of the SDA who, at the local community level, would value exclusion in the schools in order to promote their own political and religious agenda at the expense of professional teachers and administrators, amidst a city under siege, have continued to promote their exclusionary vision in the postwar era. On the one hand, their influence is restricted to the entity of the country that they politically dominate, the Federation of Bosnia and Herzegovina (FBiH), and the schools of the entity. On the other hand, in the Republika Srpska, the Serbian entity, the SDS, the Serbian nationalist party that controls the RS government, has promoted its own exclusionary vision in the schools of that entity of the divided country. Unfortunately, the political confrontation between these opposing nationalist forces continues to play out in the Dobrinja community where the struggle is seen in the reconstruction of Osman Nuri Hadžić Elementary School, which rests directly on the old frontline that became the boundary line dividing the two entities on the eastern end of the settlement.

In this regard, the school director of Osman Nuri Hadžić Elementary School, Narcis Polimac, who became director of what was then Dušan Pajić-Dašić Elementary School during summer 1992, came under fire while guiding the school into the postwar era. The 29 April 2001 headline in *Dnevni avaz*, a Sarajevo daily, read, "Stubborn Fighter for Better Future for Children of Dobrinja" (Ćatić, 2001: 18). Indeed, six years after the end of the war, Osman Nuri Hadžić still occupied administrative offices and war school classrooms that it had occupied during the years of the siege, because the original school building directly on the old frontline was in extremely bad shape and had yet to be cleared of mines, and because the boundary line that ran directly through school property was itself in dispute. Meanwhile, the other two Dobrinja elementary schools, Skender Kulenović and Ćamil Sijarić, had been rebuilt with international assistance

Teachers and students of Osman Nuri Hadžić Elementary School, formerly Dušan Pajić-Dašić Elementary School, outside their war school classrooms on the first floor of an apartment building in Dobrinja 2, six years after the end of the war. Photo by author.

monies. Nevertheless, the war school classrooms of Osman Nuri Hadžić were filled to capacity by a new generation of students of the postwar era, to include returning refugee students, and Serb and Croat children, who were taught by Bosniac, Serb, and Croat teachers.

The article appeared at a time of extreme tension in the settlement, between RS and FBiH entities over the boundary line as well as within the Canton over the ethnicity of teachers and students. With its reference to "a school in the settlement open to all Bosniacs, Serbs and Croats," the article implicitly supports Director Polimac, who is highlighted as "The Person of the Week," in his struggles with local politicians of the municipality. A portion of the article reads as follows:

> The School in Dobrinja Will Be for the Children,
> But Not Serbian, Croatian, or Bosniac.
>
> For the school in Dobrinja 1, which was assigned to the Federation of Bosnia and Herzegovina as a result of the decision of the arbitrator, Diarmuid Sheridan, they said that was the critical element in the process of arbitration. That particular school had the name Dušan Pajić-Dašić, and it used to be the biggest, the best equipped and, as people used to say, it was the most beautiful elementary school in Bosnia and Herzegovina. What is left of the school now is only a burned skeleton which reminds us of past years that Dobrinja will always remember ...
> The students, who had to study in improvised classrooms for years, classrooms which were located in some of the grocery stores, apartments, or in the premises of the community councils ... were so happy to hear that, with gratitude to the experienced and eloquent Irish judge, they were able to go back to their "old" school. After the arbitration decision was made, the students from Osman Nuri Hadžić Elementary School came to share joy together with their teachers. This joy was also shared by the parents of the 562 students who were looking forward to seeing their kids back in their normal school benches.
> That day, the school director, Narcis Polimac, a *Sarajlije*, who has been living in Dobrinja for more than fifteen years, was satisfied. He is the director of the only school in Dobrinja which does not have its own facility, and he assumed the director's position when Sarajevo and Dobrinja were the most difficult places to live in, and this was back in 1992 ... He organized classes in apartments and basements, taking into consideration the children's safety. The teachers, who at the time, had to be courageous, were risking their lives but they would still regularly come to teach. Despite those difficult conditions, (although these words are not adequate to describe the conditions at the time), this elementary school had two generations of graduating students ...

As Mr. Polimac explained, in this "new" school, he does not want anything more than this school used to have from before ... Mr. Polimac and his students did not have a chance to see their "new" school yet. They are waiting for more peaceful days, with the hope that they will be accepted in a more humane way, from those who used to live in the part which belonged to Republika Srpska. It has not been the case yet. We strongly believe that this school will never again be called a Serbian school, as used to be the case, and it will also not be called Croatian or Bosniac. They want this school to be a children's school, open to all elementary school children in Dobrinja. It is quite certain that it will not be difficult to "make" such a school in the settlement open to all Bosniacs, Serbs and Croats. Arbitrator Sheridan certainly took this into consideration when he drew the boundary lines.

Those who believe in coexistence should look at the example of this director's persistence and help, that many years of children's dreams to have classes in comfortable benches become true. The children surely deserve it, as well as their parents, who are looking forward to return to their pre-war apartments in Dobrinja 1 and 4. (Ćatić, 2001: 18)

The boundary line dispute was settled when, on 24 April 2001, the arbitrator, "the eloquent Irish judge," Diarmuid Sheridan, ruled in favor of the Bosnian Federation, effectively moving the boundary line between the two entities that ran through school property back into what the Serbs referred to as Serbian Sarajevo. The ruling restored approximately 750 housing units to the Federation and integrated the greater part of both Dobrinja 1 and Dobrinja 4 formerly divided along the frontline (CRSP, 2004). With the arbitrator's decision, and the clearing of mines from school property, efforts to rebuild the school began in earnest.

Although stories appeared citing reconstruction assistance by various international donors to include, most notably, the Chinese and Japanese, the reconstruction of the school was accomplished solely by the United States Agency for International Development (USAID).[1] Construction was approved for implementation by USAID on 30 April 2001, and actual construction began on 31 October 2001. During the construction process, workers found a tunnel that had been dug under the building during the war which delayed the project and, while the area had previously been demined five times, unexploded ordnance was found during construction on at least three occasions. "Since protection of school children is a major concern, USAID agreed to begin removal and screening of 15 to 20 cm of soil for UXO [unexploded ordnance]." Demining was completed by 26 April 2001, and the construction process was completed by 20 June 2002 (CRSP, 2004).

Osman Nuri Hadžić Elementary School began classes in its new school building on its new school premises for the 2002-2003 school year, the first time that elementary students could walk onto the school grounds for classes since April 1992 and the beginning of the war and the effective end of the 1991-1992 school year. The opening ceremony to mark the return of students and teachers to the school was delayed until 9 December 2002, for "objective reasons," for which Narcis Polimac apologized in his speech to honor the occasion. After the series of initial greetings, Director Polimac offered a brief history of the school and the significance of the new school during the postwar era:

> First of all I would like to introduce you to this institution to which you have come today.
>
> The elementary school was built in 1985, right after the Olympic

Demining of Osman Nuri Hadžić Elementary School in 2001, six years after the end of the war. The school grounds were demined on at least six occasions prior to the reconstruction of the school building which began on 31 October 2001 and, under the direction of the United States Agency for International Development (USAID), was completed on 20 June 2002. The school officially opened for the 2002-2003 school year, ten years after the beginning of the war and the premature end of the 1991-1992 school year. Photo courtesy of Mevsud Kapetanović.

Games when, at the time of the construction of Dobrinja, the need to build a new school arose. I mean, as the community was expanding, the number of students was growing, and very soon the school reached a number of over 2,000 students, and by the year 1992, this was the largest school in Bosnia and Herzegovina.

On 15 April, when schooling was suspended due to war hostilities, the school had over 2,600 students and was the largest school in Bosnia and Herzegovina. As you already know, at the beginning of April 1992 when the war started, the students had to leave this school building and pull back deep into the community due to security reasons. However, the break in schooling lasted a very short time, until March 1993 when, thanks to the Ministry of the then Republic of Bosnia and Herzegovina, we organized teaching and started work with children in earnest. Up until then, the so-called stairway schools [were organized] which, however, did not have an official form and, as I said, through the Ministry's instructions which we received at the beginning of 1993, we started work in earnest. Throughout the entire war we worked in basements, business offices, and rooms inappropriate for teaching, but at least we managed to have all the kids finish the school year, and at the end of the war, we were practically issuing diplomas which were fully valid and which enabled children to continue regular schooling upon the end of the war.

When the war ended in 1995, just like all students and teachers in the city and wider, we expected the reconstruction of our school building. We were expecting the day when we will return to our school. However, in contrast to all other schools, our students waited the longest for this period. Unfortunately, due to political problems linked to this region, we are the last school in Sarajevo Canton to enter this wonderful space, thanks first of all to USAID which invested the money, and which enabled the children of Dobrinja, this part of Dobrinja, to finally get the conditions they deserve ...

So today we have an opportunity to mark this day when we received a new school building, thanks to the assets secured by the USAID, and today we are a school with over 500 students, much less than when schooling was suspended, but these are the conditions presented by the post-war era, and we hope that we will overcome these conditions, and we expect that during the next school year the school will have over 700 students.

The entire time our school had a multiethnic character in terms of employees. Our students were also of all nationalities just like today, and this is something we are very proud of. Unfortunately, we do not have the opportunity to see students from the neighboring entity [RS] here, but we do have students from the Federation. We hope that the political disputes will be resolved and that very soon we will have the opportunity to have students from the neighboring entity in this beautiful building. (Osnovna škola Osman Nuri Hadžić, 2002)

Upon the conclusion of his address, Director Polimac introduced Damir Hadžić, the mayor of Novi Grad Municipality, to say a few words. At the outbreak of the war, as noted in Chapter Five, Damir was a 16-year old student enrolled at the Railway School Center, and soldier who fought in the defense of the settlement from the first days of the war who, today, remembers that "the Dobrinja Teaching Center and Gimnazija Dobrinja gave him a chance to finish his education" (2001). After greeting the honored guests, Damir offered the following words, noting the difficult struggle to rebuild the school in the postwar era, and the significance of the new school, in especially poignant fashion:

> This school was attended by students from Dobrinja for a long time, and I'm sure that today's date is going to stay in their memories for a long time as the date of the new birth of their second home. Even though this school was totally devastated back in 1992, and even though many believed that it would never look as it did before, today's day will prove them wrong and will break all of their negative illusions. The generations that this school produced before, during, and after the war are most deserving of its survival and its new beginning, of the beginning of work of this new building, but it was the spirit and faith which never left them, the faith that even what was impossible is possible and that good and what is progressive can win the battle. The ugly and retrograde politics which demolished this school and did not allow its reconstruction was in vain; the desire of those who loved the school and who care about it was much stronger.
>
> Thanks to the American people, the government of the United States, His Excellency Ambassador Miller, His Excellency Ambassador Bond, in Bosnia and Herzegovina naturally, who knows how many times they have shown their affection for Bosnia and Herzegovina, this building was rebuilt. For all of us, the school is not only a school, not only a pedagogical institution, but the symbol of a new common [*zajednički*] Bosnia and Herzegovina, full of understanding and tolerance, the victory of reason as a basic life motto and most important principles.
>
> I want to send a message to everyone, but most of all to the students and teachers. Let's have a feeling for this school as the school which is going to unite us, as the school which we will be alive in, and as the place in which we are going to rejoice. Take care of this school like never before, and let's not forget that for us, however, it is much more, very much more, than simply a school. (Osnovna škola Osman Nuri Hadžić, 2002)

If the war caught Damir Hadžić at that age, and he came to "the realization that we had to live in a different community," then, as the mayor of this community divided today by old frontlines and new boundary lines, Damir clearly realizes that Osman Nuri Hadžić is "not only a school, not only a pedagogical institution, but the symbol of a new common [*zajednički*] Bosnia and Herzegovina, full of understanding and tolerance." In this regard, Damir echoes the words of Robert Donia that "common life ... necessarily includes tolerance," and, as the story of the war schools of Dobrinja is brought to its conclusion, a portion of Donia's quotation that appeared earlier in Chapter One is repeated here:

> Common life ... necessarily includes tolerance ... Like tolerance, common life presupposes that people belong to different groups and are unlikely to assimilate into an undifferentiated, homogenous whole. Sarajevans have long used the concept of neighborliness to express their respect for those of different faiths and nationalities ... Common life is neighborliness writ large. It embodies those values, experiences, institutions, and aspirations shared by Sarajevans of different identities, and it has been treasured by most Sarajevans since the city's founding. (2006: 3-4)

Viewed in Donia's terms, the struggle for common schools in besieged Dobrinja occurred within the larger struggle for common life in besieged Dobrinja. Indeed, the struggle of the Dobrinja community is representative of the struggle for the identity of the country itself during the war, a country beset by the suffering and trauma and bloodshed, embodied in division of the country into two entities. Indeed, the struggle continues into the postwar era in the Dobrinja community as well as in Bosnian and Herzegovina itself.

If the new elementary school was perceived as "a children's school open to all elementary school children in Dobrinja ... open to all Bosniacs, Serbs, and Croats," it is also clear that Narcis Polimac's view of Dušan Pajić-Dašić as a "common school" that was open to all elementary school children in the prewar era was the vision he carried for Osman Nuri Hadžić as "a common school" open to all elementary school children in the postwar era. "Our school had a multiethnic character in terms of employees, also our students were of all nationalities just like today, and this is something we are very proud of," stated Director Polimac. In this regard, the symbolism of this new elementary school suggests the vision of "a common school" and resurrects the *Sarajlije* vision of "a common life." In the process, the postwar vision of educators such as Narcis Polimac reaffirms the wartime vision of Smail Vesnić even during the intolerance of the times. Here we might recall the words of Director Polimac again, cited in Chapter One, as follows:

> We had a common school (*zajednička škola*) for everybody before the war. We had a common school for the whole region, for students from the east end of Dobrinja and from the area around Dobrinja, from Kasindo, from Bijelo Polje. We want a common school today like we had before the war. (2006)

Unfortunately, this vision of "a common school" for a "common Bosnia and Herzegovina" has yet to be realized. As mayor of Novi Grad Municipality, Damir Hadžić spoke directly to the point in his brief comments, noting that "even though many believed [the school] would never look as it did before, today's day will prove them wrong and will break all of their negative illusions ... The ugly and retrograde politics which demolished this school and did not allow its reconstruction was in vain." In a very particular sense, Mayor Hadžić was addressing the long struggle within the municipality and the canton through the postwar years to reconstruct the school on the eastern end of the settlement. To Narcis Polimac, "this was not only a school problem; this was also a settlement problem" (2006). According to Director Polimac, a number of local municipal politicians wanted to close the school which, in the postwar era, operated in ten different locations, nine garages and buildings, and one private apartment provided by a woman of Serbian nationality, in the old war school classrooms. In the process, they wanted to disperse these students to Skender Kulenović Elementary School in the middle of the settlement, and to Ćamil Sijarić at the western or opposite end of the settlement. With the closure of the Osman Nuri Hadžić Elementary School, originally built for students on the eastern end of the settlement, it was clear that any hope of those Serbian children who lived in the apartments of Dobrinja 1 and Dobrinja 4, just inside the new arbitrated boundary line, as well as Serbian children who lived just on the other side of the line, would attend the elementary schools of Dobrinja, located in the middle of the settlement, or on the opposite end, would be nonexistent.

In the words of Director Polimac:

> The worst thing was not to find understanding on the part of the local authorities, Ismet Čengić and Salko Halilović, in particular. They said I was stupid. They said I was crazy. I risked everything for the school. I broke the telephone talking to Halilović, I slammed it down. I still can't forget.

> They said, "If the Serbs need a school, they can go the elementary school in the military barracks [that was operating for Serbian children at the time].
> Damir Hadžić was a gift to us. He was very good in negotiations. He had the same ideas as us, the same ideas for the school. (2006)

The opening of Osman Nuri Hadžić for the 2002-2003 school year provided Director Polimac the opportunity to reiterate the idea of "a common school" to the Serbian population that now lived within the Federation in Dobrinja 1 and Dobrinja 4 and just across the boundary line in what is today known as Eastern Sarajevo, what used to be Serbian Sarajevo, within the Republika Srpska. To reiterate his comments once again:

> The entire time our school had a multiethnic character in terms of employees, also our students were of all nationalities just like today, and this is something we are very proud of. Unfortunately, we do not have the opportunity to see students from the neighboring Entity here, but we do have students from the Federation. We hope that the political disputes will be resolved and that very soon we will have the opportunity to have students from the neighboring entity in this beautiful building. (2002)

In a very particular sense, Narcis Polimac was addressing the long struggle between the two entities, the Bosnian Federation and the Republika Srpska, over the inter-entity boundary line that once ran through school property and delayed reconstruction of the school. With the reopening of the school for the 2002-2003 school year, attendance hovered around 500 students in grades 1-8. In his 9 December 2002 address on the opening of the school, Director Polimac cited the hope that 700 students would be in attendance for the 2003-2004 school year and noted that "on 15 April, when schooling was suspended due to war hostilities, the school had over 2600 students and was the largest school in Bosnia and Herzegovina." However, with a projected capacity of 1,100-1,200 students after reconstruction, attendance had climbed by only 100, to approximately 600 students in grades 1-8, by the 2005-2006 school year, or one-half its projected capacity (Polimac, 2006).

Indeed, the reason the school operated at one-half capacity was that the Serbian children who lived in Dobrinja 1 and Dobrinja 4, within the Bosnian Federation following the April 2001 arbitration ruling, instead went to Serbian elementary schools now located across the inter-entity boundary line in the Republika Srpska. At the same time, the Serbian children who lived just across the inter-entity boundary line within the

Republika Srpska went to Serbian elementary schools within the entity as well. In other words, Serbian parents were choosing to send their children to Serbian elementary schools located in Eastern Sarajevo today within the entity of the Republika Srpska rather than send them to Osman Nuri Hadžić, a short walk up the hill from Dobrinja 4, or a short walk down the street from Dobrinja 1. In spite of the vision of Narcis Polimac for "a common school," and his hope "that very soon we will have an opportunity to have students from the neighboring entity in this beautiful building," only five or six Serbian children attend Osman Nuri Hadžić today (Polimac, 2006).

There are three Serbian elementary schools in the immediate Dobrinja area: Jovan Dučić Elementary School in the small village of Kasindo, Petar Petrović Njegoš Elementary School in the decrepit former military barracks just outside Dobrinja, and Sveti Sava Elementary School in a new school building in the former Lukavica military barracks. There is no question that Osman Nuri Hadžić is closer to Serbian residents living in the apartment complexes of Dobrinja 1 and Dobrinja 4, and probably closer to most Serbian residents living nearby than all three Serbian schools, and certainly within walking distance. Nevertheless, most Serbian parents are choosing to make longer trips for their children, usually by car, in order to send them to exclusively Serbian schools rather than send them to Osman Nuri Hadžić to create a school of multiethnic character.

At approximately the same time that construction began on Osman Nuri Hadžić, with the purpose of rebuilding a multiethnic school along the inter-entity boundary line, Merritt Broady, the director of the Minority Reintegration and Development Office of USAID, learned that the Japan International Cooperation Agency (JICA) was in the midst of their own construction project nearby in the Republika Srpska in what was then known as Serbian Sarajevo. In fact, although discussions had begun at least as early as 1997, the Japanese agency was in the process of building an entirely new school building for Sveti Sava Elementary School in the former Lukavica Barracks at the very same time USAID was rebuilding the old school for Osman Nuri Hadžić. Broady told me that he went to meet with the Japanese on the two, mutual construction projects, and he remembered the essence of the conversation in the following terms: We asked the Japanese, "Why are you doing this?" I said to them, "You are working against Dayton. You are promoting the ethnic segregation of students" (2006).

Indeed, approximately 700 Serbian children attend Sveti Sava Elementary School today, or almost the number that would fill Osman Nuri Hadžić to its full capacity, while approximately 2,000 Serbian children attend the three exclusively Serbian elementary schools within the Republika Srpska in the immediate Dobrinja area, rather than attend the three Dobrinja elementary schools within the Bosnian Federation (Polimac, 2006). Given the wishes of the Novi Grad municipal politicians, that "if the Serbs need a school, they can go the elementary school in the military barracks," that is precisely what they have done, in spite of the best wishes of Narcis Polimac whose vision of "a common school" appears to have died on the vine, and in spite of the best wishes of Damir Hadžić whose vision of "a common Bosnia and Herzegovina" lies in danger as educators and politicians seem unable to put aside their differences so that students of the postwar generation in Dobrinja can attend "common schools" together.

I caught up with Ibrahim Sejfović, the 8th grade student who attended Seniha Bulja's "First Stairway School Dobrinja 2B" on Salvador Allende Street #5, 9, and 11, "in a building that was on the frontline," and then enrolled as a first-year student in the Electroengineering Secondary School, attending class section I/4 at Jawaharlal Nehru Street #1. Ibro somehow survived his wounds, although he still suffers the physical scars and disabilities, and has undergone intensive rehabilitation therapy, but he is now

An epigraph on a wall inside Skender Kulenović Elementary School, formerly Simon Bolivar Elementary School, reads in English: "Dobrinja: No More War." Photo by author.

a United States citizen. Over the course of our conversations, I asked him to reflect back on his school experience attending a war school in Dobrinja 2B. Today, Ibro echoes the thoughts of so many of the Dobrinja educators cited in this book, and Smail Vesnić in particular, on schooling in Dobrinja during the siege within a siege, writing of his experience attending "The Stairway School in Dobrinja":

> I attended the stairway school in Dobrinja between 1992 and 1993. The stairway school was exactly as it sounds, a makeshift academic environment located in stairways of our apartment building. Classes were usually held in what was perceived as the safest place of the stairway, the basement. The bursts of automatic weapons and nearby mortar explosions hindered paying attention in class. Nevertheless, classes were rarely skipped.
>
> On occasion students would miss a class when a parent would refuse to send his/her son or daughter to class for safety reasons.
>
> Attending the stairway school was important for students as well it was for the teachers.
>
> Whether one was teaching the class, or studying and doing homework under candlelight, their mind for that moment was not occupied

Students of Simon Bolivar Elementary School pose for their 1993–1994 class picture, along with their teacher, Elvedina Vidimlić, in front of their sandbagged, war school classroom. Photo courtesy of Mevsud Kapetanović.

with thoughts on war, shortage of food, medicine, water, safety and well-being of family, or whether the lines would hold during continuous attacks by the aggressor. Instead, the intellect focused on delivering a lesson plan, solving equations, writing essays, and making illustrations. Simply, the stairway school was a way out of the grim reality brought by war and destruction equally for both teacher and student.

In addition, attending stairway schools and learning under such a strenuous environment was seen as a form of resistance to the aggressor. We were all in the same situation and faced the same risks. My classmates and I were not old enough to fight the enemy with weapons. But we were old enough to fight the best way we could, through attendance of a stairway school. (2005)

"We didn't fight with guns," said Smail Vesnić, the man who created schooling when nothing was there. "We fought in this way, to defend our homes, our families." In the process, "we saved those kids. We moved them from the streets to the classroom, and we saved them" (2001).

Note

[1] Merritt Broady, the office director of the Minority Reintegration and Development Office, United States Agency for International Development (USAID), was an instrumental figure in the reconstruction of Osman Nuri Hadžić Elementary School. I cited him, along with Edward Kadunc, the former director of USAID in Bosnia and Herzegovina, for their efforts in the reconstruction of Treća gimnazija, the secondary school in Novo Sarajevo, and the subject of my previous book. The efforts of dedicated people such as Merritt Broady in the reconstruction of the schools in postwar Bosnia are no small matter and, upon his retirement, his good work should not go unrecognized.

References

Ajanovič, Azra, "Kako saznati istinu" [How to Know the Truth], *Monografija: Djeca i škole rastu zajedno, 1992-1998*. (Sarajevo: Dom štampe dd Zenica, n.d.) 40.

Alaupović, Davor, "'Orlovima' ulaz zabranjen" [No Entry for "White Eagles"], *Večernje novine* (30 June 1992) 8–9.

Andrić, Ivo, *Bosnian Chronicle*, translated by Joseph Hitrec (New York: Arcade Publishing, 1993).

Andrić, Jelena, Personal correspondence to author (n.d.).

Babić, Fuad, "Naredba" [Order], Unpublished Document (27 August 1992).

Babić, Fuad, "Naredba o osnivanju Nastavnog centra" [Order concerning the Establishment of a Teaching Center], Unpublished Document (3 August 1992).

Baraković, Ekrem, Personal interview by author, Sarajevo (14 June 2001).

Bećirović, Hajriz, *Dobrinjska ratna drama* [Dobrinja War Drama], (Sarajevo: Jedinstvena organizacija boraca BiH "Unija veterana," 2003).

Bećirović, Hajriz, Personal interview by author, Sarajevo (14 July 2004).

Bećirović, Hajriz, Personal interview by author, Sarajevo (16 July 2004).

Bećirović, Hajriz, Personal interview by author, Sarajevo (5 May 2006).

Berman, David M., *The Heroes of Treća Gimnazija: A War School in Sarajevo, 1992-1995* (Lanham, MD: Rowman and Littlefield, 2001).

Berman, David M., Personal journal, Unpublished Document (1995).

Bešlija, Hajrija, Atija Fako, Hajrija Jahić, and Melita Sultanović, "Pedagoški patriotizam" [Pedagogical Patriotism], *Bosansko-hercegovački školski glasnik* 1:2 (February 1995) 22-23.

Broady, Merrit, Personal communication to author, Sarajevo (18 June 2006).

Bulja, Seniha, "Dnevnik rada: Haustorska škola 'S. Aljendea' Br: 9" [Work Journal: Salvador Allende Stairway School No. 9]. Unpublished Document (June 1992).

Bulja, Seniha, "Haustorska škola: model vaspitno-obrazovnog rada na Dobrinji" [The Stairway School: A Model of Socialization-Educational Work in Dobrinja], Paper presented at *Školstvo u ratnim uslovima* Symposium, Sarajevo (18 April 1994) (August 1993).

Bulja, Seniha, "Obavijest o školskim područjima" [Notice concerning School Regions], Unpublished Document (10 January 1993).

Bulja, Seniha, Personal interview by author, Sarajevo (19 April 2001).

Bulja, Seniha, Personal notes (2001).

Bulja, Seniha, "Zapisnici sa sjednica nastavničkog vijeća osnovnog obrazovanja i vaspitanja Nastavnog centra Dobrinja" [Minutes from the Meetings of the Teacher's Council of Elementary Education and Socialization of the Dobrinja Teaching Center], Unpublished Document (November 1992).

Burg, Steven L., and Paul S. Shoup, *The War in Bosnia-Herzegovina: Ethnic Conflict and International Intervention* (Armonk, NY: M.E. Sharpe, 2000).

Burić, Halil, Personal interview by author, Sarajevo (10 June 2001).

Burns, John F., "U.N. Aid Convoy Reaches Desperate Sarajevo Suburb," *New York Times* (13 July 1992) A6.

Burns, John F., "Where Olympians Once Stayed, Bosnians are Living Under Siege," *New York Times* (18 June 1992) A1, A16.

Ćar, Smail, Personal interview by author, Sarajevo (11 May 2006).

Ćatić, Indira, "Uporni borac za bolju budućnost djece Dobrinje" [Stubborn Fighter for Better Future for Children of Dobrinja], *Dnevni avaz* (29 April 2001) 18.

Community Reintegration and Stabilization Program (CRSP) in Bosnia-Herzegovina, *Final Progress Report* (Sarajevo: Parsons Global Services, 2004).

Crkvenčić-Bojić, Jasna, editor, *Stanovništo Bosne i Hercegovine: narodnosni sastav po naseljima* [Population of Bosnia and Herzegovina: Ethnic Composition by Settlements (Zagreb: Državni zavod za statistiku Republika Hravatska, 1995).

Đapić, Renko, Melita Sultanović, Hajrija Jahić, Đula Ćerimagić, Aida Lomigora, and Mirsada Liskovića-Muftić, "Ratne traume djece

Dobrinje" [War Traumas of the Children of Dobrinja], *Psihosovijalna pomoć učenicima ii roditeljima u ratu: Zbirka tekstova ii radnih materijala sa seminara I simpozija* (Sarajevo: Grafički atelje "OSKAR," March 1997) 17-33.

Dizdarević, Zlatko, "Songs in Dobrinja," *Sarajevo: A War Journal* (New York: Henry Holt. 1994) 157–159.

Drakulić, Slavenka, Afterword to Dzevad Karahasan, *Sarajevo: Exodus of a City* (New York: Kodansha International, 1994) 113-123.

Dučić, Amil, "Svaki 14. maj je pun tuge i bola" [It's much sorrow and pain every 14 May], *Oslobođenje* (29 April 2006) 18.

Dwork, Deborah, *Children with a Star: Jewish Youth in Nazi Europe* (New Haven, CT: Yale University Press, 1991).

Džemidžić, Muhamed., "Novi masakr na Dobrinji" [New Massacre in Dobrinja], *Oslobođenje* (13 July 1993) 1.

Džemidžić, Muhamed, "Podmuklo—iz Lukavice" [Treacherously—from Lukavica], *Oslobođenje* (2 June 1993) 3.

Efendić, Hadžo, "Dobrinja je simbol otpora" [Dobrinja is a Symbol of Resistance], *Dobrinja—Ratne novine* 11 (June 1993) 5-6.

Fazlagić, Mirsad, Personal communication to author, Sarajevo (27 March 2006).

Gimnazija Dobrinja, "Ljetopis gimnazije" [Annals of the Gymnasium], Unpublished Document (1992-1995).

Gimnazija Dobrinja, Unpublished Documents (1992-1995).

Gimnazija Dobrinja, "Zalmonica za dodjelu paketa" [Request for Allocation of Packets], Unpublished Document (11 June 1993).

Gimnazija Dobrinja, "Zalmonica za dodjelu porodičnih paketa za nastavnike Gimnazije na Dobrinji" [Request for Allocation of Family Packets for Teachers of the Gimnazija in Dobrinja] (26 May 1993).

Gimnazija Dobrinja, "Zapisnici sa sjednica: Nastavničko vijeće, Gimnazija" [Minutes from the Meetings: Teacher's Council, Gimnazija], Unpublished Document (1992-1995).

Green, Linda, *Fear as a Way of Life: Mayan Widows in Rural Guatemala* (New York: Columbia University Press, 1999).

Grozdanović, Emir, "Rat sam gledao samo u filmovima" [I Saw War Only in Films], *Putokazi: List Nastavnog centra Dobrinja* 1:1-2 (March 1993) 12.

Hadžić, Damir, Personal interview by author, Sarajevo (21 June 2001).

Hadžić, Ismet, Personal interview by author, Sarajevo (15 May 2001).

Hajrulahović-Talijan, Mustafa, "Juzni bedem grada" [Southern Defense of the City], *Dobrinja—Ratne novine* 11 (June 1993) 5.

Hall, Brian, *The Impossible Country: A Journey through the Last Days of Yugoslavia* (Boston: David R. Godine, 1994).

Hasanbegović, Dijala, "Čarobna svjetiljka," [Magical Lamp], *Monografija: Djeca i škole rastu zajedno, 1992-1998.* (Sarajevo: "Dom štampe dd Zenica, n.d.) 54.

Haverić, Ismail, "Izvrsenje Rjesenja broj: 03-374-140 o privremenom koristenju poslovnog prostora za Gimnaziju Dobrinja" [Implementation of Solution Number 03-374-140 Concerning Temporary Utilization of Workspace for Gimnazija Dobrinja], Unpublished Document (22 September 1993).

Hedl, Dragutin, "Ahmići Cover Up Exposed," *Balkan Crisis Report* [Online], Institute for War and Peace Reporting 145 (2 June 2000) http://www.iwpr.net/index.pl?archive/bcr/bcr_20000602_1_eng.txt

Hoare, Marko Attila, *How Bosnia Armed* (London: Saqi Books, 2004).

Hodžić, Muhamed, Personal communication to author, Sarajevo (23 July 2001).

Hodžić, Sefko, "Stvaranje legendi" [Creating Legends], *Oslobođenje* (20 April 1997) 12.

Hromadžić, Mehmed, "Dobrinja—otpisano naselje!" [Dobrinja—Settlement Written Off!], *Oslobođenje* (8 May 1992) 3.

Hromadžić, Mehmed, "Doktori" [Doctors], *Oslobođenje* (20 May 1992) 5.

Hromadžić, Mehmed, "Novi Aušvic" [New Auschwitz], *Oslobođenje* (17 May 1992) 6.

Hromadžić, Mehmed, "Poklati, Rastjerati, Zastrašiti" [To Slaughter, To Scatter, To Intimidate], *Oslobođenje* (7 May 1992) 5.

Hromadžić, Mehmed, "Ptice su pobjegle" [The Birds Flew Away], *Oslobođenje* (22 May 1992) 5.

Hromadžić, Mehmed, "Školska godina nije izgubljena" [The School Year is not Lost], *Prosvjetni list* 48:831 (June 1993) 3.

Huskić, Belma, "Rat je velika čekaonica nasilne smrti u koju je pretvoren svijet" [War is a Large Waiting Room of Violent Death into Which the World has Turned], Unpublished Document, Treća gimnazija (27 July 1995).

Ilić, Lidija, "Bilo jedno agresivno pseto" [There was an Aggressive Dog], *Putokazi: List Nastavnog centra Dobrinja* 1:1-2 (March 1993) 12.

Ilić, Lidija, "Kniga" [The Book], Unpublished Document, Osnovna škola Skender Kulenović (1992-1995).

JP Geodetski zavod BiH, "Sarajevo—Plan Grada" [Sarajevo—Plan of the

City], Četvrto dopunjeno izdanje (1993).
Jabučar, Abdulah, "Organizacija škola u ratu" [Organizing Schools in the War]. *Bosanksko-Hercegovački školski glasnik* 1:1 (August 1994) 4-5.
Jabučar, Abdulah, *Zbirka propisa iz oblasti obrazovanja* [Collection of Regulations from the Field of Education] (Fojnica: Svjetlost-Fojnica, 1997).
Jahić, Hajrija-Šahza, "Pedagoški patriotizam" [Pedagogical Patriotism], *Glasnik* [The Messenger] 1:2 (February 1995) 22-23.
Jahić, Hajrija-Šahza, Personal interview by author, Sarajevo (20 May 1998).
Jahić, Hajrija-Šahza, "The War Schools of Sarajevo," *Schools War Children: Sarajevo*, edited by Kirsten Wangebo (Copenhagen: Royal Danish School of Educational Studies, 1996) 11-27.
Jakić, Behija, Personal interview by author, Sarajevo (19 May 1998).
Jakić, Behija, Personal interview by author, Sarajevo (13 July 2004).
Jansen, Jonathan, "In Search of Liberation Pedagogy in South Africa," *Journal of Education* 172:2 (1990) 62-71.
Kapetanović, Faiza, "Saopštenje na temu 'ratne škole' (na temelju diljela iskustava iz rada haustorske 'ratne' škole 'Krin' u ulici M. Oreškovića 9—Dobrinja)" [Reporting on the Theme of the 'War School' (on the Basis of Partial Experience from the Work of the 'Lily' Stairway 'War' School on M. Oreškovića Street #9—Dobrinja]. Paper presented at *Školstvo u ratnim uslovima* Symposium, Sarajevo (18 April 1994) (October 1993).
Kapetanović, Mevsud, Personal photographs (n.d.).
Kapetanović, Mevsud, Personal video (n.d.).
Kardos, Susan M., "'Not Bread Alone': Clandestine Schooling and Resistance in the Warsaw Ghetto during the Holocaust," *Harvard Educational Review* 72:1 (Spring 2002) 33-66.
Kermish, J., "Origins of the Education Problem in the Ghetto," *Yad Vashem Bulletin* 12 (December 1962) 28-34.
Kermish, Joseph, editor, "The School System," *To Live and Die with Honor! ...: Selected Documents from the Warsaw Ghetto Underground Archives "O.S." [Oneg Shabbath]* (Jerusalem: Yad Vashem, 1986) ARI/74:500-515.
Kermish, Joseph, editor, *To Live with Honor and Die with Honor! ...: Selected Documents from the Warsaw Ghetto Underground Archives "O.S." ["Oneg Shabbath"]* (Jerusalem: Yad Vashem, 1986).
Koshi, Luljeta, Personal communication to author, Sarajevo (3 July 2004).

Koshi, Luljeta, Personal communication to author, Sarajevo (11 July 2004).
Kujundžić, Amra, Unpublished Document, Osnovna škola Skender Kulenović (1992-1995).
Kujundžić, Azra, "Izvještaj o radu" [Work Report], Unpublished Document (30 April 1993).
Kujundžić, Azra, Personal interview by author, Sarajevo (13 July 2004).
Kujundžić, Azra, Personal Journal, Unpublished Document (1992-1993).
Kujundžić, Azra, "Spisak nastavnog osoblja sa kojim raspolaže u ovom trenutku Kvadrant C5 (zajedno sa Aerodromskim naseljim)" [List of Teaching Personnel Available at This Moment in Quadrant C5 (Together with the Airport Settlement], Unpublished Document (13 September 1992).
Kujundžić, Enes, Personal communication to author, Sarajevo (8 May 2001).
Kumalić, Ismet, "Odluka o osnivanju Kulturno-informativnog centra Dobrinja" [Decision on Opening the Dobrinja Cultural-Information Center], Unpublished Document (1 April 1993).
Kumalić, Ismet, "Osnivanje Kulturno-informativnog centra Dobrinja" [Opening the Dobrinja Cultural-Information Center], Unpublished Document (9 April 1993).
Kurtović, Senka, "Svaka kuća prva linija" [Every Home the Frontline], *Oslobođenje*, European Weekly Edition (5 December 1995) 6.
Maček, Ivana, *War Within: Everyday Life in Sarajevo under Siege* (Uppsala: Acta Universitatis Upsaliensis, 2000) Uppsala Studies in Cultural Anthropology 29.
Makarević, Asja, Unpublished Document, Osnovna škola Skender Kulenović (1992-1995).
Makarević, Dino, "Naš poklik za svijet bez straha!" [Our Cry for a World without Fear], *Monografija: Djeca i škole rastu zajedno, 1992-1998*. (Sarajevo: "Dom štampe dd Zenica, n.d.) 51.
Mann, Carol, *Une Banlieue de Sarajevo en Guerre: Les amazones de la 'kuca' ou La resistance des femmes de Dobrinja* [A Sarajevo Suburb in War: The Amazons of the 'Home' or the Resistance of the Women of Dobrinja] (Paris: Ecole des Hautes Etudes en Sciences Sociales, 2000).
Miskin, Sabiha, Personal interview by author, Sarajevo (12 July 2001).
Muhamedagić, Adila, "Odluka o osnivanju Nastavnog centra" [Directive concerning the Establishment of a Teaching Center], Unpublished

Document (3 August 1992).
Muhović, Muslija, Personal interview by author, Sarajevo (17 June 2001).
Muratović, Ivona, "Preživjeti na pošten način" [Surviving in an Honest Manner], Unpublished Document, Osnovna škola Skender Kulenović (1992-1995).
Musagić, Mujo, "Ratne škole u Bosni i Hercegovini" [War Schools in Bosnia and Herzegovina], Personal correspondence to author (24 August 1998).
Musić, Omer, Personal interview by author, Sarajevo (20 June 2001).
Mustajbegović, Saida, "Dobrinjske škole: Iz inata su zvonila zvona" [Dobrinja Schools: The Schoolbells Rang from Spite], *Dani* 251 (2002) http://www.bhdani.com/archiva/251/t25138.shtml
Nastavni centar Dobrinja, "Almanah" [Almanac], Volumes I and II, Unpublished Document. (1992-1993).
Nastavni centar Dobrinja, "Haustorska škola ulice Emila Zola" [The Stairway School of Emile Zola Street], Unpublished Documents (1992).
Nastavni centar Dobrinja, "Podaci o nastavnicima učenicima: Srednjih škola, šk. 1992/93 god." [Data on Teachers and Students: Secondary School, 1992-1993 School Year], 3 Volumes, Unpublished Document (1992-1993).
Nastavni centar Dobrinja, "Programska osnova rada nastavnog centra u šk. 1992/93 god." [Basic Work Program of the Education Center in the 1992-1993 School Year], Unpublished Document (November 1992).
Nastavni centar Dobrinja, "Spisak radnika Nastovnog centra koji su primili bonove za ishranu (ručak) za November 1992" [List of Workers of the Teaching Center who have received Vouchers for Canteen Meals (Lunch) for November 1992], Unpublished Document (12 November 1992).
Nastavni centar Dobrinja, Unpublished Documents (1992-1995).
Nordstrom, Carolyn, and Antonius C.G.M. Robben, editors, *Fieldwork under Fire: Contemporary Studies of Violence and Survival* (Berkeley, CA: University of California Press, 1995).
Nordstrom, Carolyn, and JoAnn Martin, editors, *The Paths to Domination, Resistance, and Terror* (Berkeley, CA: University of California Press, 1992).
Općina Novi Grad, "Odluka o obrazovanju mjesnih zajednica u naselju

Dobrinja" [Decision on Education of Local Communities in the Settlement of Dobrinja], (4 April 1998).

Općina Novi Grad, Općinska služba za opću upravu i lokalnu samoupravu, Odsjek za mjesne zajednice, "Struktura stanovnistva na Dobrinji" [Composition of the Population in Dobrinja], Unpublished Document (1991).

Oslobođenje, "Gimnazija otvara na Dobrinji?" [Gimnazija Opens in Dobrinja?], (28 August 1992) 6.

Oslobođenje, "Granatama od 152 MM po Sarajevu" [(With) 152 mm Shells on Sarajevo] (17 October 1993) 1.

Oslobođenje, "Masakr na Dobrinji" [Massacre in Dobrinja], (2 June 1993) 1.

Oslobođenje, "Masakr pred školom" [Massacre in Front of School], (10 November 1993) 1.

Oslobođenje, "Nastavu prilagoditi ratnim uslovima" [Instruction to be Adapted to Wartime Conditions], (10 September 1992) 8.

Oslobođenje, "Novi napad na Sarajevo" [New Attack on Sarajevo], (19 October 1993) 1.

Oslobođenje, "Opet masakr u Sarajevu" [Massacre Again in Sarajevo], (11 November 1993) 1.

Oslobođenje, "Rat određuje termin" [War Determines the Term], (8 September 1992) 4.

Oslobođenje, "Sarajevo se branilo napadom" [Sarajevo Defended Itself from Attack], (14 May 1992) 1.

Oslobođenje, "'Školsko zvono' za srednjoškolce" ["School Bells" for Secondary Schools], (8 February 1993) 4.

Osnovna škola Dušan Pajić-Dašić (Osman Nuri Hadžić), "Ljetopis škole" [Annals of the School], Unpublished Document (1992-1995).

Osnovna škola Osman Nuri Hadžić (Dušan Pajić-Dašić), "Otvaranje škole" [The Opening of School], Videotape (9 December 2002).

Osnovna škola Simon Bolivar (Skender Kulenović), "Almanah" [Almanac], Unpublished Document (1992-1995).

Osnovna škola "Skender Kulenović (Simon Bolivar), *Monografija: Djeca i škole rastu zajedno, 1992-1998.* [Monograph: Children and Schools Grow Together, 1992-1998] (Sarajevo: "Dom štampe dd Zenica, 1998).

Pavelić, Davorin, Personal interview by author, Zenica (5 March 1995).

Pavelić, Davorin, Personal interview by author, Sarajevo (19 July 2001).

Pawełczyńska, Anna, *Values and Violence in Auschwitz: A Sociological*

Analysis, Catherine S. Leach, translator (Berkeley, CA: University of California Press, 1979).

Pedagoški zavod, "Informacija o početku nastave u srednjim školama, 92-93 godine" [Information on the Beginning of Instruction in Secondary Schools, 1992-1993], Unpublished Document (April 1993).

Pedagoški zavod, "Program rada u ratnim uslovima za 1992" [Work Program in Wartime Conditions for 1992], Unpublished Document (September 1992).

Pedagoški zavod, "Zaduženja škola po mjesnim zajednicama (šk. 93/94 godine)" [Assignment of Schools by Local Community (93/94 School Year], Unpublished Document (1993-1994 School Year).

Pedagoški zavod and Nastavni centar Dobrinja, "Programska osnova rada nastavnog centra u 1992" [Basic Work Program of the Education Center in 1992], Unpublished Document (July 1992).

Petrović, Ruza, "The National Composition of Yugoslavia's Population, 1991," *Yugoslav Survey* 23:1 (1992) 1-24.

Pijetlović, Gordana, editor, *Putokazi: List Nastavnog centra Dobrinja* [Highways: Gazette of the Dobrinja Teaching Center] 1:1-2 (March 1993).

Polimac, Lejla, Personal correspondence to author (19 June 1996).

Polimac, Narcis, Personal interview by author, Sarajevo (26 April 2006).

Porča, Selver, ed., *Dobrinja—Ratne novine* [Dobrinja—The War Newspapers] 6 (January 1993).

Porča, Selver, ed., *Dobrinja—Ratne novine* [Dobrinja—The War Newspapers] 16-17 (November-December 1993).

Porča, Selver, ed., "Herojska Dobrinja: jeste vitezovi, jeste i gazije" [Heroic Dobrinja: You are Knights, You are '*Gazije*'"], *Dobrinja—Ratne novine* 22 (September 1995) 1-6.

Pravidur, Zlatan, "Obezbjedjivanje prostora za izvodjenje instruktivne nastave za učenike koji su završili I i II razred srednje škole (dva prostora) [Securing Spaces for Carrying Out Instructive Teaching for Students Who Completed the First and Second Class of Secondary School (Two Spaces)], Unpublished Document (16 September 1992).

Resulović, Alija, "Naselje nesalomivih" [Unbreakable Settlement], *Dobrinja—Ratne novine* 11 (June 1993) 17.

Rohde, David, *Endgame—The Betrayal and Fall of Srebrenica: Europe's Worst Massacre since World War II* (Boulder, CO: Westview, 1998).

Salihbegović, Ismet, Unpublished Document (19 October 1994).

Salihbegović, Ismet, "Zapisnik sa sastanka održanog 11.10.1994. godine"

[Minutes for a Meeting Held on 11 October 1994], Unpublished Document (17 October 1994).

Sejfović, Ibrahim, Personal correspondence to author (20 September 2005).

Sejfović, Mensur, Personal communication to author, Columbus, Ohio (20 May 2005).

Službeni list RBiH [Official Gazette of the Republic of Bosnia and Herzegovina], "Odluka o upisu učenika u osnovne i srednje škole i o početku nastave u školskoj 1992/93 godini" [Decision on the Registration of Students in Elementary and Secondary Schools and the Beginning of Instruction in the 1992–1993 School Year], 4:92 (18 September 1992).

Smajlović, Mustafa, "Kako izvajati život" [How to Carve Out a Life], *Večernje novine* (1-2 April 1995) 14.

Smajlović, Mustafa, "Škole će nositi imena naših književnika" [The Schools Will Carry the Names of Our Writers], *Dobrinja danas*. 28 (10 April 1994) 1.

Šobot, Ilija, Personal interview by author, Sarajevo (21 May 2001).

Sultanović, Melita, "Organization and Maintenance of School System during the Civil War in Sarajevo 1992-1995," *Schools War Children: Sarajevo*, edited by Kirsten Wangebo (Copenhagen: Royal Danish School of Educational Studies, 1996) 7-10.

Sultanović, Melita, Personal interview by author, Sarajevo (1 June 1998).

Tabaković, Sabiha, editor, "Ubice u školskim klupama" [Killers in School Benches], *Dobrinja—Ratne novine* 1 (31 August 1992) 15-16.

Taussig, Michael, *The Nervous System* (New York: Routledge, 1992).

Taussig, Michael, *Shamanism, Colonialism, and the Wild Man: A Study in Terror and Healing* (Chicago: University of Chicago Press, 1987).

Todorov, Tzvetan, *Facing the Extreme: Moral Life in the Concentration Camps*, Arthur Denner and Abigail Pollak, translators (New York: Henry Holt and Company, 1996).

Topalović, Eso, "Denis Bosankić: Više od dječaka" [Denis Bosankić: More than a Boy], *Dobrinja—Ratne novine* 12-13 (July-August 1993) 14.

Treća gimnazija, "Školski ljetopis" [School Annals], Unpublished Document (1992-1995).

Večernje novine, "Škola za zločine" [School for Crime], (2 June 1992) 6.

Vesnić, Smail, "Dostava elaborata o otvaranju Gimnazije na Dobrinje"

[Delivery of a Development Plan concerning the Opening of the Gymnasium in Dobrinja], Unpublished Document (26 August 1992).

Vesnić, Smail, "Modifikacija i primjena linearno programirane nastave u Gimnazije Dobrinja u Sarajevu" [Modification and Application of Linear Programmed Instruction in Gimnazija Dobrinja in Sarajevo], Paper presented at *Školstvo u ratnim uslovima* Symposium, Sarajevo (18 April 1994) (August 1993).

Vesnić, Smail, "Obezbjedjivanje prostora (učionica) za učenike srednjih i osnovnih skola u Dobrinji 2-A" [Securing Premises (Classrooms) for Students of Secondary and Elementary School in Dobrinja 2A], Unpublished Document (22 November 1992).

Vesnić, Smail, "Obezbjedjenje učeničkog prostora za potrebe osnovnog i srednjeg obrazovanja" [Securing Student Premises for the Needs of Elementary and Secondary Education], Unpublished Document (29 September 1992).

Vesnić, Smail, Personal interview by author, Sarajevo (17 April 2001).

Vesnić, Smail, Personal interview by author, Sarajevo (29 June 2001).

Vesnić, Smail, "Ratni nastavni centar Dobrinja" [The Dobrinja War School Center], *Glasnik* 1:1 (August 1994) 17-20.

Vesnić, Smail, "Ratni nastavni centar Dobrinja" [The Dobrinja War School Center], *Naša škola* 43:1 (1996) 87-92.

Vesnić, Smail, "Rješenje o upisu Gimnnazije u sudski Registrar" [Solution Concerning the Registration of the Gimnazija in the Judicial Register], Unpublished Document (13 April 1993).

Vesnić, Smail, "Zahtjev za obezbjednje učeničkog prostora za izvodjenje nastave u osnovnom obrazovanju" [Request for Security of Student Premises for Carrying Out Instruction in Elementary Education], Unpublished Document (15 November 1992).

Vesnić, Smail, "Zamolnica za preispitivanje odredaba Odluke Savjeta Mjesne zajednice Dobrinja br. 03/93." [Request for Reconsideration of the Provisions of the Decision of the Council of the Dobrinja Local Community Number 03/93], Unpublished Document (15 April 1993).

Vidović, Dajana, Personal communication to author, Sarajevo (27 March 2006).

Vidović, Dajana, and Bojana Vidović, Personal communication to author, Sarajevo (1 April 2006).

Višnjić, Miodrag, *Mesna zajednica u političkom sistemu socijalističkog samou-*

pravljana [The Local Community in a Political System of Socialistic Self-Governance] (Belgrade: "KOSMOS," 1979).

Vuilliamy, Ed, *Seasons in Hell: Understanding Bosnia's War* (New York: St. Martin's Press, 1994).

Vuksanović, Mladen, *From Enemy Territory: Pale Diary (5 April to 15 July 1992)* (London: SAQI in association with the Bosnian Institute, 2004).

Index

A

Academy of Arts, 36
Adrović, Binasa, 95, 101, 106
Adžanela, Fehim, 95, 106
Ahmići, 4
Ajanović, Azra, 207
Alamerović, Ermin, 167-168
Alaupović, Davor, 39
Alcalaj, Sven, 124
Alipašino polje, 125, 198
Aljičević, Kemal, 62
Andrić, Ivo, 19-20, 24, 124, 195
Andreja Andrejevića Street (See Georgi Dmitrova Street)
Andrić, Jelena, 21
Arkanovci, 58
Armed Forces of Bosnia and Herzegovina (OSBiH) (See Army of the Republic of Bosnia and Herzegovina
Army of the Republic of Bosnia and Herzegovina (ARBiH), xviii, xxiv, 3-4, 6, 32, 35, 37, 66, 68-70, 73, 75, 80, 105, 130, 156, 166-167, 169, 172
Army of the Republic of Bosnia and Herzegovina, 5th Hill Brigade, 130, 170, 174
Army of the Republic of Bosnia and Herzegovina, 5th Motorized Brigade, 39, 159, 170, 172, 188, 200, 210
Army of the Republic of Bosnia and Herzegovina, 1st Corps, 37, 173
Army of the Republic of Bosnia and Herzegovina, 1st Dobrinja Brigade, xxiv, 32-33, 35, 52, 59, 61, 69, 73, 112, 125, 130, 170, 173-174
Army of the Republic of Bosnia and Herzegovina, Military Unit 5453, Military Unit 5021-Sarajevo, 168

Army of the Republic of Bosnia and Herzegovina, 155th Hill Brigade, 39, 170
Arnauti, 4
Auschwitz, 25-26

B

Babić, Fuad, 44, 59-60, 62, 70, 75, 125
Babino, 4
Bahar, Kenan, 168
Bajanović, Badrudin, 86
Bajraktarević, Rabija, 62
Bakić-Hayden, Milica, xviii
Balić, Mirsada, 95, 101, 106, 119
Balkan Task Force, 6
Baraković, Ekrem, 14
Basic Work Programs/Work Programs, Dobrinja War School Center, 44, 71-75, 80, 89, 94, 97, 102-112, 114-124, 126, 128-130, 132-133, 140, 144, 153, 169
Baščaršija, xix
Bećirović, Hajriz, xxiv, 10, 19, 22, 37, 49-50, 56-57, 61-63, 67-69, 73
Belgrade, 15
Belko, Mirsad, 171, 174
Bešić, Adis, xxvi
Bešlija, Hajrija, et al., 45
Bihać, 204
Bijelina, 38
Bijelo polje, 18, 219
Bistrik Local Community, 136
Bitka za ranjenike Street, 97
Bjelave, xvi
Blue Route (Plavi put), 2-7
Bolić, Saudin, 172
Bond, Ambassador Clifford G., 217
Bosankić, Denis, 170-172
Bosna River, 2
Bosnian Army (see Army of the Republic of Bosnia and Herzegovina)
Bosnian Krajina, 4, 200
Bosnian Republic (see Republika Bosna)
Bosnian Serb Army (BSA), 5-6, 37, 56, 67, 70
Brčko, 204
Broady, Merritt, 221
Bučan, Ema, xxv
Bukva, Aida, 203
Bulja, Seniha, xxi-xxii, 10, 25, 51, 56, 74, 81, 84-88, 90, 93-94, 96, 99, 101, 106,

110-112, 129, 149, 152, 155, 168, 208, 211, 222
Burg, Stephen L., and Paul S. Shoup, 60
Burić, Halil, xxi, 19, 31-33, 36, 57, 66, 74, 169-170, 206, 211
Burkett, Gaye, xviii
Burlović, Bojana, xix
Burlović, Maja, xix
Burlović, Sanja, xix
Burns, John F., 67-70
Burstin, Barbara, xxvii
Bušić, Ivana, xxvi
Butmir, xv, 2, 6-7, 17

C

Calgary, 168
Čalija, Maria, 95
Ćamil Sijarić, 200
Ćamil Sijarić (Nikola Tesla) Elementary School, xxiii, xxviii, 200, 212, 219
Ćar, Smail, 32-33, 36, 38, 108
Ćatić, Indira, 212-214
Čehić, Subhija, 74
Čengić, Ismet, 206, 219
Centar Municipality, 124
Center for Peace, 206
Četverta (Fourth) gimnazija, 124, 136, 140
Children's Embassy (Djecija ambasada), 51
Churchill, Winston, 59
City Assembly (Sarajevo), 126-128
City Secretariat for Education (Sarajevo), xvii, 36, 80, 111, 123, 129-130, 144, 146, 149-150, 153, 185, 197, 208
Civil Defense (CZ) Headquarters, 44, 59-60, 70, 99-100, 122, 125, 184-185, 189, 210
Clandestine (Ghetto) Schools, 27-29
Clinton, President William, 6
Colombia, 31
Columbus, Ohio, xix
Common School (Zajednička škola), 18, 207-223
Common Life (Zajednički život), 15, 18, 217-218
Concentration Camps, xxvii, 24-27, 30
Coordination Board for Dobrinja and the Airport Settlement, 59, 61-64, 67, 80, 111
Cornell University, xxv
Ćosić, Elvir, 95

Creativus, Youth Center for Communication and Creative Learning, xxv
Crkvenčić-Bojić, Jasna, 15
Croatian Defense Council (HVO), 194
Croatian Democratic Union (HDZ), 184
Croatian Republic of Herceg-Bosna (See Hrvatska Republic Herceg-Bosna)
Cultural Information Center (CIC), 184-187, 189, 209

D

Dačić, Alija, 67-68
Danka Mitrova Street, 100
Đapić, Renko, 164-165
Dayton Agreement (General Framework Agreement for Peace in Bosnia and Herzegovina), 69, 206, 221
Decision on the Registration of Students in Elementary and Secondary Schools and the Beginning of Instruction in the 1992-1993 School Year, 78
Delalić, Elizabeta, xxvi
Demirović, Samir, 85
Dizdarević Zlatko, 24, 43
Dmitrović, Edina, 151
Dnevni avaz, 212
Dobrinja 1, xxiv, xxv, 7, 16, 50, 94-95, 99, 102, 106, 119, 122, 155, 159, 166, 169, 178, 181, 213-214, 219-221
Dobrinja 2, xv, 16, 17, 22-23, 35, 85-88, 90, 94-95, 100-102, 106, 110, 115-116, 119-120, 122, 132, 146, 151, 155-159, 168-169, 173, 178, 181, 212, 222-223
Dobrinja 2B Stairway School (See Salvador Allende Stairway School)
Dobrinja 3, 16-17, 75, 94-95, 99, 102, 106-107, 115-116, 119-120, 122, 154, 159, 161, 168-169, 181, 200, 214
Dobrinja 4, xxiv, 16, 19, 23, 50-51, 70, 92, 94-95, 181, 219-221
Dobrinja 5, 40-41, 46, 92, 94, 101-102, 106, 115-116, 119, 122, 152, 154, 169
Dobrina-Butmir (D-B) Tunnel, 173
Dobrinja danas, 199
Dobrinja-Ratne novine (Dobrinja-The War Newspapers), 39, 52, 84, 170-172
Dobrinja River, 2, 166
Dobrinja War School Center (Teaching Center), xvi-xvii, xx-xxiv, xxvii-xxviii, 10, 19-20, 31-32, 35, 42, 44, 59-61, 63-65, 68, 70-77, 80-81, 84, 87-88, 91-112, 114-133, 136, 140-142, 144-145, 152, 156, 158-163, 165-166, 172, 174, 177, 182, 186-197, 199-200, 204-206, 208, 210, 217
Dobrinja War School Center, Elementary Education Section, xxi, 10, 74, 84, 91, 93-112, 117, 130, 144, 204, 208, 211
Dobrinja War School Center, Higher Education Section, xxi, 31, 66, 74, 169, 211
Dobrinja War School Center, Personnel Training Section, xxi

Dobrinja War School Center, Preschool Section, 74
Dobrinja War School Center, Scientific Research Section, xxiii, 34
Dobrinja War School Center, Secondary Education Section, xxi, 33, 74, 114-124, 128-130, 133, 140-142, 144, 152-153, 168, 208, 211
Dobrinjski spectar, 148
Donia, Robert J., 13-15, 218
Drakulić, Slavenka, 24-25
Drew, Colonel S. Nelson, 6
Druga (Second) gimnazija, 124, 154, 165
Dubrovnik, xviii
Dučić, Amil, 58
Dušan Pajić-Dašić (Osman Nuri Hadžić) Elementary School, xxiii, xxviii, 18, 23, 33, 76, 84-85, 94, 99, 101-102, 149, 151-152, 159, 167, 177-180, 192, 200-203, 212-213, 218
Dwork, Deborah, 29, 31
Džemidžić, Muhamed, 161, 164
Džiho, Dževad, 62
Džinović, Reuf, 85

E

Eastern Sarajevo, 220-221
Economics Secondary School, 141-142, 155
Eferdić, Hadžo, 39
Electroengineering Secondary School, 126, 155, 167, 222
Emile Zola Stairway School, 88, 155
Emile Zola Street, 88
Esad Pašalić Street, xviii

F

Fazlagić, Mirsad, 57
Federal Institute for Statistics, xxvi
Federation of Bosnia and Herzegovina (FBiH), 211, 213-214, 220, 222
5th Hill Brigade (See Army of the Republic of Bosnia and Herzegovina)
5th Motorized Brigade (See Army of the Republic of Bosnia and Herzegovina)
1st Corps (See Army of the Republic of Bosnia and Herzegovina)
1st Dobrinja Brigade (See Army of the Republic of Bosnia and Herzegovina)
FIVA Studio, xxv, 11
Florida International University, xviii
Foča, 38
Franca Prešerna Street, xxi, 66
Franca Rozmana Street, 91

Frasure, Robert C., 6
Free Sarajevo, 7, 80
Fulbright Scholar Award, xvii-xix, xxvi

G

Georgi Dimitrova (Andreja Andrejevića) Street, xix, 37
Gimnazija Dobrinja, xvi, xx, xxii, xxiv, 36, 39, 40, 42, 44, 64, 76, 113–114, 120, 124-133, 135-136, 138-142, 144-149, 153-155, 159-161, 166-168, 172, 174, 178-182, 184-185, 187-194, 196-197, 204-206, 208-211, 217
Gimnazija Dobrinja, Management and Supervisory Board, 210-211
Glamoć, 38
Goražde, 204
Grada Kalgarija (Calgary City) Street, 168
Green, Linda, 11, 13, 19, 58
Grozdanović, Emir, 47
Guatemala, 11
Guidelines on Educational Activities of Preschool Institutions, Elementary and Secondary Schools During the State of War, 43, 48, 111, 147, 203
Gunić, Fatima, 197
Gunić, Vehid, 197

H

Habibe Stočević Street, 69
Hadžić, Damir, xxiv, 42, 67, 173-175, 217-220, 222
Hadžić, General Ismet, 10, 22-23, 33, 36, 51, 59-61, 68-69, 75, 125, 159, 168, 170, 186, 188, 210
Hadžić, Jasmina, xxv
Hadžići, 5
Hajir, Dr. Youssef, 168
Hajrulahović-Talijan, Mustafa, 37
Halilović, Salko, 206, 219
Halilović, Smail, 92, 94, 115, 131-132
Hall, Brian, 14, 56
Hasanagić, Haris, 85
Hasanagić, Nedim, 86
Hasanbegović, Dijala, xxx-xxxi
Haverić, Ismail, 187, 189
Hayden, Milica Bakić (See Bakić-Hayden, Milica)
Hayden, Robert, xviii
Hayden, Stefan, xviii
Hedl, Dragutin, 4

Hoare, Marko Attila, 49-50
Hodžić, Muhamed, 53
Hodžić, Sead, xxvi
Hodžić, Sefko, 39
Hodžić, Smail, xxvi
Holbrooke, Richard, 6
Holocaust, xxvii, 27, 31, 34
Hrasnica, 5-6, 22, 49
Hrasno, xxvi, 125
Hrić, xix
Hromadžić, Mehmed, 10, 25, 36-37, 51-52, 149-150
Hrvatska Republika Herceg-Bosna (Croatian Republic of Bosnia-Herzegovina), 4-5
Huskić, Belma, 21

I

Ibrišimović, Nedžad, 65
Ilić, Lidija, xxix, 9, 113
Ilidža, 2, 124, 136, 141, 182
Immigration Solutions LLC, xix
Institute for Researching Crimes against Humanity, xxviii, 198
Isaković, Fahrudin, 150, 185
Islam Relief, 210
Islamic Religious Community, 210
Ithaca, NY, xxv
Ivice Marušića Ratka Street, 107, 158

J

Jabučar, Abdulah, 43, 44-45, 48-49, 111, 147, 203
Jabučar, Faruk, xxiii, 76, 99, 152
Jahić, Hajrija-Šahza, 44-45, 52, 64, 66, 81, 85
Jajce, xviii
Jakić, Behija, xv-xvi, 10, 18-19, 35, 125, 129, 196
Jamak, Nisveta, 119, 154
Jansen, Jonathan, 43
Japan International Cooperation Agency (JICA), 221
Jašarević, Munir, 210
Jawaharlal Nehru Street, 93, 155, 167-168, 222
Jelovac, Ilhan, , 163-164
Jovan Dučić Elementary School, 221

243

K

Kadrić, Ismar, 172
Kadunc, Edward, 224
Kapetanović, Faiza, 88-90
Kapetanović, Mevsud, xxv, 7, 16-17, 23-24, 38, 40-41, 53, 55, 69, 90, 104, 108, 157, 162-164, 166, 191, 195, 215, 223
Kapo, Sahir, 203
Karadžić, (Doctor) Radovan, 26, 52, 54-55
Karahasan, Dževad, 24
Kardos, Susan M., 27, 29, 31
Kasindo, 18, 219, 221
Kasindolska cesta (Road), 57-58
Kasindolski Stream, 2
Kasumagić, Larisa, xxv
Kedaš, xix
Kermish, Joseph, 28-29, 31, 34
Kiseljak, 4, 10-11
Knežević, Gordana, 164
Kodić, Izet, 189
Kordić, Miroslav, xxv, 33, 65, 141
Koshi, Bekim, 51
Koshi, Belma, 51
Koshi, Besnik, 51
Koshi, Luan, 51
Koshi, Luljeta, xxv, 23, 50-51
Koshi, Sabaheta, 51
Koševo Hospital, 57
Koste Abraševića Street, 97, 159
Kovač, Nikola, 146
Kovaći Local Community, 136
Krajišnik, Momčilo, 55
Kreso, Adila Pašalić (See Pašalić-Kreso, Adila)
Kreso, Mirsad, xviii-xix
Kreševo, 4-5
Krilić, Ajdin, 163-164
Krin Stairway School (See Lily Stairway School)
Krivošić-Tanasić, Mahira, 119
Kruzel, Dr. Joseph, 6
Kržalo, Adnan, 203
Kujundžić, Amra, 83, 97
Kujundžić, Azra, xxiii-xxiv, 95-99, 101-102, 106-107, 156, 158-159, 161, 186, 202, 208

Kujundžić, Emina, 97
Kujundžić, Enes, xxiii, 34, 74, 211
Kula Prison, 51, 58, 68
Kulenović, Mihridžan (Mimica), 33
Kulenović, Senada, 140
Kumalić, Ismet, 161, 184-186, 206
Kurtović, Senka, 60
Kusmuk, Vlastimir, 55
Kustura, Mersa, xxvi

L

Lalić, Želimir, xxvi
Lašva River, 4
Law on the Completion of Teaching in the 1991-1992 School Year in Elementary, Secondary, and Higher Schools, 48
Lily (Krin) Stairway School, 88-90
Little Guys, 65
Local Communities (Mjesna zajednica, MZ), xvi, 16-17, 46, 93, 109, 112, 136-139, 156, 184-187, 189, 197, 200, 206, 210
Lokve, 5
Louis Pasteur Street, 96, 107
Lukavica, 22, 55, 58, 68, 161, 165, 221

M

Maček, Ivana, 12
Maglaj, 204
Mak Dizdar Street, 158
Makarević, Asja, 177
Makarević, Dino, 1
Malešević, Mirjana, 146
Mandić, Drago, 190
Mann, Carol, 13
Manojlović, Vojo, 53-54
Marka Oreškovića Street, 88
Mavrak, Mirjana, xviii-xix
Mavrak, Ranko, xviii-xix
Maya, 11
Middle Bosnia, 3, 4
Miljacka River, xv, 124
Miller, Ambassador Thomas J., 217
Milošević, Slobodan, 52

Ministry of Education and Science, FBiH, xx, xxiii, 36
Ministry of Education and Science, Sarajevo Canton, xxvi
Ministry of Education, Science, Culture, and Sport, RBiH, 30, 34, 43, 48, 59, 71, 77-80, 93, 105, 109, 111, 116, 123, 126-128, 146, 156, 187, 216
Ministry for War Veterans, Sarajevo Canton, xxiv, 57
Miraščija, Mirsada, 71
Miro Popara Local Community, 46
Mirvić, Adnan, 161
Miskin, Sabiha, xxii, 184, 209-210
Mladić, Ratko, 6, 56
Mojmilo (Hill), xv, 2, 7, 16-18, 25, 51, 56, 70, 154, 162, 168, 177, 180
Montina, Severin, xxiii, 74, 211
Mostar, 200
Mount Bjelasnica, 4-5
Mount Igman, xv, 2-6, 11, 16-19, 173, 195
Mount Trebević, 2, 5, 18, 55
Muhamedagić, Adila, 60
Muhić, Elma, 162
Muhović, Muslija, 31-32
Muminović, Professor, 130
Muratović, Ivona, 143
Musagić, Mujo, 30, 32-33, 206
Musić, Aida, xxiii, xxviii, 152, 156, 158-159, 198
Musić, Omer, 37, 68-69, 156
Mustabegović, Saida, 42

N

National Library of Bosnia and Herzegovina, xxiii, 34
National Security Council, 6
Nedžarići, xv, 36, 46, 57-58, 67-68, 154, 169, 188, 190
New York Times, 67
Nikola Demonja Street, 93, 167-168
Nikola Tesla, 200
Nikola Tesla (Ćamil Sijarić) Elementary School, xxiii, xxviii, 76, 84, 94, 99, 102, 152, 200
Niš Commandos, 67
Nordstrom, Carolyn, and Antonius C.G.M. Robben, 12
Nordstrom, Carolyn, and JoAnn Martin, 12
Notice concerning School Regions, 93, 101
Novi Aušvić (New Auschwitz), 25
Novi Grad Municipality (Općina Novi Grad), xxiv, xxvi, 16-17, 46, 59, 61, 63, 76, 125-128, 136, 175, 185-187, 189, 198, 200, 217, 219, 222

Novi Grad Municipality, Municipal Secretariat for Business, Public Services, General Administration and Budget, 187, 189
Novi Grad Municipality, Property Rights Services, Survey Business and Real Estate Land Registry, xxvi
Novi Grad Municipality, Section for Local Community and Local Government, xxvi
Novi Grad Municipality, Survey Institute of Bosnia and Herzegovina (JP Geodetski zavod BiH), xxvi
Novi Grad Municipality, War Presidency, 61-62, 64, 75-76, 80, 127
Novi Travnik, 4
Novinarsko naselje Local Community, 16
Novo Sarajevo Municipality, 35, 77, 124, 139, 190, 224
Nuhanović, Asad, 72-74, 92

O

October Revolution Street, 94, 100
O'Malley, Eileen, xviii
Omladinskih Radnih Brigada (Youth Work Brigade) Street, 93, 100
155th Hill Brigade (See Army of the Republic of Bosnia and Herzegovina)
Oneg Shabbat Archives, 28-29
Order concerning the Establishment of a Teaching Center, 59
Oslobođenje, 25, 36, 51-52, 60, 76-79, 126-127, 149-150, 161, 163-164, 193-194, 198
Osman Nuri Hadžić, 200
Osman Nuri Hadžić (Dušan Pajić-Dašić) Elementary School, xxiii, xxviii, 18, 200-204, 212-222, 224
Otoka Local Community, 198
Ovčina, Safet, 65, 92

P

Pale, 26, 54-55
Park Prinčeva, xix
Party for Democratic Action (SDA), 49, 184, 210-211
Pašalić-Kreso, Adila, xviii-xix
Pašič, Mediha, 65
Patriotic League (PL), 49-50
Pavelić, Davorin, 22
Pavelić-Đurović, Svetlana, 4
Pawełczyńska, Anna, xxvii, 34
Pazarić, 4-5
Peco, Huso, 95

247

Pedagogical Academy, 95-96, 115
Pedagogical Institute Sarajevo (Inter-Municipal), xxix, 35, 44-45, 52, 59, 60, 63-64, 66, 71, 79-81, 85, 105, 108-109, 112, 126, 129, 135-136, 199
Pejović, Momcilo, 54
Pentagon, 6
Pero Kosorić School Center (Školski centar Pero Kosorić), 125, 136, 141
Pero Kosorić Square, 125
Peta (Fifth) gimnazija, 124-125, 136, 140-141
Petar Drapšina Street, 94
Petar Petrović Njegoš Elementary School, 221
Petrović, Ruza, 14
Pijetlović, Gordana, xxviii, 65, 74
Plečić, Ahmed, 119
Polimac, Lejla, 20-21
Polimac, Narcis, xxiii, 18, 33, 76, 99, 151-152, 159, 206, 212-222
Popović, Mirko, xxvi
Popović, Steve, 54
Porča, Selver, 172
Pravidur, Zlatan, 66, 74, 114, 117, 122
Prcić, Husein, 119
Prelog, Vladimir, 124
Prištinska Street, xx-xxi, 37, 67, 69, 156, 195
Prkosa Street, 40
Prosvjetni list, 30, 149
Provisional Self-Help Board, 61-64
Prva (First) gimnazija, 21, 124, 154, 200
Purić, Aida, 190
Pušina, Amir, xviii-xix
Pušina, Merjem, xix
Putokazi, xxviii-xxix, 65, 68, 92

Q

Quadrant C4, 17, 19, 37, 66, 69, 84, 87, 96-98, 116-117, 156, 171, 174
Quadrant C5, xxiv, 16-17, 23, 34, 66-69, 94-99, 101-102, 106-108, 115-117, 119, 156-159, 163-164, 169, 171, 173-174, 180-181, 185, 195, 202

R

Račić, Asim, 210
Radić, Adrijana, 85
Radončić, Dževdet, 62, 68
Radović, Pavka, 52-54

Railway School Center, 142, 155, 172-174, 187, 217
Rakovica, xxv
Rašić, Hatidža, 95
Rašidović, Safia, xxvi-xxvii
Ražnjatović, Željko (Arkan), 57
Republican Fund for Secondary Education, xxiii, 74, 79, 105, 211
Republika Bosna (Republic of Bosnia and Herzegovina, RBiH), 3, 5, 14, 43, 48, 121, 131-132, 150
Republika Srpska (Serbian Republic of Bosnia and Herzegovina), 5, 26, 54-56, 175, 211, 213-214, 216, 220-222
Resulović, Alija, 39
Ringleblum, Emmanuel, 28
Rohde, David, 6
Rosa Hadživuković 1 Local Community, 16
Rosa Hadživuković 2 Local Community, 16
Rosa Hadživuković 3 Local Community, 16

S

Safet, Alihodža, 174
Salihbegović, Ismet, 208-211
Salihović, Adil, 85
Salvador Allende (Dobrinja 2B) Stairway School, 85-88, 91-93, 110, 155, 168, 222-224
Salvador Allende Street, 85-88, 110, 222
Sandžak, 200
Sarajevo Airport, 2-3, 5
Sarajevskih Ilegalaca (Sarajevo Underground Fighter) Street, 158
Sarajlije, 5, 7, 10, 13, 15, 18-21, 24, 26, 37-38, 45, 213, 218
Šatara, Safet, 86
Savatić, Alen, xxvi
School of Fine Arts, 33
Sefica Dorica Street, 57
Sejfović, Ibrahim, xix, 86, 155, 223-224
Sejfović, Mensur, 85-86
Senči, 65
Serbian Democratic Party (SDS), 184, 211
Serbian Republic (See Republika Srpksa)
Serbian Sarajevo (See Srpsko Sarajevo)
Šešelj, Vojislav, 55
Sheridan, Diarmuid, 213-214
Silajdžić, Haris, 39
Simon Bolivar (Skender Kulenović) Elementary School, xxiii-xxiv, xxviii, 13, 32-

33, 44, 52-53, 55, 70, 76, 84, 88-90, 94-95, 98-99, 102, 108, 152, 156-159, 177-178, 193, 198-200, 203-204, 222-223
Skender Kulenović, 200
Skender Kulenovič (Simon Bolivar) Elementary School, xix, xxiii, xxviii-xxxi, 1, 9, 13, 47, 83-84, 113, 143, 156-157, 163, 177, 199-200, 203-204, 207, 212, 219, 222
Škipina, Slobodan, 55
Školstvo u Ratnim Uslovima (Schooling in War Conditions) Conference, 86, 88, 147
Službeni list, 48, 79
Smajlović, Mustafa, 33, 52, 199-200
Šobot, Ilija, xxi, 33, 74, 114, 117, 119, 152, 154, 187, 189, 208, 210-211
Socialist Federal Republic of Yugoslavia (SFRJ), 14
Soko, Rade, 119
Soldier's Field (Vojničko polje), 51
South Africa, 43
Spaulding, Seth, 3
Spite House (Inat kuča), xviii
Spite Settlement (Inat naselje), 40
Srebrenica, 204
Srpsko Sarajevo (Serbian Sarajevo), 175, 214, 220-221
Stairway Schools (Haustorske škole), xxi, 75, 84-103, 106-107, 109-111, 222-224
Stanišić, Mićo, 55
Stari Grad Municipality, 124, 136, 139
Stup, 93
Stupni Do, 193-194
Sučić, Sonja, 155
Sulejman Filipović Street, 94
Sultanović, Melita, 45, 80–81
Sumbuluša Local Community, 136
Sutjeska Street, 124
Sveti Sava Elementary School, 221-222

T

Tabaković, Sabiha, 52, 54, 84
Tahirović, Rasim, 62
Tahmaz, Azra, 95, 106
Tahmaz, M., 32
Tarčin, 4-5
Taussig, Michael, 11-12, 31
Telebak, Mladen, 54

Territorial Defense (Territorijalni odbrane, TO), xxiv, 10, 35, 49-50, 54, 56, 61-63, 69, 112, 169, 173
Tetarić, Adnan, xxiv, 61-63, 66-69, 81, 108
Tetarić, Samir, 66-69
Todorov, Tzvetan, 26-27
Todorović, Radomir, 54
Tomić, Duško, 51
Topalović, Eso, 172
Topić, Senadin, 76, 99
Trade Technical Secondary School, 168
Travnik, xviii, 19-20
Trebo, Damir, 161
Treča (Third) gimnazija, xv-xvii, xxv, xxvii, 10, 14, 18, 21, 35, 77, 124-125, 136, 139-140, 151, 168, 190-192, 224
Trle, Almir, 172-173
Trle, Fata, 95, 110, 149
Tufekčić, Darije, 167

U

United Council of Anti-Fascist Youth of Yugoslavia (USAOJ) Boulevard, 23-24, 70
United Nations (UN), 2-5, 70
United Nations Children's Fund (UNICEF), xviii, 2-4
United Nations Children's Fund, Program for Cooperation in Educational Policy, Planning, and Development in Bosnia-Herzegovina, 2
United Nations Protection Force (UNPROFOR), 3, 5-6, 23-24, 38, 70, 93, 173, 193, 200
United States Agency for International Development (USAID), xix, 214-216, 221, 224
United States Agency for International Development, Minority Reintegration and Development Office, 221, 224
United States Embassy Sarajevo, Office of Public Affairs, xxvi
United States Embassy Sarajevo, Office of Public Affairs, American Reference Center, xxvi
United States Immigration and Naturalization Service (USINS), xix
University of Pittsburgh, xviii, xxv, xxvii, 2-3
University of Pittsburgh, Bosnia Management Team, 2
University of Pittsburgh, Center for Russian and East European Studies, xviii
University of Pittsburgh, Department of History, xxvii
University of Pittsburgh, Institute for International Studies in Education (IISE), 3
University of Sarajevo, xvii-xviii, 20, 31, 71, 95-96, 115

University of Sarajevo, Faculty of Criminal Science, 31
University of Sarajevo, Faculty of Electrical Engineering, 31
University of Sarajevo, Faculty of Philosophy, xvii-xviii, xxv, 20, 95, 115
University of Sarajevo, Rectorate, 71

V

Vareš, 193
Vase Butozana Street, 107, 159
Večernje novine, 32, 39, 55
Vesnić, Smail, xx-xxii, xxiv, 35, 45-46, 59-66, 68, 73-74, 81, 91-92, 99-100, 102,
    108, 110, 112, 114, 124-128, 130-131, 147-149, 152, 161, 172, 174, 184, 189,
    203, 208-209, 223-224
Vidimlić, Elvedina, 223
Vidović, Bojana, 57-58
Vidović, Dajana, 58
Vidović, Želimir (Keli), 57-58
Vilosonovo šetaliste (Wilson Promenade), 124
Višegrad, 38
Višnjić, Miodrag, 185
Visoko, 4
Vitez, 4
Vogošča, 136, 182
Vraca, 55
Vuilliamy, Ed, 164
Vuksanović, Mladen, 26, 31, 50, 54-55, 68

W

Warsaw Ghetto, 27-29
Washington, DC, xxv
White Eagles, 39
Wilno Ghetto, 29
Winter Olympic Games, 16, 70, 168
Women for Women, 206
World Bank, xxv

Y

Yugoslav Peoples' Army (JNA), 22, 37, 49-50, 70, 97

Z

Zagreb, 14
Željeznica River, 2
Zenica, 3, 4, 5
Žepa, 204
Zmaj Jove Jovanović (Gimnazijska) Street, 124